Essentials of Finance

Essentials of Finance

Edited by
Daisy Scott

MURPHY & MOORE
www.murphy-moorepublishing.com

Published by Murphy & Moore Publishing,
1 Rockefeller Plaza,
New York City, NY 10020, USA

ISBN: 978-1-63987-204-6

Cataloging-in-Publication Data

Essentials of finance / edited by Daisy Scott.
p. cm.
Includes bibliographical references and index.
ISBN 978-1-63987-204-6
1. Finance. 2. Business enterprises--Finance. 3. Corporations--Finance. I. Scott, Daisy.
HG173 .E87 2022
332--dc23

For information on all Murphy & Moore Publications
visit our website at www.murphy-moorepublishing.com

MURPHY & MOORE

Contents

Preface

Finance can be termed as the management, procurement, and study of money and investments. Personal, public, and corporate finance are the three major areas of finance. The financial system comprises the flow of capital among individuals (personal finance), government (public finance), and businesses (corporate finance). The concepts of finance originate from micro and macroeconomic theories. Its study involves the use of mathematics, econometrics, and statistical models to develop economic theories and hypothesis. It is an integral part of business, economics, markets, taxation, insurance, and other commerce fields. Financial economics and mathematics, and experimental and behavioral finance are the main theories of this discipline. This book is a valuable compilation of topics, ranging from the basic to the most complex advancements in the field of finance. From theories to research to practical applications, case studies related to all contemporary topics of relevance to this field have been included herein. This book is a resource guide for experts as well as students.

Significant researches are present in this book. Intensive efforts have been employed by authors to make this book an outstanding discourse. This book contains the enlightening chapters which have been written on the basis of significant researches done by the experts.

Finally, I would also like to thank all the members involved in this book for being a team and meeting all the deadlines for the submission of their respective works. I would also like to thank my friends and family for being supportive in my efforts.

Editor

1

Determinants of Profitability of Polish Banks: The Role of Foreign Banks

Małgorzata Pawłowska[*♣]

[♣]Szkoła Główna Handlowa w Warszawie and Narodowy Bank Polski, Economic Institute

ABSTRACT: The aim of this study is to examine the effect of bank-specific and macroeconomic determinants of bank profitability in Poland using an empirical framework that incorporates the traditional Structure-Conduct-Performance (SCP) hypothesis as well as the Relative Market Power (RMP) hypothesis. This paper also examines the overall effect that financial structure and macroeconomic conditions had during the global financial crisis of 2008. Finally, this paper tests the effect of foreign capital on the profitability of Polish banks and attempts to determine if there is a link between the context of the parent banks and the profitability of their affiliates during the global financial crisis of 2008 and the debt crisis in the Eurozone. Empirical results based on panel data sets containing both micro-level and macro-level data are ambiguous, and we found evidence of the RMP hypothesis only. Furthermore, this paper found a positive correlation between the context of parent banks and the profitability of their affiliates. Finally, we determined that the profitability of commercial banks in Poland was contingent upon the business cycle.

Keywords: bank profitability, market power, market structure, Polish banks, foreign banks, business cycle

[*]Corresponding Author. Email: mpawlo1@sgh.waw.pl

Introduction

The profitability of banks is a subject of great interest in bank management, financial markets, bank supervision, and academics. This interest is driven by increasing globalization and consolidation within the banking sector. Globalization is changing the ownership structure of banking sectors around the world, and the Polish banking sector is no exception. Foreign banks may not only enhance the availability of credit by directly lending to domestic firms or households, but they may also increase competition between banks. Furthermore, in many countries (including Poland), we observed an increased trend toward bank disintermediation.

Currently, the profitability of commercial banks in Poland is influenced by a large number of internal and external factors: consolidation, technological processes, changes in regulation, and the real economy. However, the Polish banking sector is relatively small in comparison to the other countries in the European Union (EU) because it is only worth 85% of the country's GDPand has relatively simple, traditional business models that are dominated by foreign banks.[1] As of the end of 2012, the share of banks with predominantly foreign capital was approximately 65% whereas it was approximately 15% at the end of 1997 (cf., Figure 1). The parent financial institutions of Polish banks were located mostly in Western Europe (Austria, Belgium, Greece, Germany, France, Italy, Netherlands, Portugal, and Spain) and in the United States (cf., Figure 2). Finally, the financial crisis and the increase in systemic risk associated with cross-border links between large banks gave rise to activities aimed at reforming the post-crisis institutional system, and this reform included the systemically important banks (G-SIFIs). The fact that some of the banks on the list of G-SIFIs are also parent banks of Polish banks is significant for their affiliates (e.g., Unicredit Group and Crédit Agricole Group are parent banks in the Polish banking sector).[2]

The aim of this study is to estimate the effect of market structure on the performance of banks in Poland during the financial crisis of 2008 – after the Lehman Brothers failure. This paper will also examine the overall effect of financial structure and macroeconomic conditions to determine whether financial development and business cycles affect the profits of Polish banks. Finally, this paper attempts to determine if there is a link between the context of parent banks and the profitability of their affiliates.

In order to test the traditional Structure-Conduct-Performance (SCP) hypothesis, this paper empirically investigates the effect of market structure as it relates to profitability and has a particular focus on whether banks that are operating in concentrated markets generate more profit or not. Aside from the traditional SCP hypothesis, this paper also tests the Relative Market Power (RMP) hypothesis created by Smirlock (1985). Smirlock posited that

[1]The average for EU-27 countries is about 400% (e.g., Bijlsma and Zwart, 2013; Polish Financial Supervision Authority, 2013).

[2]Criteria for the designation of G-SIFI's: size and international link, lack of readily available substitutes for services provided or adequate infrastructure for services, global activity (i.e., activity in many legal jurisdictions), and complexity of the activity (i.e., its effect on the financial system and the economy).

there is no relationship between concentration and profitability but that there is a relationship between a bank's market share and its profitability.

In order to carry out a quantitative assessment of the effect of market structure on banking performance, this study uses panel data sets to combine micro- and macro-statistical data covering cyclical factors and the macroeconomic environment. Panel data consisted of quarterly micro- and macro-level data, combining data for Polish commercial banks and their parent banks, and information about the macroeconomic environment for the period of 2007Q1–2013Q2. We received micro-level data for Polish commercial banks from the National Bank of Poland (balance sheets, profit and loss accounts), and we received micro-level data for their parent banks from the Bankscope database.[3] We received macroeconomic data from the Polish Central Statistical Office (CSO) and Eurostat. We analysed the change of concentration within the Polish banking industry using the Herfindahl-Hirschman indices (HHI; cf., Figure 3), and we analysed profitability in the Polish banking sector using the return on assets ratios (ROA).

This study's major contribution to the literature is to test the SCP paradigm and the RMP hypothesis in the Polish banking sector and also to examine the role of foreign capital in this context during the crisis. This study consists of two parts and a summary. The first part is a broad literature review concerning the relationship between bank profit and market structure. The second part describes the changes in profitability within the Polish banking sector and presents data, empirical models, and the results of the analysis of panel data for the period 2007Q1–2013Q2. The summary provides an overview of the empirical results and the conclusions that we made.

1 Relationship Between Bank Profitability and Market Structure

There have been recent and ongoing debates concerning the economic role of market structure and competition within the banking industry. Developments in the banking sector do not only affect banks, but are highly relevant to the economy as a whole. Accordingly, both the competition between banks and the profitability of the banking sector is of interest not just at the individual bank level, but also at a broader macroeconomic level. Dramatic changes in regulation and technology have modified the structure of the banking sectors. All of these changes have strengthened competition – especially in traditional lending activity – and have encouraged banks to diversify their sources of revenue.

The SCP model was developed by Bain (1951), and this theory states that in a market with higher concentration, banks are more likely to show collusive behaviour and their oligopoly

[3]The Bankscope database was created by Bureau van Dijk-Electronic Publishing. It contains information on balance sheets and income statements for commercial banks around the world.

rents will increase their performance (i.e., profitability). The SCP paradigm dominated until the late 1970s, and it assumed that a more concentrated system leads to less competition and therefore higher profitability. Berger (1995) advocated the traditional SCP paradigm where banks set prices that are less favourable to consumers as a result of imperfectly competitive markets. Smirlock (1985) tested an alternative explanation for these results. Specifically, he posited that there is no relationship between concentration and profitability, but rather between bank market share and bank profitability. In making this distinction he created the Relative Market Power (RMP) hypothesis. However, subsequent results of analyses based on the SCP paradigm have shown that the relationship between the structure of the market and conduct is even more complex.

The Efficient Structure hypothesis (ES) was developed by Demsetz (1973), and the ES theory states that if banks enjoy a higher degree of efficiency than their competitors, they can increase shareholder value or gain market share by reducing their prices. According to the ES, concentrated markets are those where highly effective firms (banks) operate. Efficiency is not an effect but a determinant of market structure. However, Hicks (1935) developed a theory opposite to the ES, which is known in literature as the Quiet Life (QL). According to the QL, banks with superior market strength and thus a privileged position will suffer a lower cost efficiency due to the quiet life of their managers. Generally, the QL hypothesis assumes that monopoly will reduce the pressure toward efficiency (cf. Bikker and van Leuvensteijn, 2014).

A number of studies have examined the influence of market structure based on the SCP paradigm, and several of these studies reported a positive relationship between concentration and profitability (e.g., Demirgüç-Kunt and Huizinga, 2000; Molyneux and Thornton, 1992; Goddard et al., 2004), which confirms the traditional SCP hypothesis. However, Mirzaei et al. (2013) and Maudos and De Guevara (2004) also confirmed the RMP in advanced economies. The ES hypothesis, by contrast, was confirmed by Claeys and Vander Vennet (2008). Most of the studies focusing on the macroeconomic influences on bank profitability found that the business cycle had a positive influence on the development of bank profitability and that there was a positive correlation between bank profitability and inflation (e.g., Albertazzi and Gambacorta, 2009; Bikker and Hu, 2002; Demirgüç-Kunt and Huizinga, 2000; Rumler and Waschiczek, 2010).

The majority of the studies analyzing the determinants of banks performance are focused on selected microeconomic factors. The present paper offers a broad view on the subject and takes into account many micro factors as well as cyclical components (cf. Delis et al., 2014). Comprehensive studies describing many micro factors and business cycles have been published for the Austrian banking sector (cf. Rumler and Waschiczek, 2010) and for Greek banks (cf. Athanasoglou et al., 2008).

The relationship between profitability and foreign banks has been analyzed in many papers. However, empirical research on the relative performance of domestic and foreign banks has produced ambiguous results, with some studies finding that foreign banks perform better and other studies reporting stronger performance from domestic banks (cf. Degryse and Ongena, 2008; Chen and Liao, 2011). On the one hand, Havrylchyk and Jurzyk (2011) showed that foreign banks (i.e., acquired by foreign investors) in Central and Eastern European countries are more profitable due to cost minimization and better risk management. Van Horen and Claessens (2012), however, found that foreign banks might have higher capital and more liquidity, but they have lesser profitability than domestic banks. Also, during the global financial crisis of 2008, foreign banks reduced credit more sharply when compared to domestic banks, except when they dominated the host banking systems. On the other hand, other researchers have found almost no evidence that the ownership structure of banks had an effect on their profitability (e.g., Molyneux and Thornton, 1992; Cetorelli, 2004). Furthermore, La Porta et al. (2002) concluded that a state bank follows a political rather than a social agenda.

Finally, there are not a lot of studies that take into account the relationship between the profitability of the parent banks and the situation of their affiliates in the context of determining profitability – this paper fills the gap. The paper by Pawłowska et al. (2015) found intragroup links between banking institutions after the Lehman Brothers failure in the Polish banking sector.

2 Banking Structure, Business Cycle, and Profitability of Banks - Panel Data Analysis

The profitability of commercial banks in Poland prior to and during the financial crisis was influenced by a large number of internal and external factors: consolidation, technological processes, and the real economy (cf., Figure 4). After Poland's accession to the EU, there was a clear improvement in profitability both with return on assets (ROA) and return on equity (ROE). This improvement in bank profitability was facilitated by, among others, a decrease in the share of non-performing loans in assets.[4] In 2009, the slight decrease in profitability indicators were caused by the financial crisis (see Figures 5 and 6). It should be noted, however, that the group of Polish commercial banks was not homogeneous during the first part of the crisis. There was a strong deterioration in the financial results of several banks that, in previous periods, were characterized by increasing market shares (particularly in the segment of household loans). These banks had a negative effect on the performance of the entire group (however, some banks reported an improvement in financial results as compared

[4]Since Poland's accession to the EU, the classification of non-performing loans become less restrictive. Sub-standard receivables from one to three months changed to three to six months, doubtful receivables from three to six months changed to six to twelve months, and lost receivables from the above six months to the above twelve months. See National Bank of Poland (2004).

to 2008; cf. Polish Financial Supervision Authority, 2010). In the period 2010–2014, the profitability of Polish commercial banks improved again.

2.1 Data and Model Specification

In order to test the traditional SCP hypothesis and the RMP hypothesis, as well as the effect of the macroeconomic changes on the profitability of banks in Poland, this study examined quarterly data covering the period of the financial and debt crises (1997Q4–2013Q2). This data was obtained for all commercial banks operating in Poland (i.e., Polish banks, subsidiaries of foreign institutions, and branches of foreign banking institutions)[5]. The panel data sets combined micro-level data for Polish commercial banks and macro-level statistical data covering cyclical factors, and this study used a variety of microeconomic indicators stemming from the bank data to capture changes in the economic framework, including balance sheets and income statement figures from the National Bank of Poland's balance sheet statistics. Additionally, the panel data set consisted of data from the Bankscope database, which is a source of valuable information about the foreign parent institutions of the Polish affiliates. The micro-level data from Bankscope was then merged with data on the Polish banking institutions (cf., Tables 1, 2, and 3). Macroeconomic data on the growth of GDP and inflation in Poland came from the CSO (Central Statistical Office). The panel also included macro-level data from Eurostat concerning GDP growth in the parent banks' countries.

In order to carry out a quantitative assessment of the effect of market structure on the profitability of banks in the Polish sector, the generalized method of moments (GMM) estimator was used. The GMM estimator was proposed by Arellano and Bond (1991) and generalized by Arellano and Bover (1995) and Blundell and Bond (1998).[6] This paper used the system GMM (xtabond2) procedure, which can fit two closely related dynamic panel data models (the Arellano-Bond estimator and the Arellano-Bover estimator, fully developed in Blundell and Bond, 1998). The original estimator is sometimes called difference GMM, and the augmented one is sometimes called system GMM. However, the xtabond2 procedure implements both estimators. As GMM estimators, the Arellano-Bond estimators have one- and two-step variants (Arellano and Bond, 1991; Blundell and Bond, 1998). However, using the two-step GMM estimator may impose a downward (upward) bias in standard errors (t-statistics) due to its dependence on the estimated residuals. This may lead to unreliable asymptotic statistical inference (Bond and Windmeijer, 2002; Bond, 2002; Windmeijer, 2005), especially in data samples with a relatively small cross section dimensions (Arellano and Bond, 1991; Blundell and Bond, 1998). However, the xtabond2 procedure uses a finite-sample correction to the two-step covariance matrix derived by Windmeijer (2005).

[5]The numbers of banks fluctuated in the sample due to acquisitions, liquidations, and new banks entering the market.

[6]Use of a GMM estimator also accounts for possible correlations between any of the independent variables.

Finally, taking into account the above factors, this paper used a two-step robust estimator with a correction derived by Windmeijer (2005).[7] Moreover, we used the Hansen test of over-identifying restrictions, which tests the overall strength of the instruments for a one step estimator (Arellano and Bond, 1991; Arellano and Bover, 1995; Blundell and Bond, 1998), and we used the Arellano-Bond tests for AR(1) and AR(2) in the first differences. We also performed model estimation separately to avoid any alignment of variables. In order to solve the problems arising from extreme outliers that affect estimation, all outliers were removed from each panel data set (i.e., any value below the first percentage point or above the 99th percentage point in sample distributions was removed).

2.2 The Baseline Model and Estimation (Quarterly Data Set During the Global Financial Crisis and Eurozone Debt Crisis)

In order to carry out a quantitative assessment of the effect of banking sector structure on banking profitability in the Polish sector during the crisis, a quarterly data set was used that was based on data from 2007Q4–2013Q2.

The following baseline model with ROA as the dependent variable was calculated as follows:

$$\begin{aligned} ROA_{i,t} &= \alpha + a_0 ROA_{i,t-1} + a_1 market\ structure_{i,t} + a_2 market\ power_{i,t} \\ &+ a_3 business\ cycle_{i,t} + a_4 FO_i + a_5 \left(CRI_t \times FO_i\right) + a_6 EuDCRI_t \\ &+ \sum_{j=1}^{N} b_j oth_{i,t} + \varepsilon_{i,t} \end{aligned} \tag{1}$$

where $ROA_{i,t}$ denotes the return on assets ratio for each bank i and for each quarter t.[8] The market structure measure was defined as follows:

- The concentration ratio such as the Herfindahl-Hirschman index for assets (HHI_t) for each quarter t.

In this model, the size of the banking sector was defined as follows:

- The log of total assets where the total assets are the sum of assets of all banks ($Size_t$) for each quarter t (cf., Figure 7).

Market power, the relative measure of market power, was defined as follows:

[7] In the estimations, we used lagged dependent variables as instruments.

[8] To determine the robustness, additional estimations were calculated with the return on equity (ROE) for each banking sector i for each year t as a dependent variable. The results were very similar.

- The share of bank assets in the total assets ($MP_{i,t}$) for each bank i and each quarter t.
- The share of bank loans in the total loans ($ML_{i,t}$) for each bank i for each quarter t (cf., Figure 8).

Also, as the measure of relative market power, the model also tested the affect of the size of the bank on profitability, which was defined as follows:

- The log of total assets ($LA_{i,t}$) for each bank i for each quarter t.

The model also estimated the dummy variables indicating foreign ownership as follows:

- The dummy (FO_i) that takes the values of one if a bank is foreign-owned, and takes a value of zero elsewhere for each bank i for each quarter t.

This model also controls for the effect of the global financial crisis and the Eurozone debt crisis in relation to profitability and foreign ownership. Therefore, other control dummy variables were used in regression as follows:

- The dummy variable (CRI_t) that takes the value of one if t<2010Q3 and t>=2008Q4, and zero elsewhere.
- The dummy variable ($EuDCRI_t$) that takes the value of one if t>=2010Q3 and zero elsewhere.

Therefore, the full sample was split into three intervals: (1) the global financial crisis, (2) the Eurozone debt crisis (the sample begins in 3Q 2010 and ends in 2Q 2013), and (3) the whole analyzed period (2007Q4–2013Q2).

The model also tests the effect of the business cycle on bank profitability during the crisis. The variable business cycle was defined as follows:

- GDP_t growth (yoy) and inflation growth (CPI_t) for each quarter t.

In regressions, we also used control variables (oth_{it}):

- The ratio of total deposit to total assets (DTA_{it}) for each bank i for each quarter t.
- The ratio of total loans to total assets as a measure of the magnitude of disintermediation tendencies ($LTA_{i,t}$) for each bank i for each quarter t.
- The core capital ratio ($CAR_{i,t}$) as an indicator of a bank's risk behavior (the higher the capital ratio, the greater the risk aversion) for each bank i for each quarter t.

- The share of foreign currency housing loans to the household sector in total loans ($FXHL_{i,t}$) as an indicator of banking sector development for each bank i for each quarter t.

The parameter α is a constant term, $\varepsilon_{i,t}$ denotes the error, and a_0, a_1, a_2, a_3, and b_j are the regression coefficients.

Table 4 presents the results of regressions using a two-step GMM estimator. For each of the estimations, we also reported the Hansen test results at the bottom of the table as well as the Arellano-Bond tests (AR(1) and AR(2)). The model seemed to fit the panel data reasonably well, as the Hansen-test showed no evidence of over-identifying restrictions.

In Table 4, a positive coefficient a_1 was found only in regression 3. However, a positive and significant coefficient a_1 was found for the variable $Size_{i,t}$. Also, a positive and significant coefficient a_2 was found for relative size ($LA_{i,t}$) in regressions 2–4.

Relative market power – measured in terms of the individual institution's share in total assets ($MP_{i,t}$) – had a positive and significant influence on the profitability indicators in this study. However, relative market power – measured in terms of the individual institution's share in total domestic lending ($ML_{i,t}$) – had no significant influence on the profitability indicators in this study.

This paper also found a positive effect for foreign capital on profitability during the period of the Eurozone debt crisis (estimation 5). However, for the period of global financial crisis, this paper found a negative effect for foreign capital on the profitability of Polish banks (estimations 3 and 4). Finally, this paper found a positive correlation between the context of parent banks and the profitability of their affiliates for the entire period analyzed.

Of the microeconomic control variables, we found the ratio of the core-capital to risk-weighted assets to have a significant and negative influence on bank profitability. We found that banking sector development – measured in terms of foreign currency lending – had a significant and negative influence on bank profitability. These findings indicate that foreign currency loans did not positively contribute to bank profitability. They also show the positive correlation between intermediation (i.e., grater loans in total assets) and bank profitability. However, our results show a negative coefficient between the ratio of total deposit to total assets and profitability.

Generally, this paper found positive correlations between GDP growth and inflation (CPI), and the profitability of banks throughout the entire period of analysis. This means that the profitability of banks is procyclical.

In addition to all these estimated results, this paper found evidence for RMP hypothesis. However, this paper did not find sufficient evidence to verify the SCP hypothesis.

2.3 Effect of Parent Bank Situation on Profitability of their Affiliates

Furthermore, this paper tested the effect of the parent bank condition on the profitability of their affiliates. In this case, we estimated additional regressions using the GMM estimator. The ROA of banks with a majority of foreign capital was used as the dependent variable in this model. Independent variables were taken from Bankscope and from Eurostat, and the following model with ROA as the dependent variable was calculated as follows:

$$ROAf_{i,t} = \alpha + a_0 ROAf_{i,t-1} + a_1 business\ cycle\ in\ parent\ country_{i,t} + \sum_{j=1}^{N} b_j oth_{i,t} + \varepsilon_{i,t} \quad (2)$$

where $ROAf_{it}$ denotes the return on assets ratio for each bank with a majority of foreign equity i for each quarter t.

This model tested the effect of business cycles in the parent country on foreign bank profitability during the crisis. The variable *business cycle* was defined as GDP growth in the parent country, and the measure of this growth was taken from Eurostat *(parent_GDP)* for each bank with a majority of foreign equity i for each quarter t.

In regressions, we used the following control quarterly variables (oth_{it}) from the Bankscope database:

- *parent_Total_Capital_Ratio* – The capital ratio of foreign parent institutions of Polish affiliates for each bank with a majority of foreign equity i in each quarter t.
- *parent_Net_Loas_to_Assets* – Net loans to assets ratio of foreign parent institutions of Polish affiliates for each bank with majority of foreign equity i for each quarter t.
- *parent_ROA* – ROA ratio of foreign parent institutions of Polish affiliates for each bank with a majority of foreign equity i for each quarter t.

The variable α is a constant term,ε_{it} denotes the error, and a_0, a_1, and b_j are the regression coefficients.

We constructed three regressions for three time periods: (1) the global financial crisis, (2) the Eurozone crisis of 2011–2012 (the sample begins in 3Q 2010 and ends in 2Q 2013), and (3) the entire period (2007Q4–2013Q2).

Table 5 presents the results of regressions using a two-step GMM robust estimator. For each estimation, we reported the Hansen test results at the bottom of the table as well as the Arellano-Bond tests (AR(1) and AR(2)). The model seems to fit the panel data reasonably well because the Hansen-test shows no evidence of over-identifying restrictions.

Table 5 reports the positive coefficient (a_1) (estimations 1 and 2). This means that GDP growth in the parent country of a bank operating in Poland has a significant and positive effect on its profitability in Poland for the entire period of analysis and also for the period of the global financial crisis. Also, the ratio of net loans to assets of foreign parent institutions of the Polish affiliates (*parent_Net_Loas_to_Assets*) has a positive influence on the profitability of a bank operating in Poland. This means that disintermediation tendencies in European banks have a negative effect on the profitability of their affiliates. The negative effect of the parent total capital ratio (*parent_Total_Capital_Ratio*) may mean that a higher capital ratio on average did not prevent higher profitability. This result is also relevant to the current economic policy debate about future regulatory requirements for the banking sector. Also, the ROA ratio of foreign parent institutions of Polish affiliates (*parent_ROA*) is insignificant in this model. However, in estimation 3 (during the Eurozone crisis of 2011–2012), most of the variables were insignificant.

Generally speaking, the results of the above estimations determined that the economic situation of international parent banks had an effect on the profitability of the Polish subsidiaries and branches of these banks during the global financial crisis. Those results may also support the fact that the geographical diversity of parent institutions helped the local financial system to remain relatively vigorous throughout the global financial crisis (Pawłowska et al., 2015).

Conclusions

The global financial crisis has resulted in a massive reduction in profitability for many banks in the EU. However, Poland experienced only a slight decrease in the profitability of its banking sector in the first part of the crisis (in 2009). After this, the profitability of the Polish banks increased. Generally, the results of comprehensive analyses concerning the profitability of Polish banks has confirmed the RMP hypothesis. On the one hand, this paper demonstrates a positive correlation between profitability and market structure and a positive and significant correlation between profitability and market power and also with the size of the bank.

Of the microeconomic control variables, we found that the core capital ratio has a significantly negative influence on bank profitability. Furthermore, the findings indicate that foreign currency loans did not positively contribute to bank profitability. We also found a positive correlation between intermediation (i.e., grater loans in total assets) and bank profitability. These results may show that business models based on strong lending positions were a stabilizing factor in the current financial crisis. Based on the Bankscope database, this paper found that disintermediation tendencies in European banks have a negative effect on the profitability of their affiliates. However, this paper found a negative coefficient between the ratio of total deposits to total assets and profitability.

The results show that foreign capital was a stabilizing mechanism during the entire period analyzed. However, this paper found a destabilizing impact of foreign banks during the first part of the crisis. This paper found a positive correlation between the context of parent banks and the profitability of their affiliates for entire period of analysis. These results are in line with the paper by Pawłowska et al. (2015) concerning the intragroup links between banking institutions after the Lehman Brothers failure, and they confirm these links in the context of the profitability of parent banks.

Finally, as in other countries, bank profitability is strongly influenced by cyclical developments, and this paper found a positive correlation between GDP growth and bank profit – the same effect was found for CPI indices. Finally, this paper found a positive correlation between GDP growth in the parent country and the profit of their affiliates in Poland.

References

Albertazzi, U. and Gambacorta, L. (2009). Bank profitability and the business cycle. *Journal of Financial Stability*, 5(4):393–409.

Arellano, M. and Bond, S. (1991). Some tests of specification for panel data: Monte Carlo evidence and an application to employment equations. *The Review of Economic Studies*, 58(2):277–297.

Arellano, M. and Bover, O. (1995). Another look at the instrumental variable estimation of error-components models. *Journal of Econometrics*, 68(1):29–51.

Athanasoglou, P. P., Brissimis, S. N., and Delis, M. D. (2008). Bank-specific, industry-specific and macroeconomic determinants of bank profitability. *Journal of International Financial Markets, Institutions and Money*, 18(2):121–136.

Bain, J. S. (1951). Relation of profit rate to industry concentration: American manufacturing, 1936-1940. *The Quarterly Journal of Economics*, pages 293–324.

Berger, A. N. (1995). The profit-structure relationship in banking–tests of market-power and efficient-structure hypotheses. *Journal of Money, Credit and Banking*, 27(2):404–431.

Bijlsma, M. and Zwart, G. T. J. (2013). The changing landscape of financial markets in Europe, the United States and Japan. Working Paper 774, Bruegel.

Bikker, J. A. and Hu, H. (2002). Cyclical patterns in profits, provisioning and lending of banks and procyclicality of the new Basel capital requirements. *Banca Nazionale del Lavoro Quarterly Review*, 55(221):143.

Bikker, J. A. and van Leuvensteijn, M. (2014). *A New Measure of Competition in the Financial Industry: The Performance-conduct-structure Indicator*, volume 83. Routledge.

Blundell, R. and Bond, S. (1998). Initial conditions and moment restrictions in dynamic panel data models. *Journal of Econometrics*, 87(1):115–143.

Bond, S. and Windmeijer, F. (2002). Finite sample inference for GMM estimators in linear panel data models. CeMMAP Working Paper CWP04/02, Centre for Microdata Methods and Practice, Institute for Fiscal Studies.

Bond, S. R. (2002). Dynamic panel data models: a guide to micro data methods and practice. *Portuguese Economic Journal*, 1(2):141–162.

Cetorelli, N. (2004). Real Effects of Bank Competition. *Journal of Money, Credit and Banking*, 36(3):543–58.

Chen, S.-H. and Liao, C.-C. (2011). Are foreign banks more profitable than domestic banks? Home-and host-country effects of banking market structure, governance, and supervision. *Journal of Banking and Finance*, 35(4):819–839.

Claeys, S. and Vander Vennet, R. (2008). Determinants of bank interest margins in Central and Eastern Europe: A comparison with the West. *Economic Systems*, 32(2):197–216.

Degryse, H. and Ongena, S. (2008). Competition and regulation in the banking sector: a review of the empirical evidence on the sources of bank rents. *Handbook of Financial Intermediation and Banking*, 2008:483–554.

Delis, M., Kokas, S., and Ongena, S. (2014). Foreign ownership and market power in banking: Evidence from a world sample. mimeo, University of Cyprus Department of Economics.

Demirgüç-Kunt, A. and Huizinga, H. (2000). Financial Structure and Bank Profitability. World Bank Policy Research Working Paper 2430, World Bank, Washington.

Demsetz, H. (1973). Industry structure, market rivalry, and public policy. *The Journal of Law and Economics*, 16(1):1–9.

Goddard, J., Molyneux, P., and Wilson, J. O. (2004). The profitability of European banks: a cross-sectional and dynamic panel analysis. *The Manchester School*, 72(3):363–381.

Havrylchyk, O. and Jurzyk, E. (2011). Profitability of foreign banks in Central and Eastern Europe. *Economics of Transition*, 19(3):443–472.

Hicks, J. R. (1935). Annual Survey of Economic Theory: The Theory of Monopoly. *Econometrica*, 3(1):1–20.

La Porta, R., Lopez-de Silanes, F., and Shleifer, A. (2002). Government ownership of banks. *The Journal of Finance*, 57(1):265–301.

Maudos, J. and De Guevara, J. F. (2004). Factors explaining the interest margin in the banking sectors of the European Union. *Journal of Banking and Finance*, 28(9):2259–2281.

Mirzaei, A., Moore, T., and Liu, G. (2013). Does market structure matter on banks' profitability and stability? Emerging vs. advanced economies. *Journal of Banking and Finance*, 37(8):2920–2937.

Molyneux, P. and Thornton, J. (1992). Determinants of European bank profitability: A note. *Journal of Banking and Finance*, 16(6):1173–1178.

National Bank of Poland (2004). *Financial System Development Report.* Warsaw.

Pawłowska, M., Serwa, D., and Zajączkowski, S. (2015). International Banking and Liquidity Risk Transmission: Evidence from Poland. *IMF Economic Review*, 63(3):585–605.

Polish Financial Supervision Authority (2010). *Report on the condition of Polish banks in 2009.* Warsaw.

Polish Financial Supervision Authority (2013). *Report on the condition of Polish banks in 2012.* Warsaw.

Rumler, F. and Waschiczek, W. (2010). The Impact of Economic Factors on Bank Profits. *Monetary Policy and the Economy*, (4):49–67.

Smirlock, M. (1985). Evidence on the (non) relationship between concentration and profitability in banking. *Journal of Money, Credit and Banking*, 17(1):69–83.

van Horen, N. and Claessens, S. (2012). Foreign Banks; Trends, Impact and Financial Stability. IMF Working Papers 12/10, International Monetary Fund.

Windmeijer, F. (2005). A finite sample correction for the variance of linear efficient two-step GMM estimators. *Journal of Econometrics*, 126(1):25–51.

Figure 1: Share of foreign investors (in assets) in the Polish banking sector

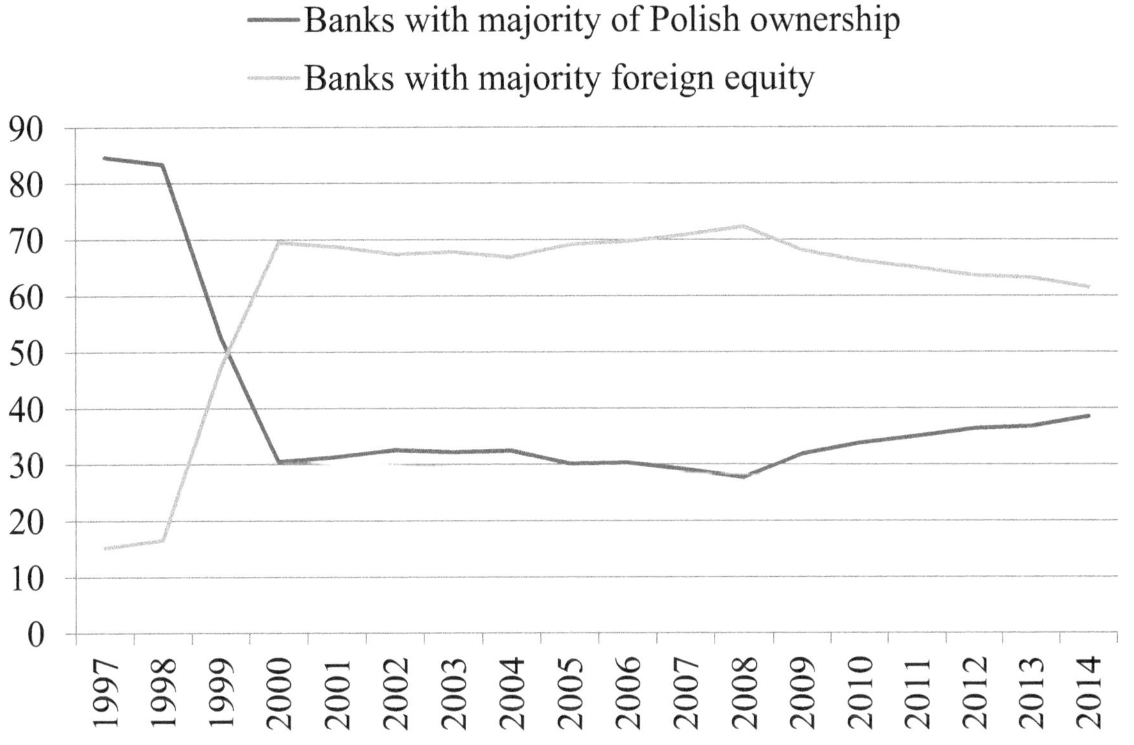

Source: Polish Financial Supervision Authority.

Figure 2: Share of foreign investors in assets of the Polish banking sector by country of origin

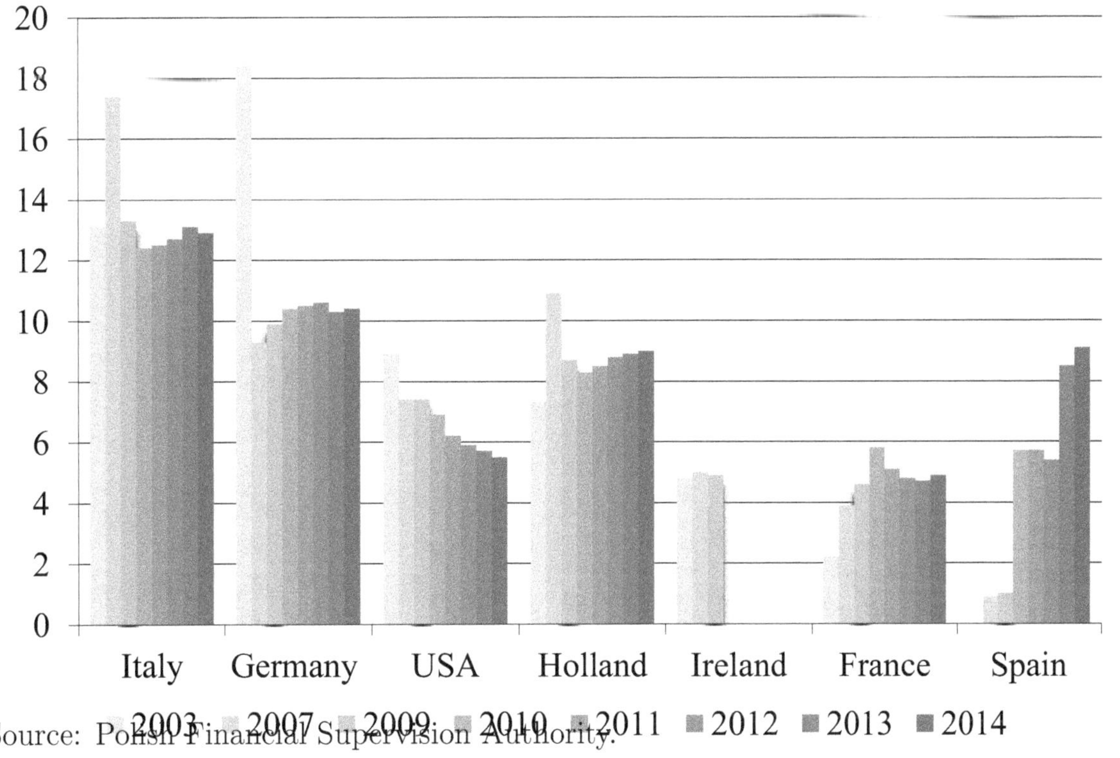

Source: Polish Financial Supervision Authority.

Figure 3: Herfindahl-Hirschman indices (quarterly)

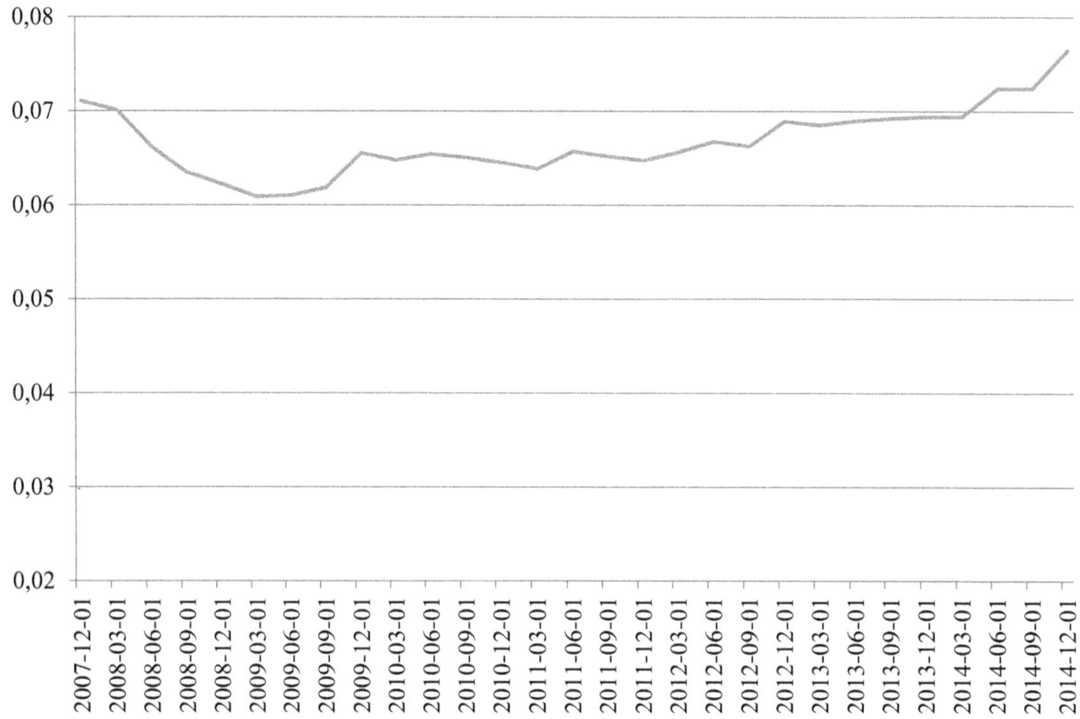

Source: NBP and author's calculations. HHI index was seasonally adjusted.

Figure 4: GDP growth and inflation rate (yoy quarterly) (%)

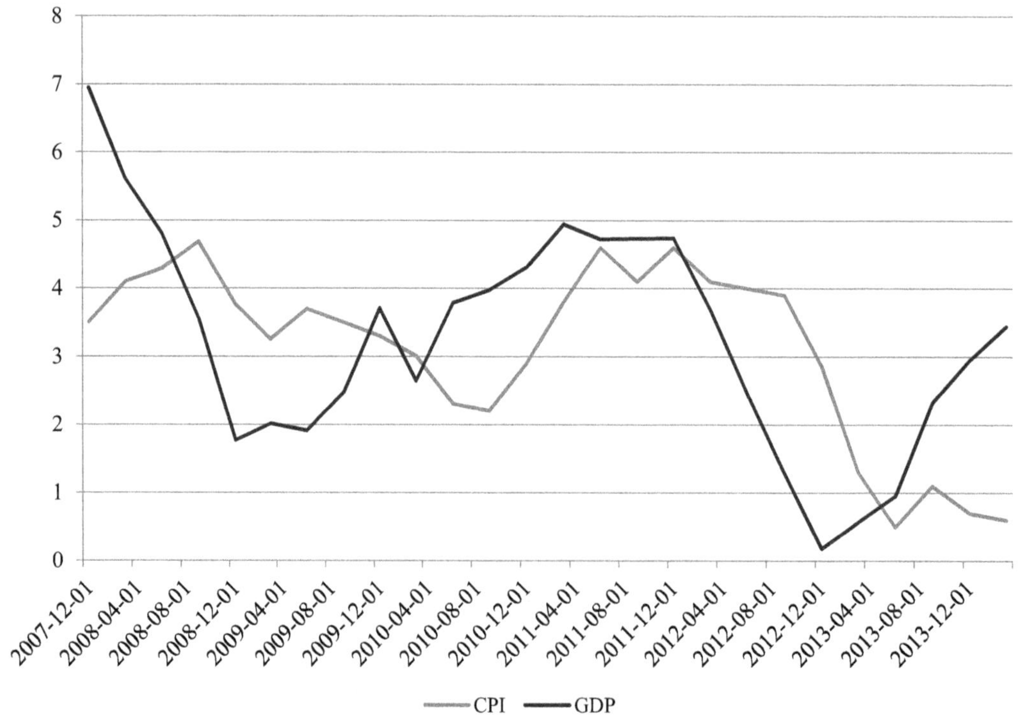

Source: NBP and author's calculations.

Figure 5: Profitability ratio in EU (ROA, in %)

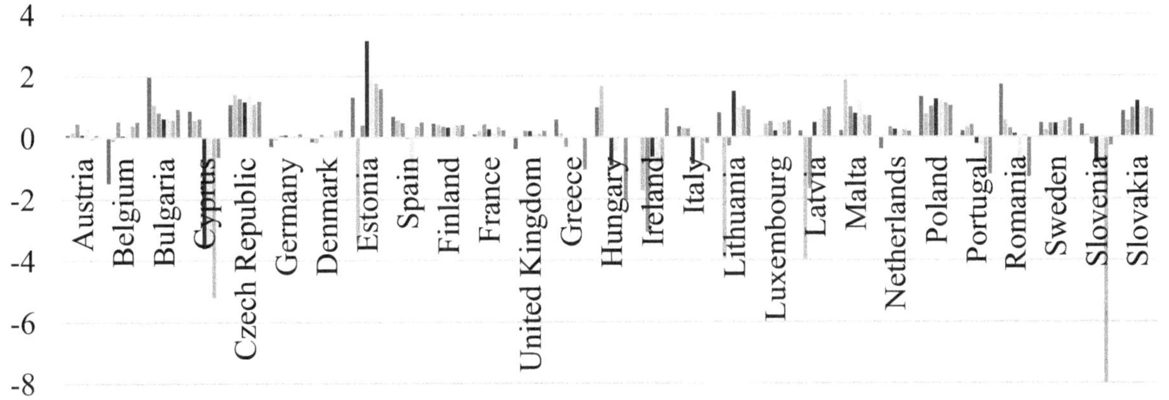

Source: European Central Bank.

Figure 6: Profitability ratio in EU (ROE, in %)

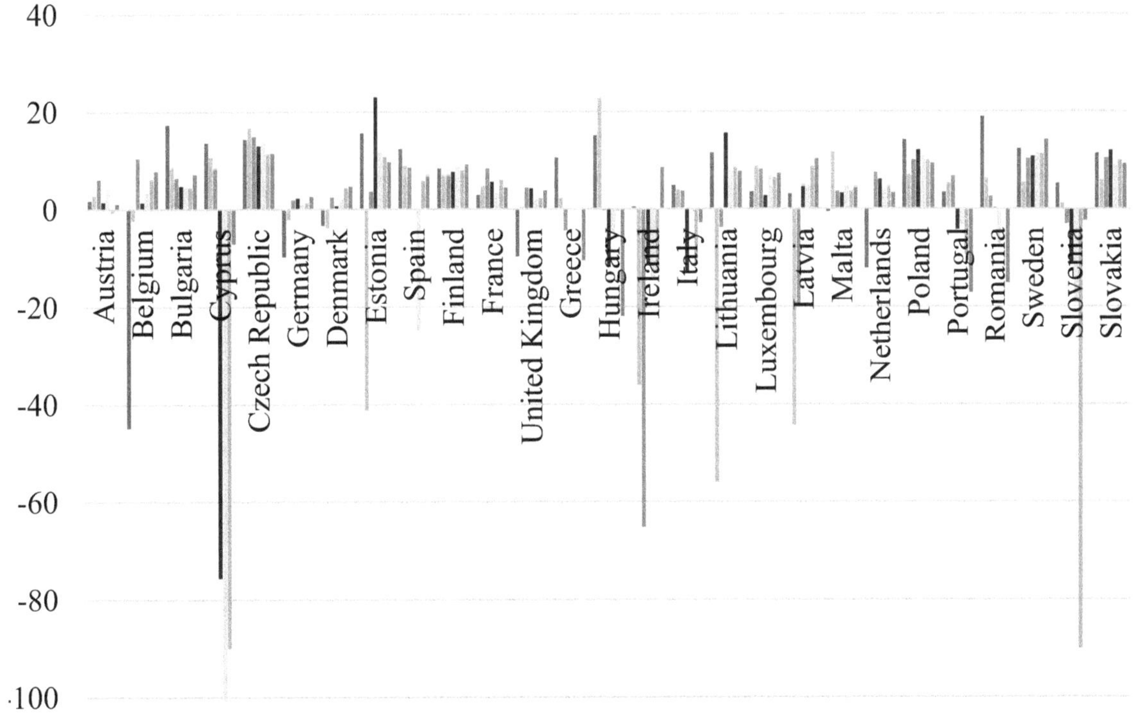

Source: European Central Bank.

Figure 7: Assets of the Polish banking sector [in bn PLN]

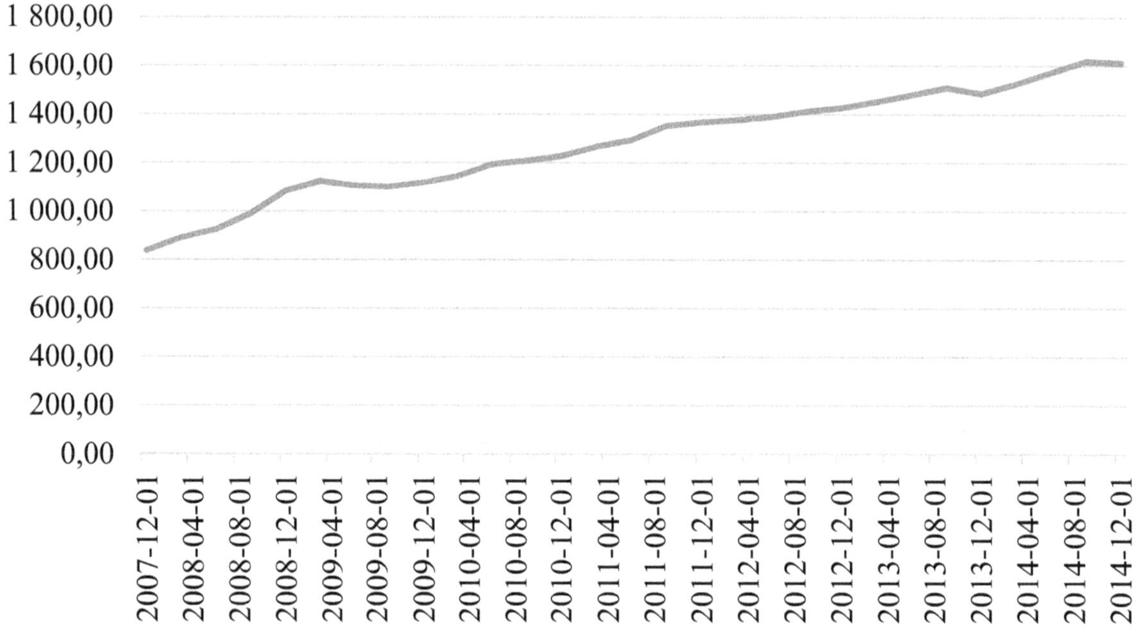

Source: Polish Financial Supervision Authority.

Figure 8: Loans for nonfinancial sector and housing loans of the Polish banking sector [in bn PLN]

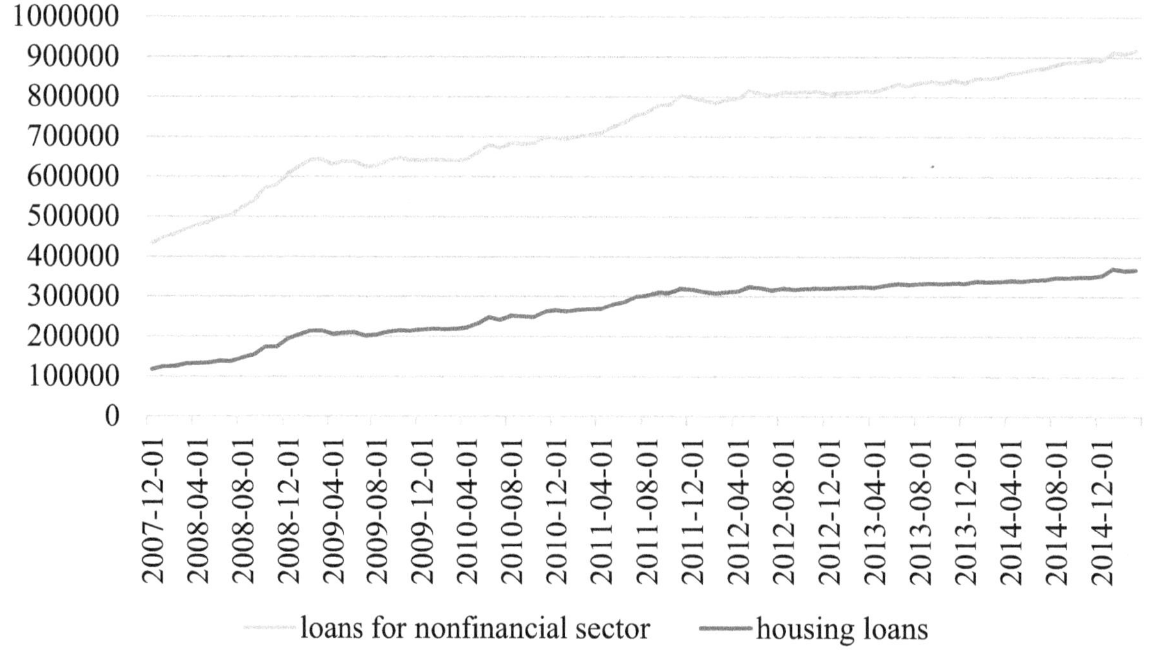

Source: National Bank of Poland.

Table 1: Summary Statistics on Bank Characteristics (quarterly data)

1. Data for all samples. Source: Author's calculations on the basis of NBP and CSO data.

	All Banks				Banks with Majority of Foreign capital			
	Mean	SD	Min	Max	Mean	SD	Min	Max
Observations	1634				1407			
Dependent Variables:								
Balance Sheet Data (for each bank i and quarter t)								
ROA Ratio(%)	-0.0246	0.20185	-2.86388	0.81991	-0.0279	0.2178	-2.8639	0.8199
ROE Ratio(%)	0.020114	0.20185	-4.731094	0.48876	0.01802	0.21173	-4.7311	0.4047
Independent Variables:								
Balance Sheet Data for Each Quarter t								
Market Structure								
Balance sheet data for each quarter t								
HHI	0.059575	0.002153	0.05599	0.06412	0.05957	0.00215	0.05599	0.06413
Log of Size of Banking Sector	27.68921	0.158017	27.3304	27.8992	27.6892	0.15798	27.3305	27.8992
Market Power								
Balance Sheet Data (for each bank i and quarter t)								
MP Ratio (%)	0.014539	0.027114	1.42e-1	0.16214	0.01236	0.022408	1.42e-1	0.16213
ML Ratio (%)	0.014539	0.027267	0	0.17197	0.01230	0.021413	0	0.15757
Log of Assets (size)	21.69478	2.438546	12.0695	26.0074	21.4947	2.492519	12.0694	25.7244
Bank-Specific Variables								
Balance Sheet Data (for each bank i and quarter t)								
Tier1 Ratio (%)	0.182737	0.165391	0.0054	3.14585	0.17869	0.161253	0.00538	3.14584
Total Loans/Assets (%)	0.777339	0.225674	0	1.47161	0.79578	0.227887	0	1.47160
Total Deposit / Assets (%)	0.346451	0.338144	0	2.52977	0.3411	0.330231	0	2.52977
FX Housing Loans / Assets (%)	0.085851	0.152134	0	0.65490	0.08676	0.1559	0	0.65490
Macroeconomics								
Data for Each Quarter t								
GDP	3.278261	1.75493	0.2	6.9	3.27721	1.75502	0.2	6.9
CPI	3.408696	1.02258	0.5	4.7	3.40863	1.02233	0.5	4.7

2. Data for Parent Banks (quarterly data). Source: Author's calculations on the basis of Bankscope and Eurostat data.

	Mean	SD	Min	Max
Observations	1257			
Independent Variables:				
parent Net Loans/Assets (%)	52.27033	23.10678	0.005	99.251
parent_Total_Capital_Ratio (%)	14.16492	5.224161	7	56.6
parent_ROA (%)	0.477185	0.866871	-6.36	8.958
parent_ROE (%)	6.934040	9.598102	-129.584	42.196
parent_Loan_Loss_Ratio (%)	2.734991	1.982544	0.021	12.44
parent_GDP	0.1164969	2.770955	-9.2	7.9

Note: This table provides summary statistics (mean and standard deviation for bank balance sheets data and macroeconomics data). Data are observed quarterly 2007Q4–2013Q2.

Table 2: Spearman's Rank Correlation Coefficients for all Variables

	ROA	MP	MPL	LA	HHI	LTA	DEP	Tier1	FXH	Size	GDP
ROA	1										
MP	0.0123	1									
MPL	0.0016	0.9797*	1								
LA	0.0183	0.9979*	0.9762*	1							
HHI	0.1035*	-0.0022	-0.02	0.0404	1						
LTA	0.1549*	-0.398*	-0.26*	-0.401*	-0.03	1					
DEP	-0.0742	0.2865*	0.1699*	0.2946*	0.0918	-0.752*	1				
Tier1	0.3373*	-0.516*	-0.569*	-0.508*	0.1660*	0.0307	0.0057	1			
FXH	-0.114*	0.7254*	0.7780*	0.7260*	0.0200	0.0844	-0.15*	-0.59*	1		
Size	0.1731*	0.0023	-0.017	0.0580	0.7752*	-0.0269	0.1115*	0.163*	0.0319	1	
GDP	-0.0110	-0.0112	-0.024	-0.0203	-0.193*	-0.0142	0.0253	0.0051	-0.006	-0.18*	1
CPI	0.0230	0.0050	-0.000	0.0104	-0.235*	0.0392	-0.016	-0.10*	0.0200	-0.003	0.4511*

Source: Author's calculations on the basis of NBP and CSO data. */ indicates significance at the 10% level.

Table 3: Spearman's Rank Correlation coefficients for Variables for Parent Banks

Data for Parent Banks	ROA_f	Parent Total_Capital_Ratio	Parent GDP	Parent ROA	Parent CTI	Parent NetLoans/Assets
ROA_f	1					
parent_Total_Capital_Ratio	0.1142*	1				
parent_GDP	0.0962*	0.2395*	1			
parent_ROA	-0.0381	0.0329	0.2724*	1		
parent_CTI	0.0268	0.2214*	0.0349	-0.5506*	1	
parent_NetLoans/Assets	-0.0056	-0.0734	-0.1615*	0.3737*	-0.6019*	1

Source: Author's calculations on the basis of Bankscope and Eurostat data. */ indicates significance at the 10% level.

Table 4: Empirical Results for Baseline Model

Variables	Estimate 1	Estimate 2	Estimate 3	Estimate 4	Estimate 5
L1.ROA	0.7359047***	0.7206154***	0.614576***	0.613027***	0.576682***
Market Structure					
HHI		-4.994079	0.9480281**	1.595917	-3.900502
Size	0.257475**	-	-	-	-
Market Power					
MP	-	11.18935*	-	-	-
ML	1.017407	-	-0.0036206	-	-
LA	-	-	-	0.058173***	0.053436***
Foreign Ownership					
FO	-0.0434477	0.0362766	-0.0019722	0.1282207**	0.372938**
$FO \times CRI$	-0.0138528	-0.004424	-0.010934*	-0.0012158*	-
$FO \times EuDCRI$	-	-	-		0.0204672*
Macroeconomics					
GDP	-	0.010461*	-	-	0.0028546**
CPI	-0.0016897	-	0.000649**	0.0496**	-
Bank-Specific Variables					
LTA	-	0.2678998***	-	0.058534**	0.2293875*
DTA	-0.0377529***	-	-0.0374935*	-	-
CAR	-	-	-0.001551***	-	-
FXHL	-	-1.508736	-	-0.780618**	-0.752328**
const	-6.80247*	-0.1833865	-0.0270513	-0.0270513	-1.35171
Hansen Test	0.974	0.824	0.961	0.974	0.661
AR(1)	0.097	0.326	0.084	0.061	0.048
AR(2)	0.196	0.426	0.196	0.343	0.330
Time Period	2007Q4-2013Q2				
Number of observations	1231	1231	1231	1231	1231
Number of gr.	86	86	86	86	86

Source: Author's calculations. ***/**/* indicate significance at the 1%/5%/10% levels respectively. All variables were seasonally adjusted. AR(1) – Arellano-Bond test for AR(1) in first differences. AR(2) – Arellano-Bond test for AR(2) in first differences. Hansen Test – the test for over-identifying restrictions in GMM dynamic model estimation.

Table 5: Effect of Situation in Parent Banks on Profitability of Foreign Banks in Poland

Time Period:	2007Q4-2013Q2	Global Financial Crisis	the Eurozone Crisis
	Estimate 1	Estimate 2	Estimate 3
L1.ROAf	0.8503813 ***	0.7812995***	0.7018803***
Macroeconomics – *Business Cycle in Parent Country*			
parent_GDP	0.009222*	0.008008**	0.0119602
Bank-Specific Variables *in Parent Country*			
parent_Total_Capital_Ratio	-0.0061702*	0.0137249	-0.0009048
parent_Net_Loas_to_Assets	0.0025147***	0.0121431***	0.002245
parent_ROA	0.0067614	0.0259831	0.0461367
const	-0.2597817	-0.4994779**	0.046968
Hansen Test	0.638	0.253	0.974
AR(1)	0.097	0.218	0.071
AR(2)	0.196	0.554	0.171
Time Period	2007Q4–2013Q2	2008Q1–2010Q1	2010Q2–2013Q2
Number of Observations	710	321	389
Number of groups	51	45	46

Source: Author's calculations. ***/**/* indicate significance at the 1%/5%/10% levels respectively. AR(1) – Arellano-Bond test for AR(1) in first differences. AR(2) – Arellano-Bond test for AR(2) in first differences. Hansen Test – the test for over-identifying restrictions in GMM dynamic model estimation.

2

The Wage Curve, Once More with Feeling: Bayesian Model Averaging of Heckit Models

Rolando Gonzales Martínez[*♣]

[♣]School of Business and Law, University of Agder, Norway

ABSTRACT: The sensitivity of the wage curve to sample-selection and model uncertainty was evaluated with Bayesian methods. More than 8000 Heckit wage curves were estimated using data from the 2017 household survey of Bolivia. After averaging the estimates with the posterior probability of each model being true, the wage curve elasticity in Bolivia is close to -0.01. This result suggests that in this country the wage curve is inelastic and does not follow the international statistical regularity of wage curves.

Keywords: model uncertainty, Bayesian model averaging, wage curve

Introduction

Blanchflower and Oswald (1990) proposed the existence of a micro-econometric association between wage level and local unemployment, portrayed as a downward-sloping "wage curve". Since evidence of a wage curve elasticity of -0.1 has been found in more than 40 countries, Blanchflower and Oswald (1995) and Blanchflower and Oswald (2005) conclude that the wage curve elasticity is an international empirical law of economics.

This paper estimates the wage curve for Bolivia and evaluates whether the elasticity of the wage curve in this country is sensitive to sample-selection and model specification: does the statistical regularity of $\hat{\theta} \approx -0.1$ changes if different control terms are included as

[*]Corresponding Author. Email: rolando.gonzales@uia.no

explanatory variables in wage curve models that adjust for the bias of considering only the working population? Bayesian model averaging was used to account for model uncertainty. Heckit models were used to account for the selection bias of estimating the wage curve with only the subpopulation of individuals that are working.

The contribution of this study to the literature is twofold. First, the estimations of wage curve elasticities have been mainly focused on developed or middle-income countries; less evidence seems to exist about the elasticity in lower and lower-middle income countries such as Bolivia. Thus, an estimation of the elasticity for Bolivia contributes to the accumulation of evidence about the value of the wage curve elasticity in developing economies with lower levels of income. Also, to the best of the author's knowledge, no study has yet considered simultaneously the effects of both sample selection and model uncertainty in estimating the wage curve elasticity with Bayesian methods.[1] Consequently, this study explores a potential methodological improvement in the econometric estimation of wage curve models.

The next section describes the methods used in the study. Section 2 presents the results and Section 3 concludes the study.

1 Bayesian Model Averaging of Heckit Models

Wage curve

The relationship between individual wages (w) and local unemployment (u), which Blanchflower and Oswald named the *wage curve*, is

$$\log w = \theta \log u + \text{controls}. \tag{1}$$

The elasticity coefficient θ has been found to be relatively constant across countries; its estimated value tends to be centered on -0.1. While the Blanchflower-Oswald finding is empirical, it is in line with the theoretical model of Campbell and Orszag (1998), who derived a dynamic efficiency wage model in which the wage elasticity with respect to employment is invariant to changes in productivity, payroll taxes, training subsidies and parameters in the training cost and quitting functions.

The empirical estimation of wage curve elasticity can be sensitive to the inclusion/ exclusion of explanatory terms, i.e., to model uncertainty. This model uncertainty implies that, for example, the elasticity estimated with a regression that takes into account formality of employment may be different from that estimated with a regression that does not take into account this variable. Moreover, some variables may affect the probability of working, but

[1]Hoddinott (1996) used a two-step approach to correct for sample selection bias in the wage equation, with data of Côte d'Ivoire, but does not treat the problem of model uncertainty.

not the wage level – for example, being the household head in the family unit – whereas other variables affect both the probability of working and the wage level – for example, education or professional experience. If different combinations of variables lead to different estimations of the wage curve models, then model uncertainty may be a problem that can affect the proper estimation of the wage dynamics.

Bayesian model averaging (BMA)

The uncertainty about which variables should be included as control terms in the calculation of the wage curve is equivalent to the uncertainty about which model specification is *correct* (in the sense of being suitable for explaining the wage-unemployment relationship) between the $\mathcal{M}_j$ $(j = 1, 2, \ldots, k)$ potential models. Bayesian model averaging (BMA) is an econometric technique that reveals the correct probability of a model specification, given the evidence provided by the data: in this case the probability of a wage curve model being correct given the data of the variables included as control terms in the sample-selection model. BMA was used *inter alia* to select the variables that affect firm default (Traczynski, 2017) or to explain the mixed evidence about the effects of oil rents on growth, which can be explained with model uncertainty according to Arin and Braunfels (2018). See Fragoso et al. (2018) for a survey of the applications of BMA.

The Bayesian posterior probability of a wage curve model $\mathcal{M}_j$ being true, conditional on a information set $\mathcal{D}$, is,

$$\mathbb{P}(\mathcal{M}_j|\mathcal{D}) = \frac{\mathscr{L}(\mathcal{D}|\mathcal{M}_j)\,\mathbb{P}(M_j)}{\sum_{i=1}^{K}\mathscr{L}(\mathcal{D}|\mathcal{M}_j)\,\mathbb{P}(M_j)} \tag{2}$$

where $\mathscr{L}(\mathcal{D}|\mathcal{M}_j)$ is the marginal likelihood for each model. Because the denominator of the previous equation is hard to calculate directly, it is common to compare two models, i and j, using the ratio of their posterior model probabilities,

$$\mathcal{P}_{ij} = \frac{\mathbb{P}(\mathcal{M}_i|\mathcal{D})}{\mathbb{P}(\mathcal{M}_j|\mathcal{D})} = \frac{\mathscr{L}(\mathcal{D}|\mathcal{M}_i)\,\mathbb{P}(\mathcal{M}_i)}{\mathscr{L}(\mathcal{D}|\mathcal{M}_j)\,\mathbb{P}(\mathcal{M}_j)}. \tag{3}$$

When equal prior weight is attached to each model, $\mathbb{P}(\mathcal{M}_i) = \mathbb{P}(\mathcal{M}_j)$, the posterior odds ratio $\mathcal{P}_{ij}$ becomes a ratio of marginal likelihoods, that is, the Bayes factor $\mathcal{B}_{ij}$,

$$\mathcal{B}_{ij} = \frac{\mathscr{L}(\mathcal{D}|\mathcal{M}_i)}{\mathscr{L}(\mathcal{D}|\mathcal{M}_j)}. \tag{4}$$

See, among others, Hoeting et al. (1999) or Koop (2003).

Asymptotic approximation to Bayes factors

Raftery (1995) proposed an asymptotic approximation to a Bayes factor $\mathcal{B}_{ij}$ through the Bayesian information criterion (BIC, see Schwarz (1978)),

$$\begin{aligned}
\mathcal{B}_{ij} &= \frac{\mathscr{L}(\mathcal{D}|\mathcal{M}_i)}{\mathscr{L}(\mathcal{D}|\mathcal{M}_j)}, && (5)\\
&= \left[\frac{\mathscr{L}(\mathcal{D}|\mathcal{M}_S)}{\mathscr{L}(\mathcal{D}|\mathcal{M}_i)}\right] / \left[\frac{\mathscr{L}(\mathcal{D}|\mathcal{M}_S)}{\mathscr{L}(\mathcal{D}|\mathcal{M}_j)}\right], && (6)\\
&= \mathcal{B}_{Si}/\mathcal{B}_{Sj}, && (7)\\
2\log\mathcal{B}_{ij} &= 2\log\mathcal{B}_{Si} - 2\log\mathcal{B}_{Sj} && (8)\\
&\approx BIC_i - BIC_j. && (9)
\end{aligned}$$

Thus, two models can be compared by taking the difference of their BIC values ($\mathcal{M}_S$ is a saturated model in which each data point is fit exactly). When the baseline model is the null model $\mathcal{M}_0$, with no independent variables, then $2\log\mathcal{B}_{ij} = 2\log\mathcal{B}_{0j}$, for $\mathcal{B}_{0j}$ the Bayes factor for the null model $\mathcal{M}_0$ against the model of interest $\mathcal{M}_j$.

Bayes factor approximation to posterior model probabilities

If $\mathcal{M}_0, \mathcal{M}_1, \ldots, \mathcal{M}_k$ models are being considered and each of $\mathcal{M}_1, \ldots, \mathcal{M}_k$ is compared in turn with $\mathcal{M}_0$, yielding Bayes factors $\mathcal{B}_{10}, \ldots, \mathcal{B}_{k0}$, then the posterior probability of $\mathcal{M}_j$, $j = 1, 2, \ldots, k$, is,

$$\mathbb{P}(\mathcal{M}_j|\mathcal{D}) = \frac{\alpha_j \mathcal{B}_{j0}}{\sum_{r=0}^{k} \alpha_r \mathcal{B}_{r0}}, \qquad (10)$$

where $\alpha_j = \mathbb{P}(\mathcal{M}_j)/\mathbb{P}(\mathcal{M}_0)$ is the prior odds for $\mathcal{M}_j$ against $\mathcal{M}_0$. A natural choice is taking all the prior odds α_j equal to 1. See Kass and Raftery (1995).

BMA estimator of the wage curve elasticity

The BMA estimator of the wage curve elasticity $\hat{\theta}_{BMA}$ is obtained by adding the estimates of θ_j in each j-model, weighted by the posterior probability $\mathbb{P}(\mathcal{M}_j|\mathcal{D})$ of each model being correct,

$$\begin{aligned}
\hat{\theta}_{BMA} &:= \mathbb{E}(\theta|\mathcal{D}, \theta \neq 0), \\
&\propto \sum\sum\nolimits_{\mathcal{A}_\theta} \mathbb{E}(\theta|\mathcal{D}, \mathcal{M}_j)\, \mathbb{P}(\mathcal{M}_j|\mathcal{D}).
\end{aligned} \qquad (11)$$

Heckman correction

Arango et al. (2010) used the Heckman (1979) correction to account for the selection bias due to estimating the wage determinants from the subpopulation of individuals who work, who are selected non-randomly and may differ from the subpopulation who do not work. The Heckman correction implies estimating a bi-equational sample selection model (henceforth, Heckit model)

$$\begin{cases} z_i^* := \mathbb{P}\left(working = 1|\mathbf{x}_j\right) = \Phi(\mathbf{x}_j'\beta_j), \\ \log w_i|z_i^* = \theta \log u + \mathbf{x}_j'\beta_j + \beta_\lambda \hat{\lambda}_i(\mathbf{x}_j'\beta_j|\sigma_2) + \nu_i, \end{cases} \tag{12}$$

where the first equation is a selection equation (a probit model) to estimate the probability of working and the second equation is the traditional wage curve, plus a correction term from the first equation, i.e., the inverse Mills ratio $\lambda_i(\mathbf{x}_j'\beta_j|\sigma_2) = \phi(-(\mathbf{x}_j'\beta_j|\sigma_2))/(1 - \Phi(-(\mathbf{x}_j'\beta_j|\sigma_2)))$. See, *inter alia*, Puhani (2000) or Cameron and Trivedi (2005). In the term $\mathbf{x}_j'\beta_j$, $\mathbf{x}_j'$ is a vector containing the $1, 2, ..., j$-control covariates and β_j are the parameters that measured the effect of each covariate on the probability of working and/or the wage level.

Model space of Heckit wage curves

The possible combinations of k-explanatory variables in a model is defined by the power set $\wp(k)$,

$$\wp(k) = \left\{\{\emptyset\}, \{x_1\}, \{x_2\}, \ldots, \{x_k\}, \{x_1, x_2\}, \ldots, \{x_1, \ldots, x_k\}\right\}. \tag{13}$$

The cardinality of $\wp(k)$ gives the total combinations of models that have to be estimated,

$$|\wp(k)| = \sum_{p=0}^{k} \binom{k}{p} = 2^k, \tag{14}$$

with $\binom{k}{p}$ the Binominal coefficient $\binom{k}{p} = \frac{k!}{p!(k-p)!}$. In the case of Heckit models, the $x_1, \ldots, x_k$ control variables can enter as explanatory terms in the selection equation, the outcome equation (the wage curve), or both. If the same variables are considered in the selection equation and the outcome equation, a total of $2^k\left(2^k - 1\right)$ Heckit wage curves need to be estimated.

2 Results

The 2017 household survey of Bolivia was used to estimate the country's wage curve elasticity. Bolivia was used as a case study because estimates of the wage curve elasticity were needed for the Computable General Equilibrium Model MAMS (*Maquette for Millennium Development Goals Simulation*) of the United Nations Development Program and the United Nations

Department of Economic and Social Affairs. See Lofgren and Diaz-Bonilla (2010) for details.[2] Geographical clustering was performed at the municipal level, thus, local unemployment is equal to municipal unemployment rates. The selection equation and the outcome equation were jointly estimated with pseudo-maximum likelihood, using expansion factors, because inconsistent estimates will result from two-stage least squares applied to the survey data.

Six control terms were considered as possible wage determinants in the outcome equation, and seven covariates were considered as possible explanatory terms of the probability of working in the selection equation of the Heckit models. In the case of the outcome equation, the possible wage determinants considered were: (1) education (measured with years of schooling), (2) experience (measured as the squared years of the individual's years of tenure in a business), (3) age, (4) gender, (5) a dummy variable equal to one if the person works in a formal business and (6) a dummy variable equal to one if the person is indigenous. For the selection equation (the probability of working), the following variables were considered as potential control covariates: (1) education, (2) age, (3) gender, (4) a dummy variable equal to one for formal businesses, (5) a dummy variable equal to one if the person is indigenous, (6) the number of family members and (7) a dummy variable equal to one if the person is a household head. These variables were selected based on data availability and also following previous studies such as Baltagi et al. (2017), who estimated the wage curve for Brazil and considered as control covariates the age of the individual, gender, race, education, the individual's years of tenure at a firm and formality of employment, among other variables available for Brazil. In Bolivia, the level of education and experience have a direct effect on the salary and on the probability of working; also, it is expected that differences in salary may exist for different age categories and between males and females. Age and gender also may affect the probability of working. Due to the high proportion of informal businesses in Bolivia, a binary variable equal to one if the worker's employment is a formal business was included as a potential control covariate for the outcome and selection equation. Also, to account for possible ethnic discrimination in salary and/or job allocation, a dummy variable equal to one was included for indigenous individuals in both equations of the Heckit models. Finally, the number of family members variable and an indicator variable for household-head individuals were included in the selection equation because higher incentives for working may exist if a person is a household-head and/or is responsible for a greater number of people in a family unit.[3] A total of $2^6(2^7 - 1) = 8128$ Heckit models were estimated with the

[2]The estimates for the MAMS model were originally obtained with data from the 2006 household survey of Bolivia, because the base year of the MAMS model was 2006. Based on the reviewer's suggestion, we updated the estimation with data from the more recent survey and, thus, this section presents results based on data from the 2017 household survey of Bolivia. In the results for 2006, the estimate of the wage curve elasticity for Bolivia was equal to 7%.

[3]A similar variable was included by Baltagi et al. (2017) as a control covariate, household type, where the response categories were couples without children, couples with children, single mother with children, and

combinations of these control terms.

Figures 1 and 2 show the results of the estimation. In Bolivia, when sample selection and uncertainty in control covariates are considered, the estimation of the wage curve elasticity is bi-modal in a range between −0.05 and 0.06. The posterior probability of the Heckit models being true is higher for negative wage curve elasticities (Figure 1), and the concentration of the Bayes factors (i.e., the model evidence) suggests that more support exists for estimations of the wage curve elasticity between −0.02 and −0.04 (Figure 2). This result is theoretically expected if higher unemployment leads to a fall in the level of wages.

Adding the estimates of θ_j in each j-model, weighted by the posterior probability of each model being correct, allows us to obtain a point estimate of the wage curve elasticity ($\hat{\theta}_{BMA}$) equal to −0.0104. This value is closer to zero than the expected statistical regularity of −0.1 reported for developing countries and suggests that the wage curve in Bolivia is inelastic.

Finally, Table 1 shows the posterior inclusion probability of the control covariates included in the Heckit models. The estimates suggest that education and gender are particularly relevant for determining the wage level, whereas age, formal employment, and being a household-head affect the probability of working.

3 Conclusion

Taking into account selection bias and model uncertainty, the estimated wage curve elasticity for Bolivia in 2017 was equal to −0.0104. This estimate (without regard to its sign) is below the absolute value of −0.1 reported as a statistical regularity of the wage curve for developing countries, and is also below the unbiased estimation of Nijkamp and Poot (2005), who performed a meta-analysis of 208 wage/unemployment elasticities from the literature to correct for publication bias and found a value of −0.07 for the wage curve elasticity.[4]

The results of the wage curve estimation for Bolivia do not provide empirical support for the burgeoning literature about non-competitive features of the job market and further suggest that the wage curve in Bolivia is inelastic. An explanation for this finding may be related to the exponential increases in the minimum wage of Bolivia since 2006, which are coupled with low levels of formal unemployment (Figure 3). In 2006, the minimum monthly wage of Bolivia was USD 62, while in 2017 the minimum wage reached USD 287, which corresponds to an increase of 363%. The increase in the minimum wage in Bolivia could have led to a reduction in the amount of labor that firms demand, increasing unemployment

---

other.

[4]The estimate for Bolivia in 2017 is also different from those obtained for other Latin American development countries by Galiani (2000), Garcia and Granados (2005), Lugo (2006), Arango et al. (2010), Cruces and Ham (2010), Ines Terra et al. (2010), Ramos et al. (2010), Carvalho Filho and Estevão (2012), Martinez (2012) or Anaya and Rodríguez-Villamil (2012).

as labor becomes more expensive. At the same time, the higher minimum wage may have stimulated the supply of labor, thereby decreasing unemployment. This is in line with Gregg et al. (2014), who suggest that in a case of wage inflexibility, real wages do not seem to respond to the varying local labor market conditions. A similar result was also put forward recently by Daouli et al. (2017), who found only a short-lived wage curve elasticity in Greece during a time of reduction in the national minimum wage and a restructuring of the collective bargaining regime in the labor market.

Future studies can employ dynamic wage curves to explore if the inflexibility of the labor market of Bolivia was indeed caused by the changes in the minimum wage. Because in Bolivia the changes in the national minimum wage were related to a change in the government, a quasi-experimental design can be used to compare models before and after the change of government in 2006. If model uncertainty is considered during the quasi-experimental estimation, Bayesian methods can be employed to provide a comprehensive and coherent framework for comparing non-nested models (Hepple, 2004).

References

Anaya, M. C. B. and Rodríguez-Villamil, C. G. (2012). An estimation of the wage curve for Uruguay. *Revista Cuadernos de Economía*, 31(36).

Arango, L. E., Obando, N., and Posada, C. E. (2010). Sensibilidad de los salarios al desempleo regional en Colombia: nuevas estimaciones de la curva de salarios. Borradores de Economía 590, Banco de la República de Colombia.

Arin, K. P. and Braunfels, E. (2018). The resource curse revisited: A Bayesian model averaging approach. *Energy Economics*, 70:170 – 178.

Baltagi, B. H., Rokicki, B., and Souza, K. B. (2017). The Brazilian wage curve: new evidence from the National Household Survey. *Empirical Economics*, 53(1):267 – 286.

Blanchflower, D. G. and Oswald, A. J. (1990). The Wage Curve. *Scandinavian Journal of Economics*, 92(2):215 – 235.

Blanchflower, D. G. and Oswald, A. J. (1995). An Introduction to the Wage Curve. *Journal of Economic Perspectives*, 9(3):153 – 167.

Blanchflower, D. G. and Oswald, A. J. (2005). The Wage Curve Reloaded. NBER Working Papers 11338, National Bureau of Economic Research, Inc.

Cameron, A. C. and Trivedi, P. K. (2005). *Microeconometrics: Methods and Applications*. Cambridge University Press.

Campbell, C. and Orszag, J. (1998). A model of the wage curve. *Economics Letters*, 59(1):119 – 125.

Carvalho Filho, I. E. and Estevão, M. M. (2012). Institutions, Informality, and Wage Flexibility: Evidence from Brazil. IMF Working Papers 12/84, International Monetary Fund.

Cruces, G. A. and Ham, A. (2010). La flexibilidad laboral en América Latina: las reformas pasadas y las perspectivas futuras. Documentos de Proyectos 291, Naciones Unidas Comisión Económica para América Latina y el Caribe (CEPAL).

Daouli, J., Demoussis, M., Giannakopoulos, N., and Laliotis, I. (2017). The wage curve before and during the Greek economic crisis. *Empirical Economics*, 52(1):59 – 77.

Fragoso, T. M., Bertoli, W., and Louzada, F. (2018). Bayesian Model Averaging: A Systematic Review and Conceptual Classification. *International Statistical Review*, 86(1):1 – 28.

Galiani, S. (2000). Wage determination in Argentina: An econometric analysis with methodology discussion. Technical report, Departamento de Economía - Universidad Nacional de La Plata.

Garcia, P. and Granados, P. (2005). La curva de salarios en Chile. Documentos de trabajo 320, Banco Central de Chile.

Gregg, P., Machin, S., and FernÃ¡ndez-Salgado, M. (2014). Real Wages and Unemployment in the Big Squeeze. *The Economic Journal*, 124(576):408 – 432.

Heckman, J. J. (1979). Sample Selection Bias as a Specification Error. *Econometrica*, 47(1):153 – 161.

Hepple, L. W. (2004). *Advances in Econometrics*, volume Volume 18, chapter Bayesian Model Choice in Spatial Econometrics, pages 101 – 126. JAI.

Hoddinott, J. (1996). Wages and Unemployment in an Urban African Labour Market. *The Economic Journal*, 106(439):1610 – 1626.

Hoeting, J. A., Madigan, D., Raftery, A. E., and Volinsky, C. T. (1999). Bayesian model averaging: a tutorial (with comments by M. Clyde, David Draper and E. I. George, and a rejoinder by the authors. *Statistical Science*, 14(4):382 – 417.

Ines Terra, M., Bucheli, M., Silvia, L., and Carmen, E. (2010). Poverty assessment from integration and employment policies in Uruguay: A CGE modelling analysis. In De Miguel, C., Duran Lima, Jose amd Giordano, P., Guzman, J., Schuschny, A., and Masakazu, W., editors, *Modeling Public Policies in Latin America and the Caribbean*, pages 175 – 273. United Nations Publications - United Nations Economic Commission for Latin America and the Caribbean and Inter-American Development Bank.

Kass, R. E. and Raftery, A. E. (1995). Bayes Factors. *Journal of the American Statistical Association*, 90(430):773 – 795.

Koop, G. (2003). *Bayesian Econometrics*. Jhon Wiley & Sons Inc.

Lofgren, H. and Diaz-Bonilla, C. (2010). MAMS: An Economywide Model for Analysis of MDG Country Strategies: Technical Documentation. Mimeo, World Bank.

Lugo, D. C. (2006). Curva salarial: una aplicación para el caso de México, 1993-2002. *Estudios Económicos*, 21(2):233 – 273.

Martinez, I. (2012). El Rol del Desempleo en la Determinación del Salario: Evidencia Empírica para Lima Metropolitana. Informe final de proyecto breve - concurso de investigación CIES, CIES.

Nijkamp, P. and Poot, J. (2005). The Last Word on the Wage Curve? *Journal of Economic Surveys*, 19(3):421 – 450.

Puhani, P. (2000). The Heckman Correction for Sample Selection and Its Critique. *Journal of Economic Surveys*, 14(1):53 – 68.

Raftery, A. E. (1995). Bayesian Model Selection in Social Research. *Sociological Methodology*, 25:111 – 163.

Ramos, R., Duque, J. C., and Surinach, J. (2010). Is the wage curve formal or informal? Evidence for Colombia. *Economics Letters*, 109(2):63 – 65.

Schwarz, G. (1978). Estimating the Dimension of a Model. *The Annals of Statistics*, 6(2):461 – 464.

Traczynski, J. (2017). Firm Default Prediction: A Bayesian Model-Averaging Approach. *Journal of Financial and Quantitative Analysis*, 52(03):1211 – 1245.

Figure 1: Histogram of the wage curve estimations and posterior probability $\mathbb{P}(\mathcal{M}_j|\mathcal{D})$ of a Heckit wage curve being true

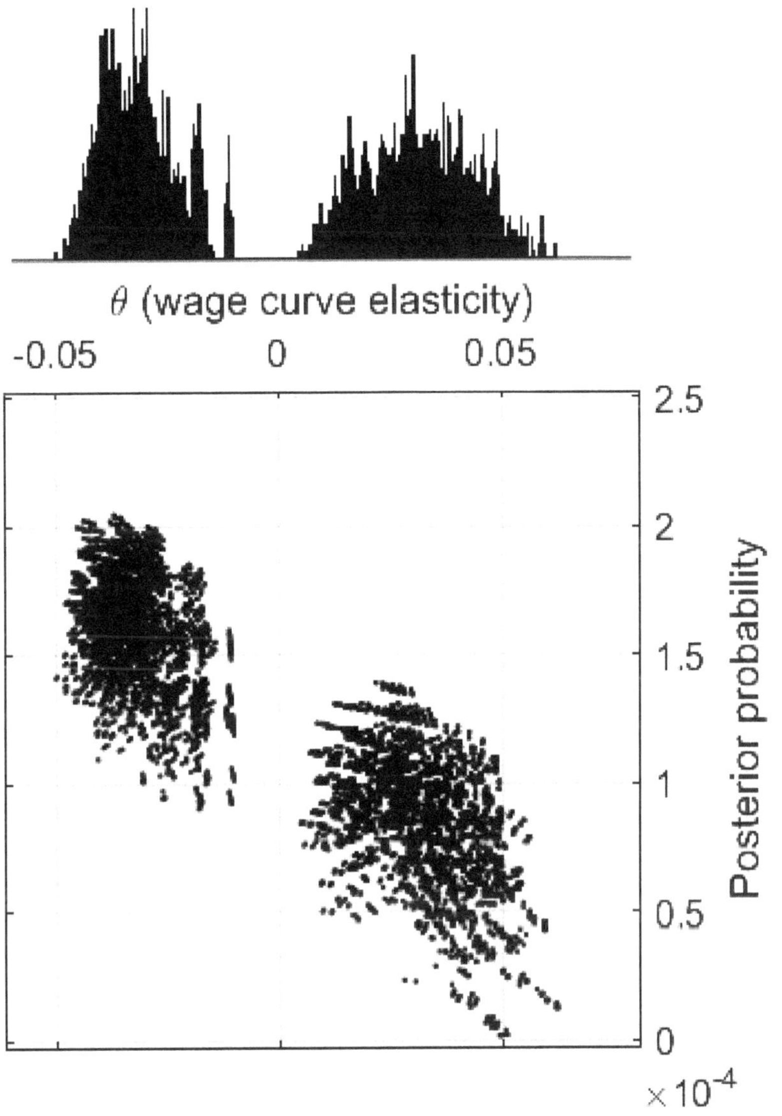

Figure 2: Bayes factors and wage curve elasticity

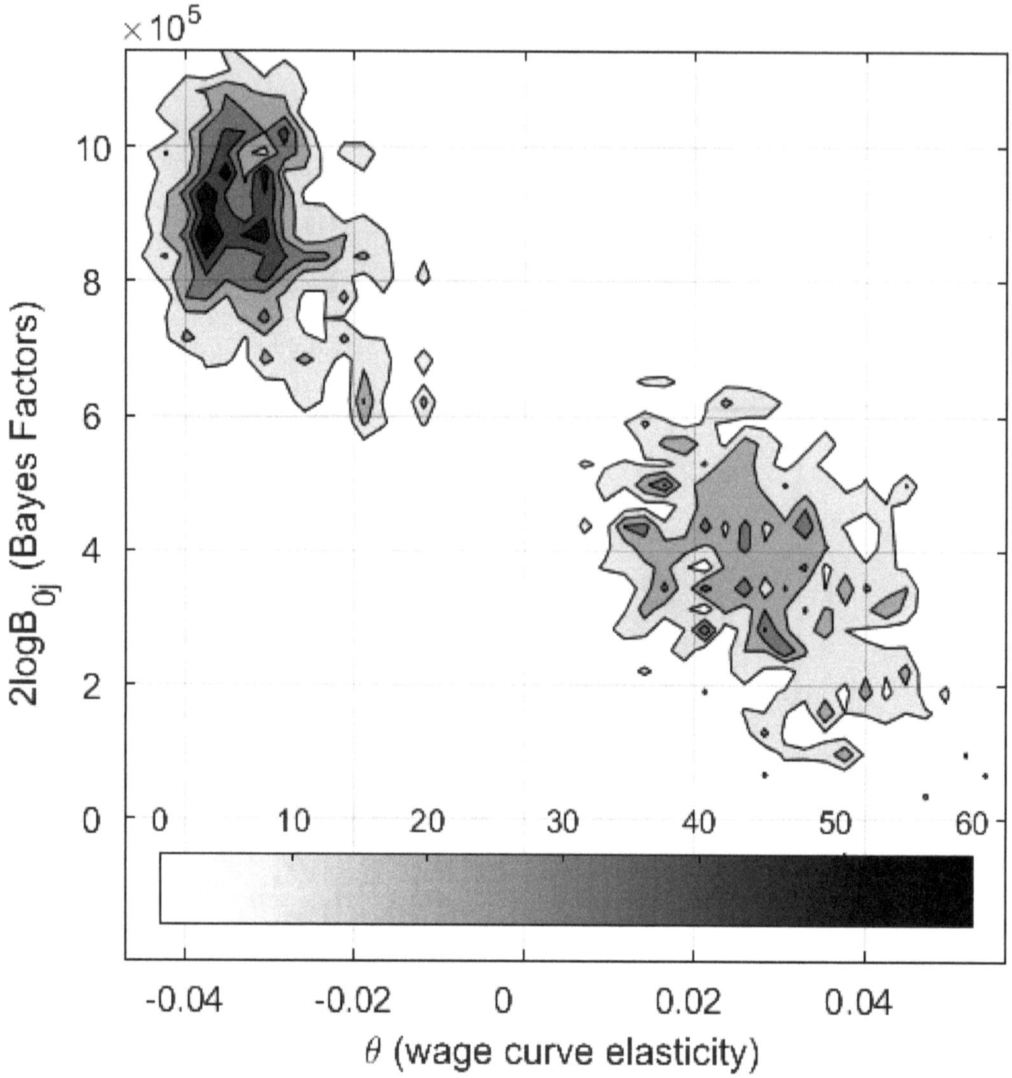

Figure 3: Minimum wage and unemployment rate in Bolivia
Source: World Bank and UDAPE

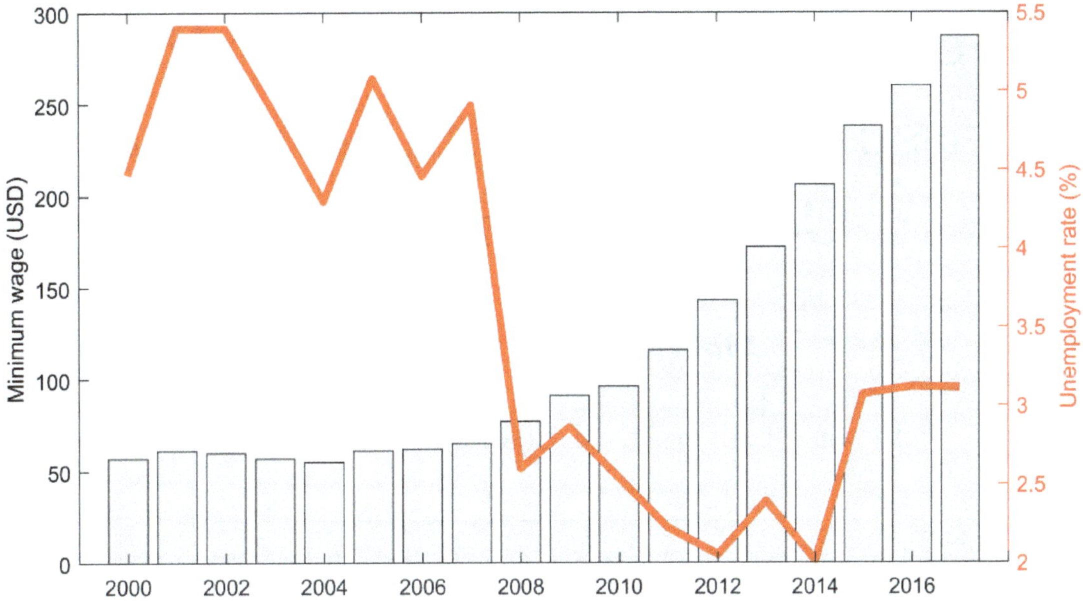

Table 1: Posterior inclusion probability of control covariates

Control	Wage curve equation	Selection equation
Education	0.649	0.506
Experience	0.511	–
Age	0.506	0.550
Gender	0.546	0.506
Fomal employment	0.523	0.537
Indigenous	0.511	0.506
Family members	–	0.506
Household-head	–	0.547

3

Neural Networks in Credit Risk Classification of Companies in the Construction Sector

Aleksandra Wójcicka[*♣]

♣ Poznań University of Economics and Business

ABSTRACT: The financial sector (banks, financial institutions, etc.) is the sector most exposed to financial and credit risk, as one of the basic objectives of banks' activity (as a specific enterprise) is granting credit and loans. Because credit risk is one of the problems constantly faced by banks, identification of potential good and bad customers is an extremely important task. This paper investigates the use of different structures of neural networks to support the preliminary credit risk decision-making process. The results are compared among the models and juxtaposed with real-world data. Moreover, different sets and subsets of entry data are analyzed to find the best input variables (financial ratios).

Keywords: credit risk, neural networks, financial ratios, credit risk decision-making process

Introduction

The history of bank systems indicates that the main reasons for decreasing potential profits or capital and the occurrence of financial difficulties are an inefficient credit granting policy, faulty credit procedures of credit norms and regulations, and insufficient collateral for loans. In a market economy, risk is a common phenomenon. However, it affects various economic

[*]Corresponding Author. Email: aleksandra.wojcicka@ue.poznan.pl

branches, and decisions made within them, to a different extent. Taking into consideration that the banking sector has gone through a tremendous evolution and that banks currently offer an impressive array of products, identifying potential 'good' and 'bad' customers is an extremely important task. The reduction of loans granted to companies of questionable credibility can significantly influence and improve banks' performance. Credit risk is broadly conceived as the probability of non-repayment of bank financial resources granted to debtors (enterprises). Every decision based on credit risk should be preceded by close scrutiny. In that analysis, the most important element for categorizing debtors as 'good' or 'bad' is a prior identification of factors that affect the condition of companies. Those factors are traditionally financial ratios.

One must keep in mind that banks constitute the link between borrowers and lenders and that the money granted to borrowers is, in fact, the money obtained by a bank from the deposits made by natural and legal persons. Accordingly, an even bigger responsibility rests with the banks to correctly choose borrowers whose creditworthiness is high. To achieve this goal, banks use different methods to assess customers' creditworthiness (i.e., the probability that the customer will pay back the full amount of the loan and all other contractual payments at a predetermined time). Usually, these methods are credit scoring methods combined with financial ratio analysis and models of discriminant analysis, the objective of which is to assign the potential debtor to one of two groups: 'good' (i.e., likely to repay money loaned) or 'bad' (i.e., unlikely to repay money loaned) customer. However, although these methods are being actively developed to make them more accurate, very often they are still too static when used alone and do not follow the latest trends in a rapidly changing economy and in market conditions, or they do not distinguish among some subtle economic or behavioral factors. Moreover, new approach credit-risk models (i.e., probability of default, standard, or reduced structural models) often appear to be too complex or too dependent on the market. Their complexity and the amount of data needed for their implementation is often a fundamental problem and a barrier to their efficient use on a larger scale.

Currently, risk analysis in the financial markets is one of the most important factors for investment analysis and new methods must be very flexible and adaptive to the changing realities of the market economy. Therefore, a growing interest in solutions such as artificial neural networks and their application to credit risk assessment is noticeable; even the smallest improvement in accuracy is a significant accomplishment. The idea of neural networks as computing processors has its origin in the way the human brain analyzes obtained data. Neural networks in the scientific literature are defined as *'a computing system made up of a number of simple, highly interconnected processing elements, which process information by their dynamic state response to external inputs'* (Hecht-Nielsen, 1988). It is important to stress that because the main characteristic of neural networks is adaptation, the above-mentioned problems are rarely a concern with these methods. Neural networks can be used in such tasks as pattern recognition, classification, and time series forecasting. They have a built-in capacity to adapt their synaptic weights to changes in the surrounding environment. In particular, a neural network trained to operate in a specific environment can be easily retrained to deal with minor changes in the operating environmental conditions (Haykin, 2011) – the biggest advantage of the method.

The present study is an applied study that uses a descriptive research strategy. A neural network (often referred to as an artificial neural network) technique is used. The main objective of the study is to deliver a useful tool (a set of financial ratios) to business practitioners (e.g., bank analysts), particularly those working in risk departments. This is achieved by meeting two interdependent goals. First, to create a novel set of financial ratios by identifying the most and least important determinants of customers' solvency in the construction sector and, consequently, of their probability of default. Second, to compare the results achieved with two different, commonly used types of neural network and their predictive abilities, on the basis of historical data.

1 Overview of neural networks' use in credit risk evaluation

Neural networks are used world-wide to analyse the scope of credit risks. Atiya (2001) presents an empirical approach based on the relationship between default and the characteristics of a firm learned from the data. The results indicated the superiority of neural networks over other techniques, as well as the need for improvements in training methods, architecture selection, and input, with the latter prompting the author to search for a better method of selection of independent input. Baesens et al. (2003) investigated how neural networks contribute to helping credit risk managers explain why a particular applicant is classified as either bad or good. They concluded that neural network rule extraction and decision trees are effective and powerful management tools, allowing the construction of advanced and user-friendly decision support systems for credit risk evaluation.

Neural networks are particularly suited to analyzing and interpreting complex and often obscure phenomena and processes (Pacelli and Azzollini, 2011). However, as with other methods, neural networks have their strengths and weaknesses, for instance, the fact that it is unknown to the researcher what kind of links and interdependencies are included in the hidden layers (Pacelli and Azzollini, 2011). Nonetheless, research shows that despite the weaknesses, neural networks perform well when data are noisy or incorrect (Angelini et al., 2008; di Tollo, 2006).

Despite much research proving neural networks' usefulness, there are also many criticisms of neural networks. The main disadvantage, which is often brought up in the literature, is the fact that a neural network acts as a 'black box.' Much information is inaccessible to the researcher. Various authors (e.g., Huang et al., 2004; Karaa and Krichene, 2012; Khemakhem and Boujelbene, 2015; Linder et al., 2004; Ogwueleka et al., 2015) have described neural networks and compared them with other modelling techniques, such as decision trees, discriminant analysis, and regression functions, also providing some opinions and critiques of the approach

As described above, many studies have been dedicated to the implementation of neural network analytical methods in business. However, very little has been said about the influence of economic sector on companies' performance and, consequently, on neural network performance and subsequent bank loan-granting decisions and potential losses due to the wrong classification of entities as good or bad credit risks. Furthermore, it is visible in companies' financial statements that the line of business has an effect on the statements' structures and figures. All the above gave the author an incentive to investigate the topic further (see also Wójcicka, 2016a,b). Therefore, choosing the unique set of variables most appropriate for a particular (industrial) sector and implementing it in a neural network is the key objective of this paper.

2 Methods

The analysis conducted for this research was based on the financial reports of Polish companies in the construction sector and the credit risk analysis method applied by one of the banks operating in the Polish market. The choice of the construction sector was dictated by the fact that companies in this sector suffered tremendously from the after-effects of the economic crisis which started in 2007-2008. Many construction sector companies (e.g., developers, main contractors, and sub-contractors) declared bankruptcy. In the tested period, defaults in the construction sector happened more often than in other sectors.[1] Hence, this is one of the sectors which caused banks a lot of trouble. Additionally, no matter how unfavorable the situation was for the banks, it also delivered much valuable data for research (e.g., data on defaulted companies or companies in distress while their situation was rapidly deteriorating soon after the positive decision of the bank). Summing up, it is beneficial to recognize the factors which can indicate future problems in the construction sector.

The tool used in the analysis was Statistica Automated Neural Networks (SANN) and the two neural network structures presented in the paper are multilayer perceptron (MLP) and radial basis function (RBF). MLP neural networks are more powerful than the single-layer

[1] The comparison of default frequency was run for the construction, trade, and industrial sectors.

models which construct linear decision boundaries. MLP can be trained as a discriminative model to yield class posteriors. There are a variety of non-linear activation functions that may be used (Migdał Najman and Najman, 2013; Osowski, 2006; Ripley, 2009; Wantoch-Rekowski, 2003; Witkowska, 2002). The RBF (multilayer and feed-forward) is often used for strict interpolation in multi-dimensional space (Osowski, 2006; Ripley, 2009; Skubalska-Rafajłowicz, 2011; Wantoch-Rekowski, 2003).[2] The main differences and similarities between the two types of neural network architecture are presented in Table 1.

The data used in the analysis were obtained from a bank operating in the Polish market, from the Commercial Court in Poznań,[3] , and from NOTORIA SERWIS (a financial data vendor in Poland). The data cover a period of six years (2009-2014). The sample contains financial statements of construction companies, which include a balance sheet, an income statement, a cash flow statement, and a statement of changes in equity. All the data (regardless of source) were verified to ensure comparability. The verification involved establishing whether the above-listed financial statements provided the data needed to calculate the 25 financial ratios (independent variables) shown in Table 2. If the statements were incomplete, then the company was rejected from the sample.

This initial set of 25 ratios was used as the entry data in the neural network learning process. Twenty neural networks, each based on one of the two chosen artificial neural network models – MLP and RBF – were estimated to determine the value of the dependent variable for the analyzed company. Then, the iterative process of reducing the set of entry data began. The first step was to calculate the correlation between each pair of ratios. Next, the pair with the highest correlation was chosen. From that pair, the ratio with the highest average level of absolute value of correlation with the remaining ratios was rejected. The resulting set of 24 ratios was then input as entry data into the neural network learning system. The same process was used to reject another ratio and that set of 23 ratios applied as entry data for the neural network. This process was continued until the results of the neural networks indicated overfitting, at which point it was stopped. Although the process of ratio selection might seem independent from the neural networks, it is not entirely so because the outcome of the neural networks' performance is its stopping point.

The dependent variable identified the company as 'good' or 'bad.' A 'bad' enterprise was defined as one that either had been declared bankrupt or where a bankruptcy petition had been filed. In turn, a company that had not been declared bankrupt and where no petition for bankruptcy had been filed was defined as a 'good' company.

The data was applied to the two chosen artificial neural network models to estimate whether the analyzed company was 'good' or 'bad.' The whole sample of unsound companies

[2]https://documents.software.dell.com/statistics/textbook/neural-networks#multilayera.

[3]The names of the companies cannot be revealed due to confidentiality restrictions.

included 408 entities. However, some financial statements were incomplete and thus made it impossible to calculate all necessary ratios. Also, to be included in the analysis, the company's financial statements had to be accessible for a minimum of three years.[4] There were 88 companies that failed to satisfy at least one of the requirements and were removed from the analysis.

For each unsound company included in the analysis, a similar healthy company was added (for a total of 320 healthy companies). Similarity was assessed in terms of belonging to the same branch of the construction sector, value of total assets, and legal form. The entire dataset – a whole, homogenous, and balanced sample of 640 companies – was divided into three groups in the following manner:

a. a learning group (80% of dataset);
b. a testing group (10% of dataset); and
c. a validation/holdout group (10% of dataset).[5]

The learning and testing groups consist of the data from the court and NOTORIA SERWIS; however, the validation group is the mix of financial statements of companies from the bank and court data, providing data of good and bad companies, respectively.

For building the models, different variants of hidden layers were used. The number of nodes in a hidden layer is selected automatically. In the output layer, the dependent variable is the category of a customer (good or bad).

3 Findings

In the process of ratio selection, the rejected ratios were as follows (in order of rejection): quick ratio, stock turnover ratio, gross profit margin ratio, equity debt ratio, short-term investments turnover ratio, equity profitability ratio, sale profitability ratio, self-financing ratio, operating ratio, sales dynamics, receivables to liabilities ratio, costs increase ratio, long-term debt ratio, debt/EBITDA, EBITDA/financial expenses, current assets turnover ratio, and operating activity profitability ratio.

It appears that the best set of ratios for MLP consists of eight following ratios (in order of importance based on the SANN sensitivity analysis): current ratio, receivables ratio, net profit margin ratio, financial surplus rate, total debt ratio, costs level ratio, assets profitability ratio, and financial leverage. However, in two instances, the MLP neural network which performed better than the other analysed MLP networks consisted of nine ratios (the additional ratio being operating activity profitability ratio).

[4]The bank requires financial statements of a company for a three-year period to assess the credit risk.

[5]A testing group tests the quality of the neural network during the learning process. The validation dataset is a separate dataset, which is not used during the learning process.

In the case of RBF, the neural network includes a slightly larger set of ten ratios, which includes the operating activity profitability and current assets turnover ratios in addition to the above eight ratios. In this case, there also were some notable exceptions in a number of ratios among the best-performing neural networks. In one case, the set was enlarged by the EBITDA/financial expenses ratio and in another, the current assets turnover ratio was removed from the set of ten.

Each learning process included 20 neural networks for each subset of ratios. The results shown in Tables 3 and 4 present the five highest quality (or best) neural networks for each model structure.[6] The networks are presented in the following way: X-Y-Z, where X equals the number of inputs, Y the number of neurons in the hidden units, and Z the number of outputs (taking values: 'healthy' and 'unsound', respectively).

In terms of the results in a learning group, it is certainly the MLP 8-11-2 network which performs the best, reaching 96.67% accuracy, although the level of accuracy of the best RBF network (10-13-2) is quite similar at 95.00%. The range in learning accuracy levels for the group of the five best networks is wider in the case of MLP (from 81.67 to 96.67, or 15 points) than in the case of RBF (from 85.0 to 95.0, or 10 points). This indicates a certain instability in the results. However, the best accuracy in the testing groups is the same (91.67%) in both types of neural network model.

The next step was to compare the performance of the best neural network of each type (i.e., MLP 8-11-2 and RBF 10-13-2) with the final set of selected ratios on a separate set of input data (the validation group) from the construction sector. This step was taken because the economy and companies' performances are undergoing a constant process of change. Very rarely, it might happen that a company would be evaluated more than once on the same set of data or that two companies were exactly the same when it came to their performance, although in general, even if a company were to have tried several times to apply for financial means from the same bank, this would probably have involved financial statements from various time periods. Therefore, the validation group used an input dataset that was separate from the learning and testing group, although included analogous financial ratios as indicated by the best neural networks. This multi-step procedure was designed to imitate a real process of credit risk validation in a bank wherein we input new data (i.e., the financial ratios of a new applicant/company) into a neural network (tool) that has already been trained in advance.

This approach proved that both types of neural network show good results; however,

[6] The term 'quality' refers to a combined measure (e.g., the expected loss from combined type I and II errors) showing the overall performance of the chosen network. The measure is calculated based on the results of the 'confusion matrix' which shows both the number of correctly classified and incorrectly classified cases per category (see more at http://documentation.statsoft.com/STATISTICAHelp.aspx?path=SANN/Ratios/SANNExamples_HRatio).

MLP performs slightly better than RBF. This was assumed on the basis of the degree of type II error, which means the degree to which banks fail to identify bad customers and instead falsely identify them as good customers, therefore accepting their applications and granting financing, which is likely to lead to a bad customer's insolvency and bankruptcy. Table 5 presents the results of type II error for both types of tested neural network.

As type II error is considered to be more significant for the banks, the results in table 5 justify the belief that MLP networks would be preferred to RBF for credit risk assessment, as the level of that type of error is lower in the case of this neural network type (10.0% compared to 13.3%). Type I error was not considered as it is less harmful for the bank. Although the rejection of good customers (if falsely identified as bad) can cause the bank to lose a significant amount of money in the form of 'lost opportunities,' this is seen as 'a virtual loss.'

The results presented in Table 5 were also compared with a real credit decision-making system (from here on referred to as the bank credit scoring method-BCSM). The sets of ratios used in MLP, RBF, and BCSM are presented in Table 6.

The BCSM uses the six following ratios: current ratio, quick ratio, financial surplus rate, total debt ratio, debt/EBITDA, and net profit margin ratio. Specified ranges for these ratios are set in advance by the bank. After calculating the required ratios and classifying them as falling into the specified range or not, a decision on the potential borrower's credit rating is made by an analyst according to the financial performance (ratios) and the analyst's experience. However, the ratios used are invariable, regardless of the line of business of the borrower. This could be a significant drawback as many sectors operate under specific conditions that may not apply to other sectors.

As seen in Table 6, the model which uses the smallest number of ratios is BCSM (six ratios). MLP uses eight ratios, and RBF uses the same set as MLP with the addition of two extra ratios. Only four ratios are shared by all three models. BCSM, based on the same set of input data, performed similarly to RBF, reaching a level of 13.33% for type II error. Therefore, the following conclusions can be drawn:

- Each tested model seems promising concerning the credit risk decision-making process as the obtained results are accurate (all of the models in the validation group exceed the level of 85%).
- A greater number of ratios used in the model does not guarantee a more accurate result; although RBF uses ten ratios, its results are slightly less accurate than, for instance, the results of MLP with eight ratios.
- On the other hand, a smaller (or in this case, the smallest) number of ratios also does not improve the results. BCSM uses the smallest number of ratios (six), but its results in the

validation group are identical to those of RBF (86.67%).

• The worse performance of BSCM, which is supposed to be tailor-made for the purpose, can be explained by the fact that it does not recognize the line of business and implements the same set of inputs (ratios) for all companies across all sectors.

• Although MLP is considered slower in learning than RBF, this fact seems to positively influence the final results, with MLP showing a higher accuracy RBF (90.0% and 86.67%, respectively).

Summing up, it is important to point out that both neural network types perform very well on a new set of data. This is both remarkable and also very useful in real life as the network is taught on historical data and then used to make decisions concerning new applications.

Another approach to selecting ratios for rejection was also implemented. It was based on a sensitivity analysis of the neural network obtained during the learning process. Sensitivity analysis in data mining and statistical model building generally refers to the assessment of the importance of each of the predictor variables in the fitted models. Given a fitted model with certain model parameters, for each predictor it presents what the effect would be of varying the parameters of the model (for each variable) on the overall model fit. In SANN, the program computes the sums of squares residuals or misclassification rates for the model when the respective predictor is eliminated from the neural net. Ratios (of the reduced model versus the full model) are also reported, and the predictors can be sorted by their importance or relevance for the particular neural network. In the research, after each process of learning, a sensitivity analysis of the input data (financial ratios) was performed. However, as useful as the tool might seem, a significant obstacle was encountered during the analysis. The problem appears when the neural network does not indicate any ratio as unnecessary which, in turn, leaves a large set of input data which, theoretically, should remain unchanged. This stopping point was reached when MLP rejected ratios until 19 remained and RBF did so until 17 remained. The results obtained by these depleted networks were of good quality. However, they did not exceed the results of either MLP 8-11-2 or RBF 10-13-2. Therefore, that path of analysis was not continued and those results are not presented. The conclusions drawn from this analysis are as follows:

1) Neural networks do not always reject the input data which might seem irrelevant.

2) Neural networks do not reject input data which seem to be duplicated (in the case of the input data from this research, for instance, two ratios: current and quick).

3) Neural networks do not always have the ability to distinguish the data, the rejection of which could improve the final results.

Concerning the above, it seems necessary to choose the input data carefully. It might also be useful to use some methods of data selection prior to neural network implementation as, according to the research, the neural network is not always able to eliminate the data, the rejection of which could improve the network's performance.

4 Conclusions

Making a wrong credit decision can result in large financial losses. Therefore, credit risk estimation and correct classification of customers is a valid, current, and significant issue. Many different ways of categorizing accounts are used, ranging from experts' opinions, credit scoring methods, Z-score models, and other individual models implemented by banks. Among these models are neural networks which, in recent years, have gained in popularity. Their performance is good, and they are effective at classifying customers and credit risks as they possess a built-in capacity to adapt their synaptic weights to changes in the surrounding environment and can be easily retrained to deal with minor changes in the operating environmental conditions. The research shows that for various structures of neural networks, different sets of variables should be used to improve the final results.

The set of input data for this study was selected from the construction sector, and proved to include information beneficial to the performance of the neural networks (MLP and RBF), particularly when compared to the results of the method used by a bank to classify customers to an appropriate group (BCSM). The analysis of the results of all three methods (two different architectures of neural networks and BCSM) indicates that banks should consider adjusting their models in relation to companies from different sectors of the economy.

The research also shows that techniques used for prior selection of input data and rejection during the process of learning are required. Neural networks with a smaller number of financial ratios delivered better results than the ones in which there were more ratios and where input data overlapped. However, the sensitivity analysis in SANN was also sufficient to achieve the goal of data selection.

One of the further directions indicated by this research is a comparative analysis among neural networks and other approaches to categorizing clients: credit scoring, Z-score models, and other classification methods (e.g., classification trees and regression). Another direction is to extend the financial analysis of ratios and to decide whether each business sector should be evaluated on a separate subset of data or whether a universal set of financial variables exists which can be used regardless of the line of business.

References

Angelini, E., di Tollo, G., and Roli, A. (2008). A neural network approach for credit risk evaluation. *The Quarterly Review of Economics and Finance*, 48(4):733–755.

Atiya, A. F. (2001). Bankruptcy prediction for credit risk using neural networks: A survey and new results. *IEEE Transactions on neural networks*, 12(4):929–935.

Baesens, B., Setiono, R., Mues, C., and Vanthienen, J. (2003). Using neural network rule extraction and decision tables for credit-risk evaluation. *Management Science*, 49(3):312–329.

Bishop, C. M. (1995). *Neural Networks for Pattern Recognition.* Oxford University Press, Inc., New York, NY, USA.

di Tollo, G. (2006). Credit Risk: A Neural Net Approach. mimeo, Università di Chieti–Pescara.

Haykin, S. (2011). *Neural networks and learning machines.* Prentice Hall; 3 edition.

Hecht-Nielsen, R. (1988). Theory of the backpropagation neural network. *Neural Networks*, 1(Supplement 1):445–448.

Huang, Z., Chen, H., Hsu, C., Chen, W., and Wu, S. (2004). Credit rating analysis with support vector machines and neural networks: A market comparative study. *Decision Support Systems*, 37(4):543–558.

Karaa, A. and Krichene, A. (2012). Credit–Risk Assessment Using Support Vectors Machine and Multilayer Neural Network Models: A Comparative Study Case of a Tunisian Bank. *Journal of Accounting and Management Information Systems*, 11(4):587–620.

Khemakhem, S. and Boujelbene, Y. (2015). Credit Risk Prediction: A Comparative Study between Discriminant Analysis and the Neural Network Approach. *Journal of Accounting and Management Information Systems*, 14(1):60–78.

Linder, R., Geier, J., and Kölliker, M. (2004). Artificial neural networks, classification trees and regression: Which method for which customer base? *Journal of Database Marketing and Customer Strategy Management*, 11(4):344–356.

Migdał Najman, K. and Najman, K. (2013). *Samouczące się sztuczne sieci neuronowe w grupowaniu i klasyfikacji danych. Teoria i zastosowania w ekonomii.* Wydawnictwo Uniwersytetu Gdańskiego.

Ogwueleka, F. N., Misra, S., Colomo-Palacios, R., and Fernandez, L. (2015). Neural Network and Classification Approach in Identifying Customer Behavior in the Banking Sector: A Case Study of an International Bank. *Human Factors and Ergonomics in Manufacturing and Service Industries*, 25(1):28–42.

Osowski, S. (2006). *Sieci neuronowe do przetwarzania informacji.* Oficyna Wydawnicza Politechniki Warszawskiej.

Pacelli, V. and Azzollini, M. (2011). An artificial neural network approach for credit risk management. *Journal of Intelligent Learning Systems and Applications*, 3(02):103.

Ripley, B. D. (2009). *Pattern Recognition and Neural Networks.* Cambridge University Press.

Skubalska-Rafajłowicz, E. (2011). *Sieci neuronowe w przetwarzaniu strumieni danych: struktury sieci i algorytmy uczenia.* Oficyna Wydawnicza Politechniki Wrocławskiej, 1 edition.

Wantoch-Rekowski, R. (2003). *Sieci neuronowe w zadaniach: perceptron wielowarstwowy.* Bel Studio.

West, D. (2000). Neural network credit scoring models. *Computers and Operations Research*, 27(11):1131–1152.

Witkowska, D. (2002). *Sztuczne sieci neuronowe i metody statystyczne: wybrane zagadnienia finansowe.* Studia Ekonomiczne - C. H. Beck. C. H. Beck.

Wójcicka, A. (2016a). Classification of trade sector entities in credibility assessment using neural networks. Econometric Research in Finance Workshop in Warsaw.

Wójcicka, A. (2016b). Neural networks in credit risk evaluation of construction sector. MZBO'16 conference in Czerniejewo.

Table 1: Comparison of multilayer perceptron (MLP) and radial basis function (RBF) neural networks

Feature of network architecture	Neural network type	
	MLP	**RBF**
Signal transmission	Feed-forward	Feed-forward
Process of building the model	One stage	Two different independent stages: • First stage: the probability distribution is established by means of radial basis functions • Second stage: the network learns the relations between input x and output y Note: The lag is only visible in RBF in the output layer
Threshold	Yes	No
Type of parameters	Weights and thresholds	• Location and width of basis function • Weights binding basis functions with output
Functioning time	Faster	Slower (bigger memory and size required)
Learning time	Slower	Faster

Source: own, on the basis of Bishop (1995); Haykin (2011); Migdał Najman and Najman (2013); Skubalska-Rafajłowicz (2011); West (2000).

Table 2: Financial ratios used as independent variables

1	Current ratio	14	Financial surplus rate
2	Quick ratio	15	Long-term debt ratio
3	Receivables ratio	16	Current assets turnover ratio
4	Stock turnover ratio	17	Short-term investments turnover ratio
5	Receivables to liabilities ratio	18	Operating activity profitability ratio
6	Gross profit margin ratio	19	Assets profitability ratio
7	Net profit margin ratio	20	Equity profitability ratio
8	Sale profitability ratio	21	Costs increase ratio
9	Costs level ratio	22	Sales dynamics
10	Total debt ratio	23	Operating ratio
11	Equity debt ratio	24	Self-financing ratio
12	Financial leverage	25	EBITDA/Financial expenses
13	Debt/EBITDA		

Note: *,**,*** denote significance at 10%, 5% and 1% levels. Standard errors in brackets.

Table 3: Highest quality multilayer perceptron (MLP) neural networks

Rank	Neutral Network	Quality (learning) %	Quality (testing) %	Function of error	Activation (hidden layer)	Activation (output)	Additional ratio
1	MLP 8-11-2	96.67	90.00	Entropy	Sinus	Softmax	-
2	MLP 8-12-2	95.00	91.67	Entropy	Sinus	Softmax	-
3	MLP 9-10-2	93.33	88.33	SOS	Logistic	Linear	Operating activity profitability ratio
4	MLP 9-13-2	86.67	80.00	SOS	Exponential	Sinus	Operating activity profitability ratio
5	MLP 8-9-2	81.67	78.33	SOS	Tanh	Exponential	-

Table 4: Highest quality radial basis function (RBF) neural networks

Rank	Neutral Network	Quality (learning) %	Quality (testing) %	Function of error	Activation (hidden layer)	Activation (output)	Additional ratio
1	RBF 10-13-2	95.00	91.67	Entropy	Gaussian	Softmax	-
2	RBF 10-12-2	93.33	91.67	Entropy	Gaussian	Softmax	-
3	RBF 10-10-2	88.33	83.33	Entropy	Gaussian	Softmax	-
4	RBF 11-14-2	88.33	81.67	Entropy	Gaussian	Softmax	EBITDA/ Financial expenses ratio
5	RBF 9-12-2	85.00	81.67	Entropy	Gaussian	Softmax	(Current assets turnover ratio)*

Note: *Without indicated ratio.

Table 5: Type II error for multilayer perceptron (MLP) and radial basis function (RBF) networks

Type of neural network	Type II error (%)
MLP	10.00
RBF	13.33

4

Evaluating Combined Forecasts for Realized Volatility Using Asymmetric Loss Functions

Giovanni De Luca[♣], **Giampiero M. Gallo**[♠], and **Danilo Carità** [*♣]

[♣]Università degli Studi di Napoli "Parthenope"
[♠]Università degli Studi di Firenze

ABSTRACT: In this work we provide the findings of a forecast combination analysis carried out on the realized volatility series of three market indexes (DAX, CAC, and AEX). Two volatility types (5 minutes, kernel) have been considered. Different loss functions suggest that forecasts computed through combining models are generally more accurate than those provided by single models. However, the choice of the latter can significantly affect the goodness of the results.

Keywords: realized volatility, forecast combinations, loss functions

Introduction

Volatility is a central parameter in many financial decisions, including the pricing and hedging of derivative products as well as the development of efficient risk management methods. Most of the volatility models presented in the literature are based on the empirical finding that volatility is time-varying and that periods of high volatility tend to cluster (Ané, 2006). The forecasting process of such an important measure represents a major issue.

*Corresponding Author. Email: danilo.carita@uniparthenope.it

In the literature there exists a wide variety of models to forecast volatility forecasts, but these are, almost by definition, simple and incomplete (Raviv, 2016). An improvement in the forecast accuracy can be achieved by combining forecasts originating from different types of models. Forecast combinations have been used successfully in empirical works in different areas such as forecasting Gross National Product, currency market volatility, inflation, money supply, stock prices, meteorological data, city populations, outcomes of football games, wilderness area use, check volume and political risks (Timmermann, 2006).

The aim of this paper is to use both single and combined models to forecast the daily realized volatility one step ahead for a one-year period. Thereafter we will compare predicted values with actual data using a number of loss functions. To carry out our analysis, we have used data on realized volatility of three market indexes (DAX, CAC, and AEX) for the period 2008 to 2016.

The remainder of the paper is organized as follows. Section 1 describes the data, the models adopted, and the loss functions used for evaluating the different forecasts. Section 2 presents the results of the analysis while Section 3 concludes the paper.

1 Data and Methodology

This study focuses on the realized volatility of three European market indexes:

- DAX 30 (*Deutsche Aktienindex 30*) is a blue chip stock market index consisting of the 30 largest German companies trading on the Frankfurt Stock Exchange;

- CAC 40 (*Cotation Assistée en Continu*) represents a capitalization-weighted measure of the 40 largest among the 100 companies with the highest market capitalizations on the Euronext Paris;

- AEX (*Amsterdam Exchange Index*) is a stock market index composed of Dutch companies that trade on the Euronext Amsterdam; it includes 25 most frequently traded securities on the exchange.

The time series of the indexes are provided by the Oxford-Man Institute of Quantitative Finance by means of its own website (http://realized.oxford-man.ox.ac.uk/data). For each asset, the dataset contains the realized volatility collected every 5 minutes, the realized kernel volatility (in both cases denoted by rv_t), and the daily returns (denoted by r_t), covering the period from January 1, 2008 to Dezember 31, 2016.

Three different models have been chosen to create the single forecasts:

1. *Asymmetric Multiplicative Error Model* (AMEM) (Engle, 2002; Engle and Gallo, 2006), which for a basic (1,1) order has the following structure:

$$\begin{aligned} rv_t &= \mu_t \xi_t \\ \mu_t &= \omega + \alpha_1 rv_{t-1} + \beta_1 \mu_{t-1} + \gamma D_{t-1} rv_{t-1} \end{aligned} \quad (1)$$

   with $\omega > 0$, $\alpha_1 \geq 0$, $\beta_1 \geq 0$, $\alpha_1 + \beta_1 < 1$. D_t as a dummy variable that takes the value of 1 if the $r_t < 0$ and 0 otherwise;

2. *Asymmetric Power Multiplicative Error Model* (APMEM), which for the usual (1,1) order is given by:

$$\begin{aligned} rv_t &= \mu_t \xi_t \\ \mu_t^{\delta} &= \omega + \alpha_1 rv_{t-1}^{\delta} + \beta_1 \mu_{t-1}^{\delta} + \gamma D_{t-1} rv_{t-1}^{\delta} \end{aligned} \quad (2)$$

   with $\omega > 0$, $\alpha_1 \geq 0$, $\beta_1 \geq 0$, $\alpha_1 + \beta_1 < 1$, $\delta > 0$. This model is a generalization of the basic MEM and is strictly related to the Asymmetric Power ACD model (cf., Fernandes and Grammig, 2006);

3. *Asymmetric Heterogeneous AutoRegressive Model* (AHAR), that is the HAR model with a leverage effect term (Corsi, 2009):

$$rv_t = c + \beta^{(d)} rv_{t-1} + \beta^{(w)} rv_{t-1}^{(w)} + \beta^{(m)} rv_{t-1}^{(m)} + \gamma D_{t-1} rv_{t-1} + \epsilon_t^{(d)} \quad (3)$$

   where (d) stands for the time horizons of one day, $[rv_{t-1}^{(w)}]$ is the weekly realized volatility, which at time t is given by the average:

$$rv_t^{(w)} = \frac{1}{5}\left(rv_t^{(d)} + rv_{t-1d}^{(d)} + \cdots + rv_{t-4d}^{(d)}\right) \quad (4)$$

   and $rv_{t-1}^{(m)}$ is the monthly realized volatility which at time t is given by the average

$$rv_t^{(m)} = \frac{1}{22}\left(rv_t^{(d)} + rv_{t-1d}^{(d)} + \cdots + rv_{t-21d}^{(d)}\right) \quad (5)$$

As a preliminary analysis, in Figure 1 we compare the forecasts obtained using the three models mentioned above for the year 2016 (colored lines) with the actual values of the volatility (dashed black line) for the DAX 5-minute series. The chart shows that all models react satisfactorily to positive peaks of volatility, whereas they are not able to achieve a suitable degree of accuracy when volatility reaches a local minimum. This issue, which is common also to the other observed time series, can be overcome by combining the forecasts of two models, as we will see later.

The combined methods are based on the following two combination models:

- *comb1* model, based on a simple unconstrained ordinary least squares estimation of the weights. The one-step-ahead forecast is given by

$$rv_T(1) = \alpha + \beta_1 f_T^{(1)}(1) + \beta_2 f_T^{(2)}(1) \tag{6}$$

  with $f_T^{(1)}(1)$ and $f_T^{(2)}(1)$ denoting, respectively, the first and second model forecasts;

- *comb2* model, with the combination given by

$$rv_T(1) = \alpha + (\beta_1 + \delta_1 D_{t-1}) f_T^{(1)}(1) + (\beta_2 + \delta_2 D_{t-1}) f_T^{(2)}(1) \tag{7}$$

  which includes a dummy variable, D_t, that takes the value 1 if rv_t is lower than rv_{t-1} and 0 otherwise. The ratio of this choice is given by considering that, as we have mentioned before, the forecast of volatility is often far from the actual realized volatility while the latter is decreasing.

1.1 Loss Functions

To compare the results of the combined schemes with those that can be obtained by exclusively relying on a single model, we have computed three loss functions:

1. *Mean Square Error*(MSE), given by

$$MSE = \frac{\sum_{i=1}^{n} (rv_{T+i} - rv_{T+i-1}(1))^2}{n} \tag{8}$$

   with rv_{T+i} being the observed value of the realized volatility and $rv_{T+i-1}(1)$ as the one step ahead forecast for time $T+i$, $i = 1, \ldots, n$;

2. *Quasi-Likelihood*(QLIKE), defined as

$$QLIKE = \frac{1}{n} \sum_{i=1}^{n} \left[\frac{rv_{T+i}}{rv_{T+i-1}(1)} - \ln \left(\frac{rv_{T+i}}{rv_{T+i-1}(1)} \right) - 1 \right] \quad ; \tag{9}$$

3. A new measure called Asymmetric MSE(AMSE), given by

$$AMSE = \frac{1}{n} \sum_{i=1}^{n} \left(1 + \left(\frac{{\epsilon_{T+i}}^2}{rv_{T+i}} \right)^m I(\epsilon_{T+i} > 0) \right) {\epsilon_{T+i}}^2 \tag{10}$$

where $\epsilon_{T+i} = rv_{T+i} - rv_{T+i-1}(1)$. This measure is an extension of the MSE: each term of the sum reduces to ${\epsilon_{T+i}}^2$ when the indicator function is 0 (overestimation of the volatility) and is given by $\left(1 + \left(\frac{{\epsilon_{T+i}}^2}{rv_{T+i}}\right)^m\right) {\epsilon_{T+i}}^2$ when the indicator function is 1 (underestimation of the volatility).

We decided to build up a new loss function for the evaluation of forecasts for two reasons. First, as we have already said, AMSE is more suitable than MSE when it comes to assessing forecasts that underestimate the volatility as it penalizes underestimation to a greater extent. Second, it can be shown that AMSE is able to perform more reasonably than QLIKE, one of the most widely used loss functions in the volatility forecasting literature (Patton, 2011).

Figure 2 displays a graphic comparison of QLIKE with MSE and two versions of its asymmetric modification, the first with power term $m = 1$ and the second with $m = 2$. On the x-axis we have depicted the relative deviations of the forecasts from the true value (which amounts to 2 in this case), whereas on the y-axis we have represented the relative difference of the loss functions between the cases of underestimation and overestimation of the same size. As expected, MSE appears as a flat line because it is a symmetric loss function. In contrast, QLIKE and AMSE start to rise almost immediately, particularly QLIKE which, as evidenced by the sharp slope of the red line, is able to reach very high values. However, the AMSE loss function appears distinctly smoother than QLIKE (especially when $m = 1$), indicating that AMSE is well-balanced and also more regular than the QLIKE loss function.

For computing the forecast combinations, we start by splitting the data into an estimation and training set and a test set. The former is again split into two parts, the first being used to estimate the parameters of the model, the second (the training period) to estimate the weights to be attributed to the single forecasts. The test set is used to evaluate the different models. We have chosen to take into account two different training periods in our analysis: a four-year training period and a three-year training period. For instance, with a four-year training period, we estimate the parameters of the models using observations from January 2, 2008 to December 31, 2011, then compute one step ahead forecasts from January 2, 2012 to December 31, 2015; these forecasts are used to estimate the weights of the combinations; finally, the one step ahead forecast for January 2, 2016 is produced. Then, we estimate the parameters of the models using observations from January 3, 2008 to January 2, 2012, compute one step ahead forecasts from January 3, 2012 to January 2, 2016 to estimate the weights of the combinations, and the one step ahead forecast for January 3, 2016 is produced.

2 Comparisons among forecasting models

In this section we will show the results of our analysis. For each model we display the values of the three loss functions mentioned above for both the forecasts and the observed values.

Because two of the three single models we have used (AMEM and APMEM) are very similar to each other, we present first a comparison between AMEM and AHAR, then between APMEM and AHAR, along with the combined schemes we described in Section 1.

2.1 AMEM vs. AHAR

The order of the two single models is defined using the Ljung-Box test on the residuals of the in-sample analysis of the two models. We have selected an AMEM (1,1) for the DAX dataset, an AMEM (1,2) for CAC and AEX, and an AHAR with a second lag term (rv_{t-2}) for all datasets.

Table 1 shows the results for the first comparison, i.e., AMEM (1,1) and AHAR models, along with combined forecasts, using DAX data. We can see that the *comb2* model performs very well for almost all indicators; only QLIKE prefers the AMEM (1,1) model.

The findings provided in Table 2 for the CAC dataset are very similar to those for the DAX dataset. Indeed, there are only two differences: QLIKE prefers *comb2* for rv kernel with a training period of four years instead of AMEM (1,2); and AMSE with $m = 1$ prefers the AMEM model for rv 5 minutes with a training period of three years, instead of *comb2*.

The results for the AEX dataset (Table 3) are not so different from the others. The *comb2* model predominates, but the AMEM (1,2) also performs well, particularly according to QLIKE (in three cases out of four).

2.2 APMEM vs. AHAR

In this subsection we assess if a generalization of the AMEM basic model is able to improve the accuracy of the combined forecasts. According to the Ljung-Box test, we use an APMEM (1,1) for DAX and an APMEM (1,2) for CAC and AEX.

As shown in Table 4, we have observed an actual improvement in the combined forecasts. Compared to the findings shown in Table 1, in 14 cases out of 16 the loss functions appoint the smallest value to a combination. Even according to QLIKE, *comb2* is preferred over APMEM half the time.

As we expected, the improvement that occurred for the DAX dataset moving from AMEM to APMEM holds for CAC as well, even if it is less significant. Indeed, the results shown in Table 5 are almost the same as those that we see in Table 2 in terms of loss functions choices. However, this time AMSE ($m = 1$) selects the *comb2* model for all volatility measures and training periods.

Observing the Table 6, we can gladly see that, compared to the Table 3, the transition from AMEM to APMEM has caused a consiistency of the loss functions. Almost all loss functions suggest choosing *comb2*. The single model APMEM (1,2) thas has only been chosen with the use of the by QLIKE statistic. Overall, these are the same findings that are seen in Table 5.

2.3 Accuracy of Forecasts

So far we have evaluated the available forecasts by means of the numerical values provided by the loss functions. Before doing so, however, we need to assess if the forecast series are different from a statistical point of view. To this end, we have used a conditional predictive ability (CPA) test of Giacomini and White (2006) to make pair-wise comparisons among all forecasting models ($\alpha = 0.05$). The null hypothesis is that the two models under comparison have the same predictive accuracy. Because *comb2* has proved to be the best combination scheme in most cases, we tested if it is more accurate than the other models as our alternative hypothesis.

Tables 7-9 provide the findings of the analysis according to the three datasets. At first glance, we observe some similarities among the comparisons. In more detail, we find that the two combination schemes, *comb1* and *comb2*, show the same equal conditional predictive ability for all models, market indexes, types of realized volatility, or the training periods, except for kernel estimates with a training period of four years using the CAC dataset. Regarding the other comparisons, the alternative hypothesis was rejected for *comb2* and AMEM twice in DAX, once in CAC, and three times out of four in AEX. The same applies for *comb2* and APMEM. Finally, AEX data depict an equal forecast accuracy also between *comb2* and AHAR when *rv* 5 minutes with a three-year training period is involved. In all other cases, the CPA test provides evidence that *comb2* has a better predictive ability than the other models.Tables 7-9 especially make it clear that *comb2* outperforms AHAR in almost all situations, except for the AEX case mentioned before.

3 Conclusions

In this paper, we demonstrate that an improvement in the accuracy of forecasts of a measure of volatility, namely realized volatility, can be achieved by combining predictions originating from several models. We forecast the daily realized volatility one step ahead for a one-year period with three single models (AMEM, APMEM, AHAR) and two combinations (*comb1*, *comb2*). Subsequently, we compare predicted values and actual data using a number of loss functions. We find that combining the AHAR model with APMEM instead of AMEM causes an enhancement in the quality of the forecasts computed using combination schemes, especially the *comb2* model, which proves to be the best model in most situations. This finding holds for the DAX, AEX, and (to a lesser extent) CAC datasets, and for all training periods. However, after carrying out a CPA test to assess the forecasting accuracy, we found that the *comb2* model, in almost all cases, was as accurate as *comb1* and, in half the cases, as accurate as AMEM and APMEM. Furthermore, *comb2* outperforms the AHAR model in almost all situations, allowing us to reject the null hypothesis of equal unconditional predictive ability.

References

Ané, T. (2006). An analysis of the flexibility of asymmetric power GARCH models. *Computational Statistics and Data Analysis*, 51(2):1293–1311.

Corsi, F. (2009). A simple approximate long-memory model of realized volatility. *Journal of Financial Econometrics*, 7(2):174–196.

Engle, R. (2002). Dynamic conditional correlation: A simple class of multivariate generalized autoregressive conditional heteroskedasticity models. *Journal of Business and Economic Statistics*, 20(3):339–350.

Engle, R. and Gallo, G. (2006). A multiple indicators model for volatility using intra-daily data. *Journal of Econometrics*, 131(1):3–27.

Fernandes, M. and Grammig, J. (2006). A family of autoregressive conditional duration models. *Journal of Econometrics*, 130(1):1–23.

Giacomini, R. and White, H. (2006). Tests of conditional predictive ability. *Econometrica*, 74(6):1545–1578.

Oxford-Man Institute of Quantitative Finance (2017). Realized Library. http://realized.oxford-man.ox.ac.uk/data.

Patton, A. (2011). Volatility forecast comparison using imperfect volatility proxies. *Journal of Econometrics*, 160(1):246–256.

Raviv, E. (2016). Forecast combinations in R using the ForecastCombinations package. A Manual.

Timmermann, A. (2006). Forecast combinations. *Handbook of Economic Forecasting*, 1:135–196.

Figure 1: Comparison among observed realized volatility (5 minutes) for year 2016 and AMEM (1,1), APMEM (1,1), and AHAR forecasts – DAX dataset.

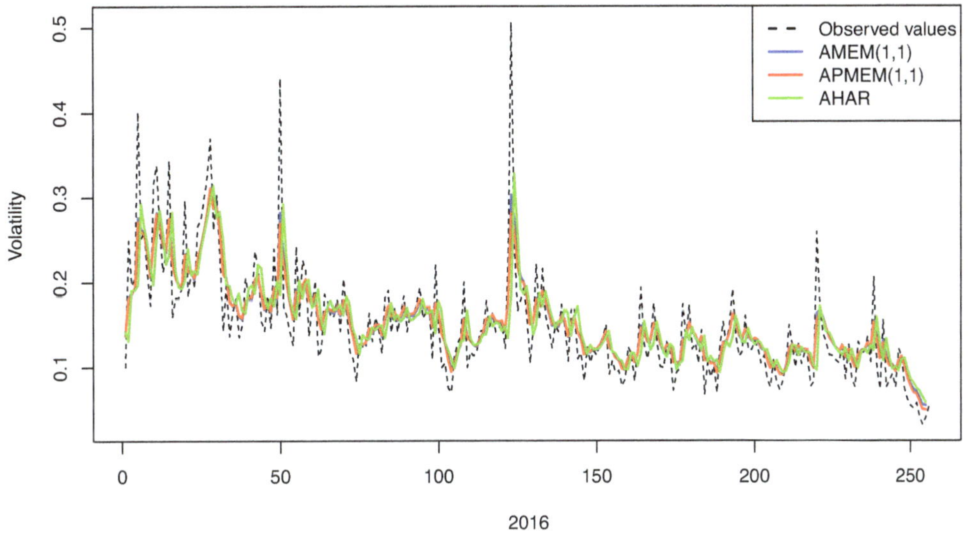

Figure 2: Comparison of MSE, QLIKE, AMSE (m=1,2) loss functions computed on a series h of evenly spaced forecasts from 0 to 2.

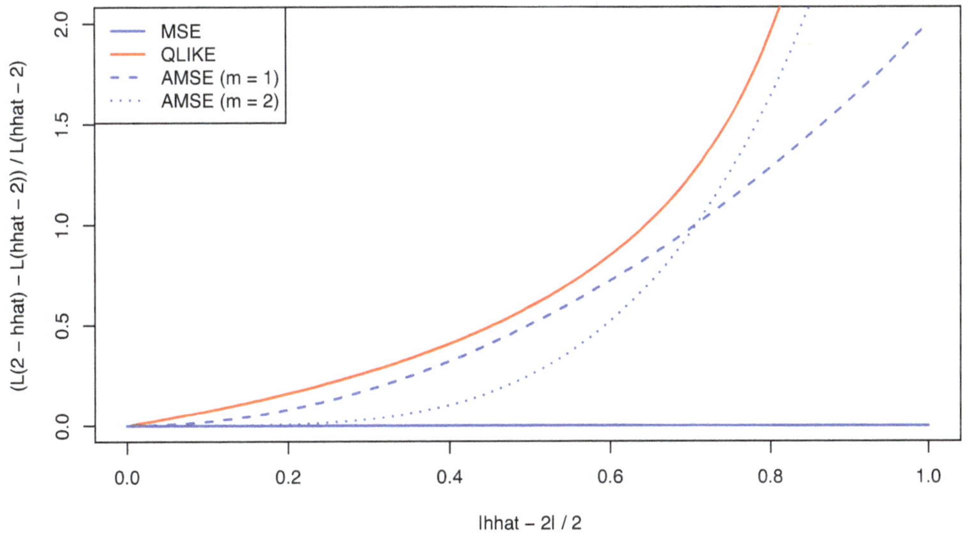

Table 1: Comparison of AMEM (1,1), AHAR, and combination schemes (smallest values in bold) – DAX dataset.

		MSE				QLIKE			
Series	Training period	AMEM (1,1)	AHAR	comb1	comb2	AMEM (1,1)	AHAR	comb1	comb2
rv 5min	4 years	0.254	0.293	0.252	**0.248**	**4.231**	4.979	4.285	4.246
	3 years	0.254	0.293	0.254	**0.250**	**4.231**	4.979	4.393	4.338
rv kernel	4 years	0.206	0.251	0.204	**0.200**	**3.505**	4.312	3.552	3.508
	3 years	0.206	0.251	0.206	**0.203**	**3.505**	4.312	3.639	3.594
		AMSE ($m = 1$)				AMSE ($m = 2$)			
Series	Training period	AMEM (1,1)	AHAR	comb1	comb2	AMEM (1,1)	AHAR	comb1	comb2
rv 5min	4 years	0.271	0.316	0.271	**0.268**	0.257	0.298	0.255	**0.251**
	3 years	0.271	0.316	0.273	**0.270**	0.257	0.298	0.257	**0.254**
rv kernel	4 years	0.217	0.267	0.216	**0.212**	0.207	0.254	0.206	**0.201**
	3 years	0.217	0.267	0.218	**0.215**	0.207	0.254	0.208	**0.204**

Table 2: Comparison of AMEM (1,2), AHAR, and combination schemes (smallest values in bold) – CAC dataset.

		MSE				QLIKE			
Series	Training period	AMEM (1,2)	AHAR	comb1	comb2	AMEM (1,2)	AHAR	comb1	comb2
rv 5min	4 years	0.243	0.292	0.241	**0.239**	**3.809**	4.660	3.845	3.836
	3 years	0.243	0.292	0.243	**0.242**	**3.809**	4.660	3.884	3.891
rv kernel	4 years	0.240	0.295	0.238	**0.233**	3.855	4.810	3.889	**3.834**
	3 years	0.240	0.295	0.239	**0.236**	**3.855**	4.810	3.925	3.895
		AMSE ($m = 1$)				AMSE ($m = 2$)			
Series	Training period	AMEM (1,2)	AHAR	comb1	comb2	AMEM (1,2)	AHAR	comb1	comb2
rv 5min	4 years	0.268	0.325	0.269	**0.267**	0.249	0.301	0.248	**0.246**
	3 years	**0.268**	0.325	0.270	0.270	0.249	0.301	0.249	**0.249**
rv kernel	4 years	0.264	0.325	0.264	**0.260**	0.245	0.303	0.244	**0.240**
	3 years	0.264	0.325	0.265	**0.263**	0.245	0.303	0.245	**0.242**

Table 3: Comparison among AMEM(1,2), AHAR, and combination schemes (smallest values in bold) – AEX dataset.

		MSE				QLIKE			
Series	Training period	AMEM (1,2)	AHAR	comb1	comb2	AMEM (1,2)	AHAR	comb1	comb2
rv 5min	4 years	0.251	0.293	0.250	**0.247**	**3.925**	4.706	3.969	3.960
	3 years	**0.251**	0.293	0.251	0.251	**3.925**	4.706	4.007	4.023
rv kernel	4 years	0.219	0.257	0.218	**0.213**	3.854	4.677	3.898	**3.834**
	3 years	0.219	0.257	0.219	**0.216**	**3.854**	4.677	3.933	3.886
		AMSE ($m = 1$)				AMSE ($m = 2$)			
Series	Training period	AMEM (1,2)	AHAR	comb1	comb2	AMEM (1,2)	AHAR	comb1	comb2
rv 5min	4 years	0.288	0.343	0.289	**0.287**	0.263	0.313	0.263	**0.261**
	3 years	**0.288**	0.343	0.290	0.291	**0.263**	0.313	0.264	0.265
rv kernel	4 years	0.241	0.286	0.241	**0.237**	0.224	0.266	0.224	**0.218**
	3 years	0.241	0.286	0.242	**0.239**	0.224	0.266	0.224	**0.221**

Table 4: Comparison among APMEM (1,1), AHAR, and combination schemes (smallest values in bold) – DAX dataset.

		MSE				QLIKE			
Series	Training period	APMEM (1,1)	AHAR	comb1	comb2	APMEM (1,1)	AHAR	comb1	comb2
rv 5min	4 years	0.249	0.293	0.248	**0.245**	4.165	4.979	4.177	**4.156**
	3 years	0.249	0.293	0.250	**0.247**	**4.165**	4.979	4.267	4.232
rv kernel	4 years	0.203	0.251	0.202	**0.198**	3.464	4.312	3.469	**3.429**
	3 years	0.203	0.251	0.203	**0.200**	**3.464**	4.312	3.546	3.506
		AMSE ($m = 1$)				AMSE ($m = 2$)			
Series	Training period	APMEM (1,1)	AHAR	comb1	comb2	APMEM (1,1)	AHAR	comb1	comb2
rv 5min	4 years	0.267	0.316	0.266	**0.265**	0.252	0.298	0.251	**0.249**
	3 years	0.267	0.316	0.268	**0.266**	0.252	0.298	0.253	**0.251**
rv kernel	4 years	0.214	0.267	0.213	**0.210**	0.205	0.254	0.203	**0.200**
	3 years	0.214	0.267	0.215	**0.213**	0.205	0.254	0.205	**0.202**

Table 5: Comparison among APMEM (1,2), AHAR, and combination schemes (smallest values in bold) – CAC dataset.

		MSE				QLIKE			
Series	Training period	APMEM (1,2)	AHAR	comb1	comb2	APMEM (1,2)	AHAR	comb1	comb2
rv 5min	4 years	0.246	0.292	0.243	**0.240**	**3.833**	4.660	3.880	3.855
	3 years	0.246	0.292	0.245	**0.242**	**3.833**	4.660	3.931	3.913
rv kernel	4 years	0.241	0.295	0.239	**0.234**	3.865	4.810	3.903	**3.840**
	3 years	0.241	0.295	0.241	**0.236**	**3.865**	4.810	3.948	3.903
		AMSE ($m = 1$)				AMSE ($m = 2$)			
Series	Training period	APMEM (1,2)	AHAR	comb1	comb2	APMEM (1,2)	AHAR	comb1	comb2
rv 5min	4 years	0.272	0.325	0.271	**0.268**	0.252	0.301	0.250	**0.247**
	3 years	0.272	0.325	0.273	**0.271**	0.252	0.301	0.252	**0.249**
rv kernel	4 years	0.266	0.325	0.265	**0.261**	0.247	0.303	0.245	**0.240**
	3 years	0.266	0.325	0.267	**0.263**	0.247	0.303	0.247	**0.243**

Table 6: Comparison among APMEM (1,2), AHAR, and combination schemes (smallest values in bold) – AEX dataset.

		MSE				QLIKE			
Series	Training period	APMEM (1,2)	AHAR	comb1	comb2	APMEM (1,2)	AHAR	comb1	comb2
rv 5min	4 years	0.256	0.293	0.252	**0.247**	**3.946**	4.706	4.001	3.975
	3 years	0.256	0.293	0.253	**0.250**	**3.946**	4.706	4.049	4.039
rv kernel	4 years	0.219	0.257	0.218	**0.213**	3.855	4.677	3.902	**3.831**
	3 years	0.219	0.257	0.219	**0.215**	**3.855**	4.677	3.942	3.886
		AMSE ($m = 1$)				AMSE ($m = 2$)			
Series	Training period	APMEM (1,2)	AHAR	comb1	comb2	APMEM (1,2)	AHAR	comb1	comb2
rv 5min	4 years	0.292	0.343	0.293	**0.288**	0.267	0.313	0.266	**0.261**
	3 years	0.292	0.343	0.294	**0.292**	0.267	0.313	0.267	**0.264**
rv kernel	4 years	0.241	0.286	0.242	**0.237**	0.224	0.266	0.224	**0.219**
	3 years	0.241	0.286	0.242	**0.239**	0.224	0.266	0.225	**0.221**

Table 7: Percentage of superiority in forecasting accuracy of *comb2* using CPA test (pair-wise comparisons against AMEM, APMEM, AHAR and *comb1*) – DAX dataset.

f_1	f_2	DAX rv 5 min. 4 years t.p.	DAX rv 5 min. 3 years t.p.	DAX rv kernel 4 years t.p.	DAX rv kernel 3 years t.p.
comb2	AMEM	0.016	0.178	0.007	0.129
comb2	AHAR	0.004	0.015	0.002	0.007
comb2	comb1	0.119	0.170	0.076	0.127
comb2	APMEM	0.015	0.156	0.005	0.096
comb2	AHAR	0.003	0.009	0.002	0.005
comb2	comb1	0.130	0.193	0.076	0.113

Table 8: Percentage of superiority in forecasting accuracy of *comb2* using CPA test (pair-wise comparisons against AMEM, APMEM, AHAR and *comb1*) – CAC dataset.

f_1	f_2	CAC rv 5 min. 4 years t.p.	CAC rv 5 min. 3 years t.p.	CAC rv kernel 4 years t.p.	CAC rv kernel 3 years t.p.
comb2	AMEM	0.036	0.142	0.006	0.034
comb2	AHAR	0.000	0.001	0.000	0.000
comb2	comb1	0.187	0.397	0.046	0.161
comb2	APMEM	0.044	0.107	0.008	0.036
comb2	AHAR	0.000	0.001	0.000	0.000
comb2	comb1	0.132	0.212	0.041	0.120

Table 9: Percentage of superiority in forecasting accuracy of *comb2* using CPA test (pair-wise comparisons against AMEM, APMEM, AHAR and *comb1*) – AEX dataset.

f_1	f_2	AEX rv 5 min. 4 years t.p.	AEX rv 5 min. 3 years t.p.	AEX rv kernel 4 years t.p.	AEX rv kernel 3 years t.p.
comb2	AMEM	0.074	0.538	0.024	0.153
comb2	AHAR	0.035	0.076	0.007	0.017
comb2	comb1	0.217	0.764	0.065	0.104
comb2	APMEM	0.051	0.233	0.024	0.135
comb2	AHAR	0.024	0.052	0.006	0.014
comb2	comb1	0.171	0.484	0.078	0.144

5

Corporate Governance and Efficiency of Rural and Community Banks (RCBs) in Ghana

Eric Fosu Oteng-Abayie*♣, Anthony Affram♠, Henry Kofi Mensah♠

♣Department of Economics, Kwame Nkrumah University of Science and Technology, Ghana
♠School of Business, Kwame Nkrumah University of Science and Technology, Ghana

ABSTRACT: Corporate governance crises that occur in the banking sector normally cripple economies and bring many hardships to individuals, corporate entities, communities, and the nation at large. In this study, we sought to examine the level of technical efficiency and productivity growth of rural and community banks (RCBs) and the impact of corporate governance indicators on the RCBs' efficiency performance in Ghana. A sample of 70 out of 140 RCBs was selected based on the ARB Apex Bank's performance ratings and data availability. Data envelopment analysis (DEA) was used to determine the technical efficiency scores of the selected RCBs. In the second stage of the analysis, these computed efficiency scores were regressed on the corporate governance variables to assess the effects of the latter. The findings from the DEA approach show that 11% to 20% of the sampled RCBs in Ghana operate close to the efficiency frontier, whereas the majority–about 65% to 81%-underperformed within the study period of 2007 to 2013. The study further established that the number of board members, frequency of board meetings, and corporate social responsibility have significant influence on RCB efficiency.

Keywords: data envelopment analysis, technical efficiency, corporate governance, rural banks, Ghana

*Corresponding Author. Email: efoteng-abayie.socs@knust.edu.gh

Introduction

Good corporate governance is increasingly acknowledged as a significant driver of long-term investment and has become a crucial subject in financial circles. Such governance has become necessary for any organization serious about optimizing its performance. The literature on this subject also contains evidence of a positive correlation between the level of corporate governance and bank crises. Bank crises are argued to be a long-term result of a series of bad corporate decisions. Decisions critical for bank survival, including incentives, performance targets, provision of internal controls, and strategy, are all taken by the board of governors. As a result, corporate governance is seen as a vital key to understanding institutional efficiency and productivity. On the international front, cases such as Enron, WorldCom, Pacific Gas and Electricity Company, and Barings Bank are commonly cited. In Ghana, Atobease Rural Bank, DKB Finance, Merchant Bank, and Noble Dream Microfinance are commonly cited examples of the negative repercussions of weak corporate structures. In July 2018, the Bank of Ghana also cited corporate governance practices as the underlying factor for the collapse of seven commercial banks in Ghana between 2016 and 2018.

Adnan et al. (2011) indicate the need for strong corporate structures in the banking sector. A number of studies have thus attempted to assess the effect of corporate governance on bank performance. Recent additions include Fidanoski et al. (2014), Ameer et al. (2010), Tahir (2015), Poudel (2013), and Rao and Desta (2016). A common observation made from these extant studies is that banks rely too much on accounting indices to evaluate corporate performance. However, accounting indices are always single-factor input or output measures of performance and may be considered as "just scratching the surface" It is particularly useful to measure performance from multiple activities because financial institutions combine multiple inputs to produce different financial outputs.

Meanwhile, since the inception of rural banking in Ghana, concerns about limited capacity and liquidation threats, amidst fierce competition from the commercial banks, remain rife. Several rural and community banks (RCBs) have been closed down by the Bank of Ghana due to financial difficulties. In 2012 alone, 15 RCBs were classified as distressed, and 19 others were identified as mediocre banks. A 2012 Bank of Ghana report indicates that a total of 23 distressed RCBs have been shut down by the central bank since 2007 (Oteng-Abayie, 2017). These developments suggest a strong link between corporate governance and RCB performance. Despite the recent interest in corporate governance, studies of its effects on rural banking performance remain few. To the best of our knowledge, the deficit is even larger when the Ghanaian context is considered. Empirical research on the subject is largely non-existent, with the exception of Bokpin (2013) for commercial banks and other studies that focused only on rural bank efficiency and productivity (see Adusei, 2016; Oteng-Abayie, 2017).

The purpose of this paper is to examine the effects of several attributes of corporate governance, in particular, size of the board of directors and audit committee, frequency of board meetings, and corporate social responsibility, on the efficiency of RCBs in Ghana. We first estimate the technical efficiency levels and then examine the effects of corporate governance indicators on the efficiency performance of RCBs in Ghana. We employ the data envelopment analysis (DEA) approach to measure bank performance. The significance of using the DEA approach is that it allows for the assessment of bank performance using an array of output and input variables, unlike the one index performance measure that mostly characterizes the extant bank governance literature. Therefore, we can capture the real effect of corporate governance on the efficiency performance of RCBs. This study focuses on a unique dataset retrieved from the financial accounts of RCBs in Ghana from 2007-2013. Our findings from the DEA approach show that 11% to 20% of the sampled RCBs operate close to frontier efficiency, whereas the majority-about 65% to 81%-underperformed within the study period. The study established that the number of board members, frequency of board meetings, and the level of corporate social responsibility have significant influence on RCB efficiency.

The rest of this paper is organized as follows. Section 1 presents a brief literature review and the methodology is presented in the second section. Section 3 describes the data. Section 4 captures the data analysis and presentation of empirical results and the final section concludes and presents the practical implications of the study results.

1 Review of Related Literature

The evolution of thinking about corporation governance is traced to Berle and Means (1932) regarding the consequences of separating corporate control and ownership and then to Jensen and Meckling (1976) regarding agency theory. Corporate governance has been expressed as the processes and procedures through which firms are guided and controlled for effective decision-making (European Central Bank, 2004). Black et al. (2006) concluded that the way corporate governance is measured matters. Corporate governance in banks has been measured in diverse ways in the existing literature. For instance, whereas some studies use single indicators (Tanna et al., 2011; Laeven and Levine, 2009), others find it more convenient to use multiple indicators (such as board size, experience and independence of board members, and gender diversity, among others) to increase robustness of the measurement (Hartarska and Mersland, 2012; Romano et al., 2012; Huang, 2010). In this study, we use multiple indicators of corporate governance.

1.1 Corporate Governance and Efficiency of Banks

A plethora of studies exist that explore the effect of corporate governance on corporate performance (see Achim, 2016; Soba et al., 2016; Andrieş et al., 2018, for a summary of the empirical literature). The general consensus is that the effect of corporate governance on firm performance is mixed (Beisland et al., 2014). The effects are highly dependent on contextual factors as well as the measures of corporate governance and firm performance.

Gleaning from Andrieş et al. (2018) and Soba et al. (2016), studies focusing on the link between corporate governance and bank performance are growing in the literature. Earlier studies measured performance using traditional accounting-based ratios (e.g., pre-tax operating income, return on assets, market-to-book value, Tobin's Q, and the non-performing loans ratio) that are not multidimensional to studies that use robust frontier efficiency methods. Accounting-based indicators have, however, received large amounts of criticism. Therefore, with the availability of more robust mathematical programming and econometrics techniques, most recent studies have used frontier efficiency approaches to measure bank performance (Tanna et al., 2011). In Table 1, we present a summary of the empirical literature on the effects of corporate governance on bank performance. However, as shown in the table, studies that applied frontier efficiency methods are limited and their findings do not converge.

Performance measurement relying on frontier efficiency techniques such as the DEA is strongly recommended in the bank performance literature (Berger and Humphrey, 1997). The efficiency measures have several advantages over traditional indicators of performance. Efficient frontier approaches provide an overall objective numerical score and ranking, an efficiency proxy that complies with an economic optimization mechanism (Tanna et al., 2011). Also, the frontier efficiency approach simultaneously takes into account more than one input and one output of a firm, in contrast to accounting-based performance ratios (Thanassoulis et al., 1996).

Based on the reviewed empirical literature, we contribute to the existing studies by employing the frontier efficiency DEA technique to aid in determining the effect of corporate governance on bank performance. This will be the first study of its kind in the context of RCBs in Ghana.

2 Methodology

2.1 Efficiency Model

In order to investigate the empirical effect of corporate governance on the performance of RCBs, this study uses efficiency scores computed using the DEA model. The first part of the data analysis involves calculating the efficiency score of the ith RCB. DEA is a commonly applied linear programming technique used for constructing a piece-wise frontier surface that can be used to evaluate the relative efficiency of identical decision-making units (DMUs) by capturing how each of them deviates from the idealized production output of the virtual DMU. DEA may adopt either Constant Returns to Scale (CRS), as first used by Charnes et al. (1978), or Variable Returns to Scale (VRS), later used by Banker et al. (1984). DEA, under the assumption of CRS or VRS, can be estimated by applying either the input-oriented or output-oriented approach.

In the input-oriented approach, efficiency is calculated as the proportional reduction in input usage given an observed level of output, whereas under the output orientation, efficiency is calculated as the proportional increase in output level given the observed input usage. For a detailed exposition of the DEA approach, see Murillo-Zamorano (2004).

In this paper, we employ the output-oriented DEA approach, motivated by the general observation that the RCBs have been put under a different categorization based on industrial ratings, which are performance-based. Thus, assuming that all the RCBs in the sample operate at an optimal scale would be incorrect. Moreover, we execute an output-oriented DEA approach based on the simple reason that the objective of RCBs in Ghana through the years has been to mobilize rural savings and capital. The RCBs are doing this by competing with peers, commercial banks, and other financial institutions in the financial market. Recent developments have resulted in most RCBs establishing new branches, collection points, and a variety of innovative products and programmes in a bid to compete in the market. Thus, we anticipate that increasing financial output is of primary importance to RCBs in Ghana.

The DEA efficiency score for the ith RCB is calculated by solving the following linear programming problem:

$$\begin{aligned} Max\,\theta \quad & subject\,to \\ -\theta q_i + \mathbf{Q}\lambda \quad & \geq \mathbf{0}, \\ x_i - \mathbf{X}\lambda \quad & \geq \mathbf{0}, \\ \mathbf{1}'\lambda \quad & = 1, \\ \lambda \quad & \geq \mathbf{0} \end{aligned} \tag{1}$$

where y_i is a vector of outputs, x_i is a vector of inputs, $\mathbf{1}$ is an $N \times 1$ vector of ones, and λ is a $N \times 1$ vector of constants. Computed θ lies between 0 and 1. This means that when the computed efficiency score is equal to 1, then the DMU is said to be efficient and is otherwise considered inefficient. The symbol λ is the weight assigned to a DMU. Hence, θ and λ are the so called dual variables.

2.2 Determinants of Efficiency

Subsequently, computed efficiency scores are used as dependent variables and regressed on the corporate governance variables. This study adopts the pooled OLS regression model, which follows the normal OLS estimator assumptions. The model is expressed as:

$$Z_{i,t} = \alpha + h_{i,t}\beta + e_{i,t}, \quad i = 1, 2, 3 \ldots N, \quad t = 1, 2 \ldots T \tag{2}$$

where $Z_{i,t}$ is the efficiency score of each RCB at time t, $h_{i,t}$ is the vector of corporate governance indices, β is a vector of parameters, α is the constant term, and $e_{i,t}$ is the random error term. The empirical estimable equation is expressed as:

$$\theta_{i,t} = \beta_0 + \beta_1 NBM_{i,t} + \beta_2 FBM_{i,t} + \beta_3 ACS_{i,t} + \beta_4 FACM_{i,t} + \beta_5 CSR_{i,t} + e_{i,t} \tag{3}$$

3 Data

The data for this study were extracted from audited annual reports of the RCBs for the period 2007-2013, kept by the ARB Apex Bank. Based on the available data, 70 out of 140 RCBs were used for the analysis. The ARB Apex Bank serves as a central bank and regulator for rural and community banks in Ghana. The ARB Apex Bank assesses the performance of RCBs in four major rating areas as strong, satisfactory, fair, marginal, or distressed based on their capital, assets (including asset quality and asset utilization), savings/profitability, and liquidity. The sample used comprises 10 strong, 35 satisfactory, 15 fair, and 10 marginal RCBs.

3.1 Input and Output Variable Specification

This study adopts the intermediation approach because RCBs in Ghana take savings from depositors and lend them out to prospective borrowers (Paxton, 2003). Deposits and operating expenses (including interest expenses) are treated as inputs, whereas interest income and loans are treated as outputs (see Soba et al., 2016). All the variables used in the model are measured in Ghanaian Cedis. The variable descriptions and expected signs are presented in Table 2 and the descriptive statistics of the input and output variables are in Table 3.

4 Empirical Results

4.1 Technical Efficiency Estimates

Efficiency scores of all the RCBs were determined through DEA analysis. The efficiency indices were measured based on the VRS and output orientation assumptions. Table 4 gives a frequency distribution of technical efficiency scores based on the VRS-DEA output-oriented approach. The technical efficiency scores do not differ much from the VRS input-oriented approach or from the scores generated with the CRS approach (see Figures 1, 2, 3 and 4). A visualization of the trends in overall average efficiency shows that the RCBs experienced a fall in technical efficiency from 2007 to 2011 and picked up from 2011 to 2013. The period of the decline may be attributed to the global financial crises when banks experienced financial difficulties and credit crunches. All the RCBs that obtained a computed efficiency score equal to unity are regarded as fully efficient, whereas all those with scores less than 1 are referred to as inefficient. From Table 4, we observed that the annual technical efficiencies for the individual RCBs ranged from a minimum of 11.20% to a maximum of 100%. Average annual technical efficiency scores for all 70 RCBs varied from 54.28% to 69.36%, suggesting that the sampled RCBs were generally technically inefficient during the sampled period. This is also reflected in the number of technically efficient RCBs. A closer look at the annual technical efficiency scores revealed that most of the sampled RCBs received efficiency scores of 51% to 90%. Figures 1 and 2 show the average technical efficiency during the study period for each RCB. Only three of the 70 RCBs sampled achieved full technical efficiency consistently during the study period. The CRS efficiency score, which is more flexible, returns about 10 fully efficient RCBs. The least efficient bank (RCB59) achieved an efficiency score of 18.3%.

4.2 Effect of Corporate Governance on Technical Efficiency

Table 5 reports the effects of the corporate governance variables on technical efficiency (TE) of the RCBs based on equation 3. Based on the model statistics, which show a minimal Root MSE (17.793), we focus on the constant returns TE (CRS) model for interpretations. The results show that the number of board members (NBM) has a positive and significant effect on efficiency, suggesting that a large board size is more technically efficient than a smaller one. Other studies that find a positive relationship between board size and bank efficiency include Soba et al. (2016), Bokpin (2013), Poudel (2013), and Tanna et al. (2011). Anderson and Campbell (2004) also found evidence to suggest that boards of larger size monitor managers to track a reduced cost of debt. Creditors are of the view that those firms have good and efficient monitoring systems to ensure strong accounting procedures for firm performance. However, this finding is inconsistent with Jensen's agency theory, which suggests that smaller board size is beneficial for driving organizational outcomes (Jensen, 1993). Damme et al. (2016) report findings for microfinance institutions in support of the agency theory.

The frequency of board meetings (FBM) is significant at 10%, and reveals a positive influence on RCB efficiency. This is consistent with the view that boards which meet frequently may overcome the risk of information asymmetry and can address issues on time before they get out of control. Tai (2015) stated that, like board size, more frequent board meetings might lead to better firm effectiveness. Likewise, Ntim and Osei (2011) stated that there is an important and positive alliance among the performance of corporations and the series of board meetings. Moreover, experts have argued that increasing the frequency of board meetings will assist directors to keep abreast of the information on important developments happening in their firm, thereby placing them in a good position to solve budding problems quickly.

The study findings show corporate social responsibility (CSR) has a significant positive but muted influence on technical efficiency under the CRS assumption. This finding supports the view that good corporate citizenship enhances firm performance. CSR aims to hold corporations responsible for their actions and to promote a positive corporate effect on the environment and stakeholders, including consumers, employees, investors, communities, and others. Corporate governance and corporate social responsibility may reinforce each other in the search for a vision of the firm as an institution, which may create value while having regard for the welfare of stakeholders. This is in line with the observations made by Laan et al. (2008).

Audit committee size (ACS) and frequency of audit committee meetings (FACM) show no significant influence on RCB efficiency. This may be due to the lack or absence of standing audit committees in most of the RCBs in Ghana. This result is somewhat contrary to the findings of De Zoort et al. (2002), which suggest that larger audit committees tend to have better resources at their disposal than smaller ones. Klein (2002) and Kyereboah-Coleman (2008), however, revealed that there is a positive relationship between audit committee size and a firm's performance. The independent work of the audit committee has a great influence on the efficiency of the firm.

5 Conclusion

Issues regarding corporate governance are a global phenomenon and its crucial role in financial institutions must not be underestimated. Indeed, good corporate governance is a catalyst for ensuring good performance in the banking sector, in which the RCB industry is not exceptional. RCBs in Ghana have recently moved in the direction of adopting corporate governance best practices in order to boost efficiency in their operations. This study was undertaken to uncover the extent to which corporate governance affects RCB performance in Ghana. We estimated the level of efficiency of 70 sampled RCBs using the DEA technique under different assumptions. Our findings suggest that most RCBs are technically inefficient and although some RCBs had attained full efficiency at some points in the sample period, the majority of them were unable to operate at an optimal technical efficiency. In the period 2007-2011, the sampled RCBs generally suffered an efficiency decline within the period of the global financial crisis. In terms of the effect of corporate governance variables, the study recognized that the board size, frequency of board meetings, and CSR are significant predictors of RCB efficiency. The implication is that managers of RCBs must encourage regular board meetings and also increase investment in corporate social responsibility to improve their performance.

References

Achim, Monica-Violeta; Borlea, S.-N. M. C. (2016). Corporate governance and business performance: Evidence for the Romanian economy. *Journal of Business Economics and Management*, 17(3):458–474.

Adnan, M. A., Htay, S. N. N., Rashid, H. M. A., and Meera, A. K. M. (2011). A Panel Data Analysis on the Relationship between Corporate Governance and Bank Efficiency. *Journal of Accounting, Finance and Economics*, 1(1):1–15.

Adusei, M. (2016). Determinants of bank technical efficiency: Evidence from rural and community banks in Ghana. *Cogent Business & Management*, 3(1).

Ameer, R., Ramli, F., and Zakaria, H. (2010). A new perspective on board composition and firm performance in an emerging market. *Corporate Governance: International Journal of Business in Society*, 10(5):647–661.

Anderson, C. W. and Campbell, T. L. (2004). Corporate governance of Japanese banks. *Journal of Corporate Finance*, 10(3):327 – 354.

Andrieş, A. M., Căpraru, B., and Nistor, S. (2018). Corporate governance and efficiency in banking: evidence from emerging economies. *Applied Economics*, 50(34-35):3812–3832.

Banker, R. D., Charnes, A., and Cooper, W. W. (1984). Some Models for Estimating Technical and Scale Inefficiencies in Data Envelopment Analysis. *Management Science*, 30(9):1078–1092.

Beisland, L. A., Mersland, R., and Randøy, T. (2014). The Association between microfinance rating scores and corporate governance: a global survey. *International Review of Financial Analysis*, 35(C):268–280.

Berger, A. N. and Humphrey, D. B. (1997). Efficiency of financial institutions: International survey and directions for future research. *European Journal of Operational Research*, 98(2):175 – 212.

Berle, A. and Means, G. (1932). *The Modern Corporation and Private Property.* New York: Macmillan.

Black, B. S., Love, I., and Rachinsky, A. (2006). Corporate governance indices and firms' market values: Time series evidence from Russia. *Emerging Markets Review*, 7(4):361 – 379. Financial market development in the Central and Eastern European countries.

Bokpin, G. A. (2013). Ownership structure, corporate governance and bank efficiency: an empirical analysis of panel data from the banking industry in Ghana. *Corporate Governance: The international journal of business in society*, 13(3):274–287.

Charnes, A., Cooper, W., and Rhodes, E. (1978). Measuring the efficiency of decision making units. *European Journal of Operational Research*, 2(6):429 – 444.

Damme, P. V., Wijesiri, M., and Meoli, M. (2016). Governance and Efficiency of Microfinance Institutions: Empirical Evidence from Sri Lanka. *South Asia Economic Journal*, 17(2):236–247.

De Zoort, F. T., Hermanson, D. R., Archambeault, D. S., and Reed, S. A. (2002). Audit Committee Effectiveness: A Synthesis of the Empirical Audit Committee Literature. *Journal of Accounting Literature*, 21:38–75.

European Central Bank (2004). *European Central Bank. Annual Report: 2004.* European Central Bank,Frankfurt.

Fidanoski, F., Mateska, V., and Simeonovski, K. (2014). Corporate Governance and Bank Performance: Evidence from Macedonia. *Economic Analysis*, 47(1-2):76–99.

Hartarska, V. and Mersland, R. (2012). Which Governance Mechanisms Promote Efficiency in Reaching Poor Clients? Evidence from Rated Microfinance Institutions. *European Financial Management*, 18(2):218–239.

Huang, C.-J. (2010). Board, ownership and performance of banks with a dual board system: Evidence from Taiwan. *Journal of Management and Organization*, 16(2):219 – 234.

Jensen, M. (1993). The Modern Industrial Revolution, Exit, and the Failure of Internal Control Systems. *Journal of Finance*, 48(3):831–80.

Jensen, M. C. and Meckling, W. H. (1976). Theory of the firm: Managerial behavior, agency costs and ownership structure. *Journal of Financial Economics*, 3(4):305 – 360.

Klein, A. (2002). Audit committee, board of director characteristics, and earnings management. *Journal of Accounting and Economics*, 33(3):375 – 400.

Kyereboah-Coleman, A. (2008). Corporate governance and firm performance in Africa : a dynamic panel data analysis. *Studies in Economics and Econometrics*, 32(2):1–24.

Laan, G., Ees, H., and Witteloostuijn, A. (2008). Corporate Social and Financial Performance: An Extended Stakeholder Theory, and Empirical Test with Accounting Measures. *Journal of Business Ethics*, 79(3):299–310.

Laeven, L. and Levine, R. (2009). Bank governance, regulation and risk taking. *Journal of Financial Economics*, 93(2):259 – 275.

Murillo-Zamorano, L. R. (2004). Economic Efficiency and Frontier Techniques. *Journal of Economic Surveys*, 18(1):33–77.

Ntim, C. and Osei, K. (2011). The impact of corporate board meetings on corporate performance in South Africa. *African Review of Economics and Finance*, 2(2):83–103.

Oteng-Abayie, E. F. (2017). Technical efficiency and total factor productivity of rural banks in Ghana. *Cogent Economics & Finance*, 5(1):1366088.

Paxton, J. (2003). A poverty outreach index and its application to microfinance. *Economics Bulletin*, 9(2):1–10.

Poudel, Ravi Prakash; Hovey, M. (2013). Corporate governance and efficiency in Nepalese commercial banks. *International Review of Business Research Papers*, pages 53–64.

Rao, K. and Desta, K. (2016). Corporate Governance and Financial Performance: A study with reference to Commercial Banks in Ethiopia. *International Journal of Applied Research*, 2(8):551–557.

Romano, G., Ferretti, P., and Rigolini, A. (2012). Corporate Governance and Performance in Italian Banking Groups. In *"Corporate governance & regulation: outlining new horizons for theory and practice"*.

Salim, R., Arjomandi, A., and Seufert, J. H. (2016). Does corporate governance affect Australian banks' performance? *Journal of International Financial Markets, Institutions and Money*, 43:113 – 125.

Soba, M., Erem, I., and Ceylan, F. (2016). The impact of corporate governance practices on bank efficiency: A case of Turkey. *Journal of Suleyman Demirel University Institute of Social Sciences*, 25(3):305–322.

Tahir, M. W. C. W. A. (2015). Effects of Corporate Governance on Organization Performance: Evidence from Banking Sector of Pakistan. *Journal of Business and Management*, 17(3):75–82.

Tai, L. (2015). The Impact of Corporate Governance on the Efficiency and Financial Performance of GCC National Banks. *Middle East Journal of Business*, 10(1):12–16.

Tanna, S., Pasiouras, F., and Nnadi, M. (2011). The Effect of Board Size and Composition on the Efficiency of UK Banks. *International Journal of the Economics of Business*, 18(3):441–462.

Thanassoulis, E., Boussofiane, A., and Dyson, R. (1996). A comparison of data envelopment analysis and ratio analysis as tools for performance assessment. *Omega*, 24(3):229 – 244.

Figure 1: Average Technical Efficiency: VRS Output Oriented (2007-2013)

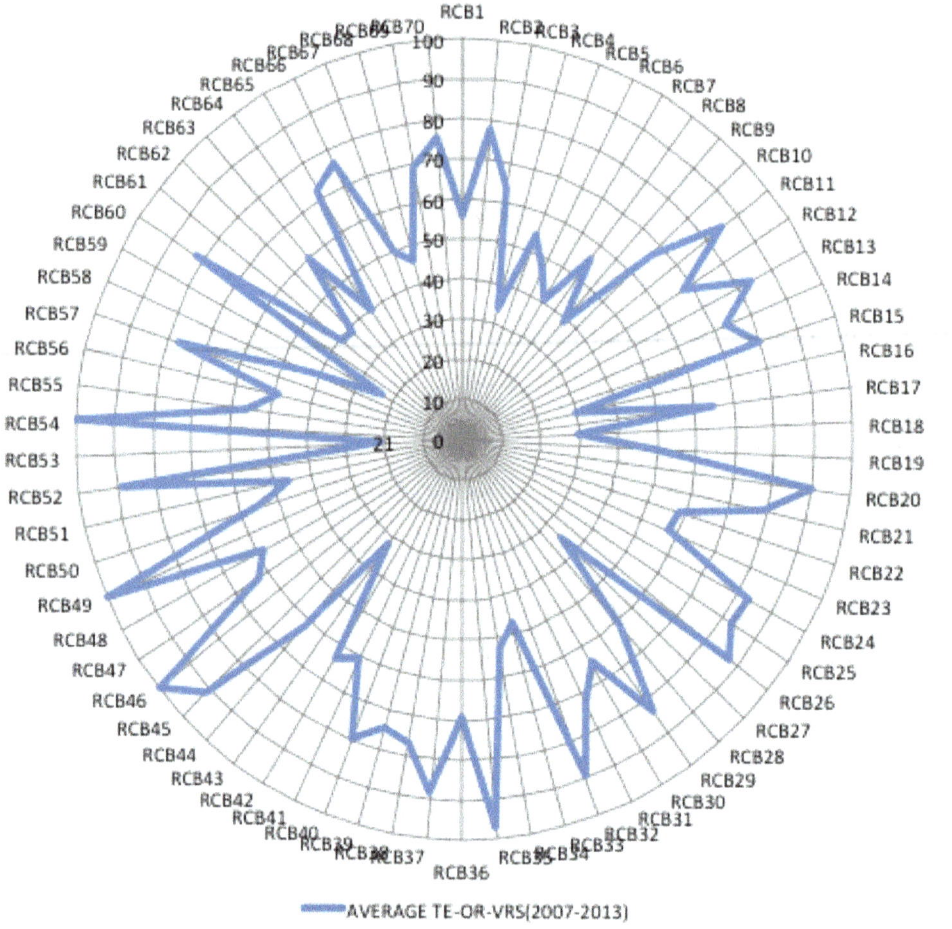

Figure 2: Average Technical Efficiency: VRS Input Oriented (2007-2013)

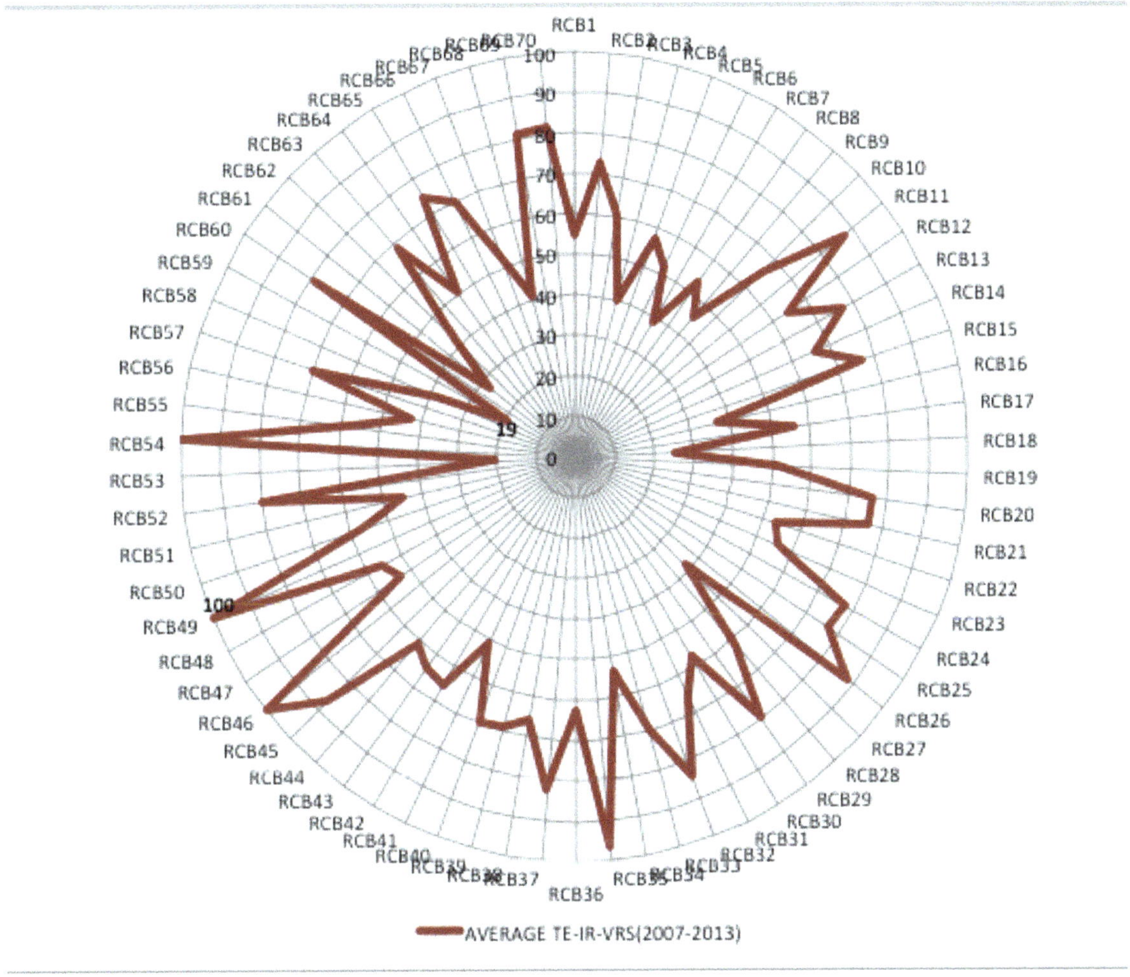

Figure 3: Average Technical Efficiency: CRS (2007-2013)

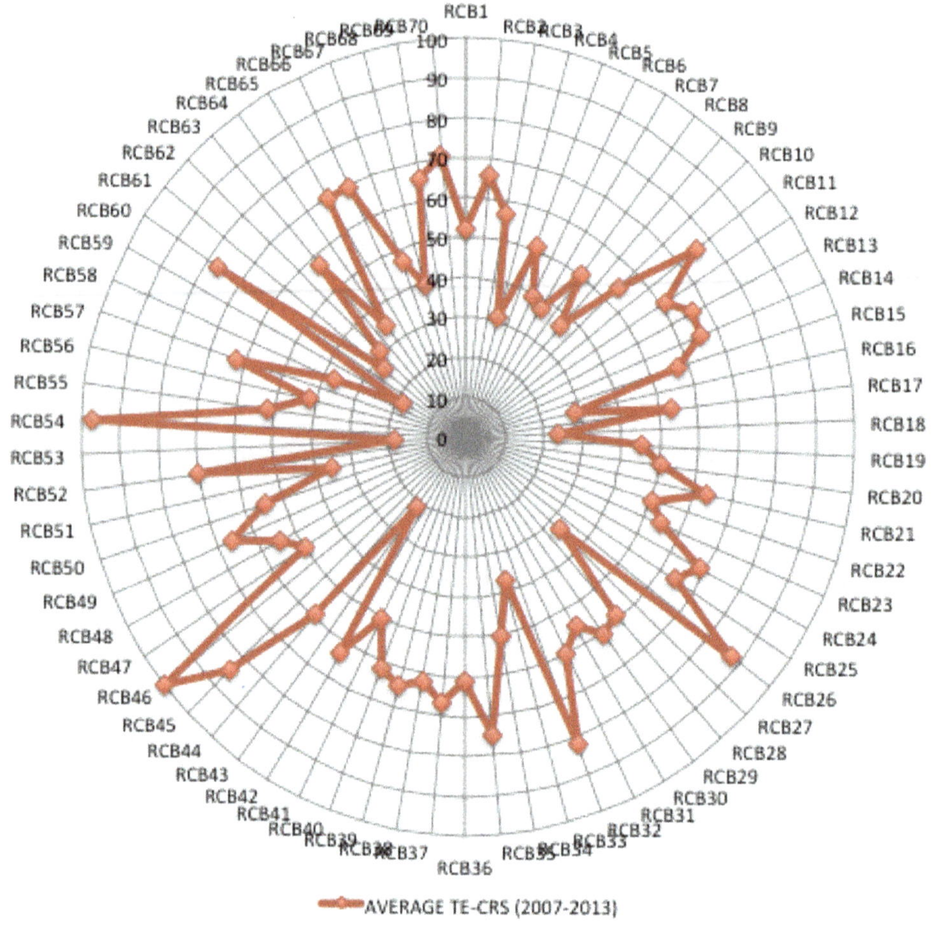

Figure 4: Trends in Overall Average Technical Efficiency (2007-2013)

Table 1: Summary of Empirical Literature on Corporate Governance and Bank Efficiency

Authors	Country and Period	Method	Bank Performance Indicator	Corporate Governance Indicators	Key Findings
Frontier efficiency studies					
Salim et al. (2016)	Australia (1999-2013)	Data Envelopment Analysis and Truncated Regression Analysis	Technical efficiency Inputs: - Interest expenses - Non-interest expenses Outputs: - Interest income - Non-interest income	- Board size - Board independence - Number of board meetings - Number of committee meetings - Ownership concentration	Positive relationship between technical efficiency and both board size and number of committee meetings
Soba et al. (2016)	Turkey (2005-2015) 10 Turkish depository banks listed in Borsa Istanbul (BIST)	Data Envelopment Analysis and Panel Regression Analysis	Technical efficiency Inputs: - Total deposits - Interest expenses - Personnel expenses Outputs: - Total loans - Interest income	- Board independence - Major shareholder - Number of committees - Board size	Board independence has a negative and significant impact on the efficiency of the banks. Major shareholder, number of committees, and board size has positive and significant relationship with bank efficiency.

Continued on the next page

Table 1: Summary of Empirical Literature on Corporate Governance and Bank Efficiency (Continued)

Authors	Country and Period	Method	Bank Performance Indicator	Corporate Governance Indicators	Key Findings
Frontier efficiency studies					
Damme et al. (2016)	Sri Lanka (2011) 36 monetary financial institutions (MFIs)	Data Envelopment Analysis and Truncated Regression Analysis	Inputs: - Operating expenses - Total employees Outputs (Financial Model): - Gross loan portfolio Outputs (Outreach Model): - Women borrowers	- Board size - Number of women on the board - CEO/Chair duality - Presence of a woman CEO on the board	Results reveal that smaller and gender-diverse boards have a positive impact on financial efficiency. MFIs in which the chief executive officer (CEO) chairs the board and a woman holds the CEO position are less efficient in terms of poverty outreach.
Andrieş et al. (2018)	17 countries of Central and Eastern Europe (2005-2012) 139 commercial banks	Data Envelopment Analysis Method	- Cost efficiency - Technical efficiency	- Corporate governance index - Risk management index - Supervisory board index	Rigorous corporate governance structures are associated with higher costs for banks and a lower level of efficiency. Tight governance mechanisms significantly increase banks' cost and technical efficiencies.

Table 1: Summary of Empirical Literature on Corporate Governance and Bank Efficiency (Continued)

Authors	Country and Period	Method	Bank Performance Indicator	Corporate Governance Indicators	Key Findings
Frontier efficiency studies					
Bokpin (2013)	Ghana (1999-2007) 25 commercial banks	Stochastic Frontier Analysis and Panel Data Analysis	- Cost efficiency - Profit efficiency Inputs: - Labor input price - Finance input price - Physical input prices Outputs: - Loans and investments	- Ownership structure - Board size - Board independence - Inside ownership	Governance (a larger board size) strongly improves profit efficiency, but slightly worsens banks' cost efficiency.
Hartarska and Mersland (2012)	60 countries 278 MFIs	Stochastic Frontier Analysis	- Cost efficiency	- Board size - CEO duality - Number of independent executives on the board	The findings of the study showed that the size of the board has a non-linear effect on firms' cost efficiency. Furthermore, we observed that CEO duality and the number of independent executives on the board negatively affects the efficiency of firms.
Tanna et al. (2011)	England (2001-2006) 17 banks	Panel Regression Analysis	- Cost efficiency Inputs: - Fixed assets - Deposits and short-term funding - Personnel expenses Outputs: - Net loans - Other earning assets	- Board size - Board independence	Positive relationship with all corporate governance variables.

Continued on the next page

Table 1: Summary of Empirical Literature on Corporate Governance and Bank Efficiency (Continued)

Authors	Country and Period	Method	Bank Performance Indicator	Corporate Governance Indicators	Key Findings
Accounting-based studies					
Al-Sahafi et al. (2015)	Saudi Arabia (2009-2012) 11 banks	Panel Regression Analysis	- Return on assets - Return on equity - Tobin's Q	- Board size - Board independence - CEO status - Audit committee - Ownership concentration	Positive relationship with board size and board independence. Negative relationship with ownership concentration.
Haider et al. (2015)	Pakistan (2008-2012)	Correlation and Linear Regression Analysis	- Return on assets - Return on equity - Earnings per share	- Board size - Number of meetings - Audit committee size	Positive relationship with all corporate governance variables
Arouri et al. (2014)	GCC countries (2010) 58 banks	Multivariate Regression Analysis	- Tobin's Q	- Family ownership - Institutional ownership - Foreign ownership - Government ownership - Board size - CEO duality	Positive relationship with family, institutional, and foreign ownership.
Al-Amarneh (2014)	Jordan (2000-2012) 13 banks	Panel Regression Analysis	- Return on assets - Operating efficiency ratio	- Ownership concentration - Institutional ownership - Foreign ownership - Board size - CEO duality	Positive relationship with board size and ownership concentration. Not significant with institutional and foreign ownership.

Continued on the next page

Table 1: Summary of Empirical Literature on Corporate Governance and Bank Efficiency (Continued)

Authors	Country and Period	Method	Bank Performance Indicator	Corporate Governance Indicators	Key Findings
Accounting-based studies					
Poudel (2013)	Nepal (2005-2011) 29 banks	Panel Regression Analysis	- Non-performing loan/total loan	- Board size - Board independence - Number of board meetings - Audit committee size - Number of audit committee meetings - Institutional ownership - Foreign ownership	Positive relationship with board size, audit committee size, and board independence.
Akpan and Riman (2012)	Nigeria (2005-2008) 11 banks	Correlation and Regression Analysis	- Return on assets - Return on equity - Non-performing loans	- Board size - CEO duality - Number of shareholders	Positive relationship with all corporate governance variables.
Tomar and Bino (2012)	Jordan (1997-2006) 14 banks	Panel Regression Analysis	- Return on assets - Return on equity	- Ownership structure - Composition of board of directors - Managerial ownership - Outstanding shares owned by members of board of directors - Number of directors appointed by the shareholders on the board	Positive relationship with compositions of board of directors and institutional ownership. Negative relationship with institutional ownership.

Continued on the next page

Table 1: Summary of Empirical Literature on Corporate Governance and Bank Efficiency (Continued)

Authors	Country and Period	Method	Bank Performance Indicator	Corporate Governance Indicators	Key Findings
Accounting-based studies					
Aygun et al. (2010)	Turkey (2006-2008) 12 banks	Correlation and Regression Analysis	- Return on assets - Tobin's Q	- Board size - Free float rate	Negative relationship between board size and return on assets. Positive relationship between Tobin's Q and return on assets. Positive relationship with free float rate.
Praptiningsih (2009)	Asian Emerging Markets (2003-2007) 52 banks	Panel Regression Analysis	- Return on assets	- Ownership concentration - Government ownership - Foreign ownership - CEO duality - Board size - Board Independence - Rating of banks by reputable ratings agencies (Big 3) - Auditing by reputable external auditor (Big 4)	Not significant relationship with board size, board independence, ownership concentration, and Big 3. Negative relationship with foreign ownership and CEO duality. Positive relationship with Big 4.
Staikouras et al. (2007)	Europe (2002-2004) 58 European banks	Panel Regression Analysis	- Return on assets - Tobin's Q	- Board size - Board Independence	Negative relationship with board size. Positive relationship with board independence.

Table 2: Summary of Variables Used in the Study

Variables	Description	Hypothesized signs
Performance variables		
Deposits	Used as an input variable and measured as the total savings deposits of members of a particular RCB	n/a
Expenses	Used as an input variable and defined as the total operating expenses, including interest expenses, of the RCB	n/a
Interest	Used as an output variable and defined as the total income	n/a
Income	due to interest payment on loans	
Loans	Volume of loans granted to members in a particular year.	n/a
Corporate Governance variables		
NBM	Number of board members (board size)	+/-
FBM	Frequency of board meetings	+
ACS	Number of audit committee members (audit committee size)	+/-
FACM	Frequency of audit committee meetings	+/-
CSR	The level of corporate social responsibility	+

Table 3: Descriptive Statistics of Input and Output Variables

Variables	N	Mean	Std.Dev	Minimum	Maximum
Deposits	490	6,569,255	7,152,924	78767.37	5.13e+07
Interest Expenses	490	1,123,206	1.38e+07	7754.22	3.04e+08
Interest Income	490	2,242,833	2.17e+07	19968	4.78e+08
Loans and Advances	488	3,438,434	3,692,280	23907.3	2.55e+07

Table 4: Frequency Distribution of Mean Technical Efficiency Scores

Frequency	2007	2008	2009	2010	2011	2012	2013
<=30	4 (5.7%)	6 (8.57%)	8 (11.43%)	8 (11.43%)	15 (21.43%)	8 (11.43%)	6 (8.57%)
31-50	10 (14.29%)	9 (12.86%)	12 (17.14%)	14 (20%)	18 (25.71%)	15 (21.43%)	16 (22.86%)
51-70	19 (27.14%)	21 (30%)	16 (22.86%)	20 (28.57%)	19 (27.12%)	20 (28.57%)	22 (31.43%)
71-90	20 (28.57%)	19 (27.12%)	19 (27.12%)	19 (27.12%)	10 (14.29%)	19 (27.12%)	10 (27.12%)
91-99	2 (2.86%)	3 (4.29%)	2 (2.86%)	3 (4.29%)	1 (1.43%)	1 (1.43%)	4 (5.7%)
100.00	14 (20%)	11 (15.71%)	13 (18.57%)	5 (7.14%)	7 (10%)	7 (10%)	11 (15.71%)
Overall Stats							
Mean score	69.36	68.57	66.39	61.34	54.28	61.92	63.67
Standard dev.	22.85	23.84	25.41	24.74	25.85	23.07	24.65
Minimum score	16.10	12	13.80	12.70	11.20	19.90	19.90
Maximum score	100	100	100	100	100	100	100

Table 5: Effect of Corporate Governance on RCB Technical Efficiency (TE)

	Efficiency Models		
Variables	**TE (OR-VRS)**	**TE (IR-VRS)**	**TE (CRS)**
Constant	46.80***	46.42***	22.63
	(15.22)	(15.86)	(14.30)
NBM	4.613**	3.888*	6.008***
	(1.950)	(1.977)	(1.829)
FBM	0.685	0.433	1.212*
	(0.708)	(0.720)	(0.669)
FACM	-2.079	-0.905	-2.671
	(2.557)	(2.613)	(2.399)
ACS	0.157	0.123	0.179
	(0.559)	(0.571)	(0.55)
CSR	0.00009	0.0003	0.0004**
	(0.0002)	(0.0002)	(0.0002)
F(5,64)	1.44	1.31	3.88***
R-squared	0.1013	0.0929	0.2325
Root MSE	18.892	19.218	17.793

6

Governance and Financial Development: Evidence from the Middle East and North Africa Region

Badry Hechmy *♣

♣University of Tunis el Manar, Faculty of Economic Sciences and Management of Tunis

---

ABSTRACT: Since the 1990s, the promotion of good governance has been a priority for major international organizations such as the International Monetary Fund and the World Bank. This article aims to estimate the effect of institutional development on financial development in MENA countries during the period 1996 to 2013. Drawing on Demetriades and Luintel (1996) and Ito (2006), the econometric approach used is based on the GMM, the autocorrelation test for errors of Arellano and Bond (1991), and the over-identification test of Sargan for dynamic panel data. The results derived from this study show a considerable delay in financial development in MENA countries compared to several other emerging countries in Asia and Latin America. Furthermore, it shows a negative effect of institutional development on financial development. This unexpected relationship between these two variables has two explanations. First, the delusory level of institutional development of some countries in the region actually remains under the threshold beyond which it begins to positively affect the financial sector. Second, the political unrest experienced by the region during the study period has encouraged the informal financial sector to the detriment of the formal sector.

Keywords: financial deepening, governance, institutional development, MENA, GMM

*Corresponding Author. Email: Badrihechmi2013@gmail.com

Introduction

There has been ongoing debate and extensive discussion about strategies to enable financial growth in developing countries. A few studies indicate that the quality and structure of financial institutions is based upon the important role of different political systems (La Porta et al., 1996), the institutional framework (Engerman and Sokoloff, 1994; Chinn and Ito, 2002), the development of telecommunications infrastructure, and computing and financial sector policies (Merton, 1992). Weak institutional development may explain the considerable delay in development of the financial sector in the Middle East and North Africa (MENA) countries compared to some emerging countries of South East Asia (such as Malaysia and South Korea) and Latin America.

In their financial and economic development and poverty reduction programs, major international organizations such as the International Monetary Fund and the World Bank provide guidelines to promote good governance. This paper reports on an analysis of the impacts of institutional and legal growth based on these guidelines, on the financial development of the MENA countries using a new econometric approach primarily based on the generalized method of moments (GMM) estimation approach for dynamic panel data models.

The remainder of this paper is divided into four sections. Section 1 summarizes the main theoretical and empirical results on the relationship between institutional development and financial deepening. Section 2 describes the empirical method used in this study. Section 3 reports and discusses the findings and Section 4 offers a conclusion.

1 Review of the Theoretical and Empirical Literature

The literature on the relationship between financial development and institutional development can be divided into three schools of thought to explain the level of financial development: the legal system, political factors, and social capital.

1.1 Legal System and Financial System: The Theory of Law and Finance

Legal and institutional frameworks can help explain the difference in the level of financial development observed between countries. In a country where the legal and judicial system strictly enforces the rights of private property, execution of contracts between economic agents, and the protection of legal rights of depositors, shareholders and investors, the financial markets will grow (La Porta et al., 1998; Beck and Levine, 2008). Indeed, such a system will restore confidence among the various economic agents (depositors, shareholders, and investors). Investors will increase their deposits with financial institutions, and this can lead to higher levels of investment. According to a study by Wurgler (2000), countries that respect the rights of creditors and shareholders benefit from an efficient allocation of credit against those countries where these rights are not respected. The less developed the judicial and legal system of a country is, causing investors and shareholders to be "afraid", the more are savings and investment levels lowered. This results in financial underdevelopment and reduces economic growth. By collecting data on firms in 20 countries, Love (2003) showed that financial constraints are more widespread in countries where the legal and judicial system is broken La Porta et al. (1998) showed that common law is more inclined to promote financial development, compared with other legal systems (French and Scandinavian).

1.2 Importance of Political Factors

Political factors can play a major role in determining the level of financial development in a country. When a group of people holds power, it creates an environment (political, institutional, and economic) that is profitable to them. The work of Rajan and Zingales (1998) showed that when the ruling class of a country is strongly constituted of landowning aristocrats, financial markets are poorly developed, but when power is largely held by businesspeople (traders, business leaders, industrialists, etc.), financial markets develop. Indeed, businesses need financial resources to boost their economic activities. They will, therefore, establish a climate or an environment conducive to attracting capital.

Based on the thesis of Myrdal (1963), Mama (2006) showed that it is necessary and desirable to establish a "strong state" and kill the "soft state" characterized by corruption, mismanagement, incompetence and inefficiency of public services, administrative delays, failure to respect laws, and misappropriation of public funds, that has prevented financial development in many African countries.[1] In a soft state, the political powers may actually destabilize the functioning of financial markets because they borrow excessively from financial institutions without repaying the credit.

1.3 The Role of Social Capital

In the social science literature, the term social capital has several connotations. The terms usually used in the definition are: cooperative norms, confidence, and networks that enable people to act collectively (Putnam et al., 1994; Knack and Keefer, 1997). The efficiency of a market economy is based on perfect information. Financial markets are imperfect and characterized by information asymmetries between lenders and borrowers (Stiglitz and Weiss, 1981).

[1]Gunnar Myrdal received the Nobel Memorial Prize in Economic Sciences in 1974.

In the presence of imperfect information situations in the financial markets, moral qualities (confidence, loyalty, etc.) can play an important role in financial development. Many exchanges between economic agents are made on the basis of confidence that enables a considerable reduction in transaction, monitoring, and information costs (Fukuyama, 1995). The loss of confidence of economic agents (depositors and lenders) resulting from the fear of non-repayment of loaned capital and distrust of institutions and financial contracts, leads to a decrease in lending to the economy, thus narrowing financial markets.

It is clear that the confidence of economic agents in established financial contracts and the economic and institutional environment plays a major role in the development of financial markets, even in the case of noncompliance with laws (Galindo et al., 2001). By analyzing the effect of confidence on financial deepening in areas of northern and southern Italy, a study by Guiso et al. (2004) found that in areas where economic agents have greater confidence in one another, individuals have easy access to credit, investment rates are high, and the use of the informal financial market is weak.

2 Empirical Method

2.1 Methodology

The generalized method of moments[2] (GMM) in dynamic panel data models, introduced by Holtz-Eakin et al. (1988) and Arellano and Bond (1991), solves the problems of simultaneity bias, reverse causality, and omitted variables. The GMM is better than the ordinary least squares estimator, because the latter is not consistent in the case of a dynamic model.[3] There are two forms of GMM estimators in dynamic panels: the first difference GMM estimator and the GMM system estimator.

The method which Arellano and Bond (1991) proposed is a GMM first difference estimator. It involves taking, for each period, the first difference of the equation to be estimated to eliminate country specific effects, and instrumenting thereafter the explanatory variables of the first difference equation by their values lagged one period or more. The model of Blundell and Bond (1998) determined a GMM system estimator that combines the first difference equations with the level equations where the variables are instrumented by their first differences. The GMM system estimator seems better than the first difference GMM estimator as the latter estimator gives more biased results in the case of finite samples when instruments are weak.

[2]Levine et al. (2000) have provided detailed arguments justifying the use of GMM.

[3]In our case, a dynamic model is a model where one of its explanatory variables is a lagged dependent variable. This delayed explanatory variable will be correlated with the model error. Due to this correlation, the estimator of the ordinary least squares (and the generalized least squares) is not consistent.

The study period ran from 1996 to 2013 and the sample was composed of 17 countries: Algeria, Bahrain, Egypt, Iran, Iraq, Jordan, Kuwait, Lebanon, Libya, Morocco, Oman, Qatar, Saudi Arabia, Syria, Tunisia, United Arab Emirates, and Yemen. The data used in this study came mainly from the World Bank database.

2.2 The Model to Estimate

The basic equation used for the econometric estimates is based on the work of Demetriades and Luintel (1996) and Ito (2006) on financial development. The dynamic equation is presented as follows:

$$FD_{i,t} = \alpha \cdot FD_{i,t-1} + \beta \cdot ID_{i,t} + \gamma \cdot X_{i,t} + u_i + \varepsilon_{i,t}, \tag{1}$$

where:

- $FD_{i,t}$: financial development in country i at time t;
- $ID_{i,t}$: institutional development in country i at time t;
- $X_{i,t}$: a vector of control variables such as GDP per capita (PIB), inflation (INF), a composite index of financial liberalization (FL);
- u_i: the country-specific effect;
- $\varepsilon_{i,t}$: the error term.

Definitions are provided in the following section for the composite variables in the dynamic equation as well as the macroeconomic variables considered in the context of this work, namely gross domestic product (GDP) per capita and inflation.

Composite index of financial development (FD). Several financial development indicators have been identified in the literature since the work of King and Levine (1993). Due to the availability of statistical data, this study makes use of only two of these financial development indicators: the money supply to GDP ratio ($M2/GDP$), and private sector credit to GDP ratio (PSC/GDP). Financial development refers to a strong mobilization of savings and the financing of the economy by financial institutions. $M2/GDP$ captures the mobilization of savings, whereas PSC/GDP is used to measure the financing of the economy. These two indicators were built from World Bank statistical data. To capture overall financial development, it seemed appropriate to calculate the composite index; the latter is obtained in the following manner:

$$FD_t = \frac{1}{2}\left(\frac{M2_t}{PIB_t} + \frac{PSC_t}{PIB_t}\right) \tag{2}$$

Index of financial liberalization (FL). We used the index of financial liberalization from the International Monetary Fund, which is calculated as the sum of the seven following indicators: credit control, interest rate controls, barriers to entry, banking supervision, privatizations, exchange control, and regulation of financial markets.

Index of institutional development (ID). Previously used by Kaufmann et al. (2006), the ID is a composite index of five institutional development indicators: control of corruption (CC), political stability (PS), rule of law (RL), regulatory quality (RQ), and government effectiveness (GE), and is obtained as follows:

$$ID_t = \frac{1}{5}(CC_t + PS_t + RL_t + RQ_t + GE_t) \tag{3}$$

GDP per capita. The variable GDP per head which captures economic growth can pose an endogeneity problem in equation (1). However, the use of GMM overcomes this difficulty. Some studies have shown that economic growth affects financial development (Schumpeter, 1934; King and Levine, 1995; Beck et al., 2000), whereas others revealed the opposite (Robinson, 1952).

Inflation (Inf). Inflation is likely to influence economic decisions, especially in terms of placement. A high inflation rate may discourage the use of financial intermediation and encourage investment in real assets (such as real estate, gold, oil, etc.). The level of inflation is often considered an indicator of financial repression, particularly because of seigniorage (McKinnon, 1973). These data come from World Development Indicators Database Archives.

3 Results and Discussion

We started with the residual autocorrelation test, the Sargan overidentification test, and stationarity test for panel data. In a second step, we conducted the estimation of results by the method of Arellano and Bond (1991). The Hansen test did not reject the hypothesis of validity of the lagged variables in levels and in differences as instruments. The residual autocorrelation test suggested that the hypothesis of no serial correlation of residuals could not be rejected.

3.1 Stationarity Test for Panel Data

We used the stationarity test of Im, Pesaran, and Shin (2003) (IPS) which is the most used due to certain relative advantages in comparison to other stationarity tests. For example, unlike the test by Levin and Lin (1993), the IPS test allows for heterogeneity of the autoregressive root and a heterogeneity regarding the presence of a unit root in the panel.

Augmented Dickey-Fuller stationarity tests were applied separately for each country in the model, which can be written as follows:

- the model without trend:

$$\Delta Y_{i,t} = \alpha_i + \rho_i Y_{i,t-1} + \sum_j \beta_{i,j} \Delta Y_{i,t-j} + \varepsilon_{i,t} \tag{4}$$

- the model with trend:

$$\Delta Y_{i,t} = \alpha_i + \rho_i Y_{i,t-1} + \delta_i t + \sum_j \beta_{i,j} \Delta Y_{i,t-j} + \varepsilon_{i,t}, \tag{5}$$

where α_i is the individual effect, $\varepsilon_{i,t} \sim N\left(0, \sigma_\varepsilon^2\right)$, $i = 1, 2 \ldots N$; $t = 1, 2 \ldots T$.
The IPS test consisted of testing the null hypothesis (H_0) of nonstationarity for all countries against the alternative hypothesis (H_1) of stationarity for at least one country.

$$H_0: \quad \rho_i = 1$$

$$H_1: \quad \rho_i < 1$$

The IPS-t statistic is the average of N-ADF individual statistics. The results of the IPS test (2002) stationary panel are shown in Table 1.

We note that all series were nonstationary when the trend was not taken into account, and they were stationary around a deterministic trend.

3.2 Results of the Model by Arellano and Bond

The lagged endogenous variable was statistically significant, assuming a positive sign, which indicated there was not a static relationship in the model, but a dynamic one. It also meant that countries that experienced an improvement in the ratio of financial development in a given year, also experienced an improvement in this ratio during the next year.

The financial liberalization coefficient was positive and significant; this result supports the thesis of McKinnon (1973) and Shaw (1973) that liberalization policy promotes financial deepening. Conscious that government intervention only allows the creation of several financial distortions, the majority of countries in the region started relative financial liberalization in the 1990s, with the help of international financial institutions. The restrictive policies adopted by MENA countries until that date, such as reserve requirements, the supervision of credit policy, and the preferred financing and administration of interest rates accompanied by high inflation rates have resulted in a reduction of loanable funds to businesses and a limit of bank competition.

The low level of institutional development of the MENA countries affects negatively and significantly their level of financial development. This result is not surprising. In fact, there is a threshold at which institutional development begins to have a positive effect on the financial sector and this threshold has not been reached by some countries in the region. The improvement of the legal and institutional framework of those countries, in recent years, with the help of international institutions, has usually taken a long time to effect.

Afterward, even for countries with relatively developed institutional frameworks, the political unrest, Gulf War, Arab Spring, and terrorism that have been experienced by the region since the early 1990s have favored the informal financial sector to the detriment of the formal sector, which has reversed the relationship normally expected between institutional development and financial development.

According to the existing literature (La Porta et al., 1997, 1998; Levine, 1998; Wurgler, 2000; Barth et al., 2003; Edison, 2003; Acemoglu et al., 2008), the financial reforms that have been adopted by MENA countries can have adverse effects on the financial system (systemic crises) in countries with less developed institutional environments. Indeed, corruption, political instability, inefficient government actions, and the unreliability of the regulatory framework for financial activities that characterize these countries in the MENA region contribute to their financial underdevelopment.

An increase in the level of GDP per capita had a positive and significant effect on financial development. This result supports the "demand following" thesis of Patrick (1966) where financial development is a consequence of economic growth. A high inflation rate had a positive effect on financial development, but not a statistically significant one. The over identification Sargan test (P = 0.1324) did not allow us to reject the hypothesis that the lagged variables were valid instruments in the model. Similarly, there is an absence of residual autocorrelation at order two (P = 0.9287) but the residual autocorrelation is present at order one (P = 0.0082), and the expected outcome for the GMM is better.

4 Conclusion

The results indicate that institutional development and financial development are negatively related. This can be explained, on the one hand, by the fact that the institutional reforms adopted by some countries in the region remain below the threshold at which the institutional development would start to have a positive effect on the financial sector, and, on the other hand, by the fact that the relationship between these two variables is perturbed by political turmoil experienced by the region during the studied period. If the level of institutional quality was high enough, most countries would have been able to improve their level of financial development.

MENA countries have an interest in implementing strategies that support the fight against corruption and political instability, and improve the effectiveness of government actions and the quality of the regulatory framework. Control of corruption, respect for democratic principles, respect for laws and the legislature are important elements related to the success of any financial policy promoting sustainable economic growth.

Finally, a limitation of this study was the inability to examine the impact of another factor often underlined by the new literature as a natural complement to the institutional environment—social capital, which is measured by the level of confidence or cooperation between individuals. Norms that produce social capital must include substantial sincerity, loyalty, cooperation, and reciprocity. The relationship between social capital and financial development can be reduced to a financial contract between creditor and entrepreneur, which requires primarily a degree of trust between agents for the respect of contract terms. Future research could be directed at providing insight into the impact of social capital, and in particular, whether a high level of social capital is likely to develop financial contracts and, consequently, the financial markets.

References

Acemoglu, D., Johnson, S., Robinson, J. A., and Yared, P. (2008). Income and Democracy. *American Economic Review*, 98(3):808–42.

Arellano, M. and Bond, S. (1991). Some tests of specification for panel data: Monte Carlo evidence and an application to employment equations. *The Review of Economic Studies*, 58(2):277–297.

Barth, J. R., Nolle, D. E., Phumiwasana, T., and Yago, G. (2003). A Cross-Country Analysis of the Bank Supervisory Framework and Bank Performance. *Financial Markets, Institutions & Instruments*, 12(2):67–120.

Beck, T. and Levine, R. (2008). *Legal Institutions and Financial Development*, pages 251–278. Springer Berlin Heidelberg, Berlin, Heidelberg.

Beck, T., Levine, R., and Loayza, N. (2000). Finance and the sources of growth. *Journal of Financial Economics*, 58(1–2):261–300.

Blundell, R. and Bond, S. (1998). Initial conditions and moment restrictions in dynamic panel data models. *Journal of Econometrics*, 87(1):115–143.

Chinn, M. D. and Ito, H. (2002). Capital Account Liberalization, Institutions and Financial Development: Cross Country Evidence. Working Paper 8967, National Bureau of Economic Research.

Demetriades, P. O. and Luintel, K. B. (1996). Financial Development, Economic Growth and Banking Sector Controls: Evidence from India. *The Economic Journal*, 106(435):359–374.

Edison, H. (2003). Testing the Links. How Strong Are the Links Between Institutional Quality and Economic Performance? *Finance and Development*, 40(2):35–37.

Engerman, S. L. and Sokoloff, K. L. (1994). Factor Endowments: Institutions, and Differential Paths of Growth Among New World Economies: A View from Economic Historians of the United States. Working Paper 66, National Bureau of Economic Research.

Fukuyama, F. (1995). *Trust: The Social Virtues and the Creation of Prosperity.* New York: Free Press.

Galindo, A. J., Chong, A., and Calderón, C. A. (2001). Structure and Development of Financial Institutions and Links with Trust: Cross-Country Evidence. IDB Publications (Working Papers) 6482, Inter-American Development Bank.

Guiso, L., Sapienza, P., and Zingales, L. (2004). The Role of Social Capital in Financial Development. *American Economic Review*, 94(3):526–556.

Holtz-Eakin, D., Newey, W., and Rosen, H. S. (1988). Estimating Vector Autoregressions with Panel Data. *Econometrica*, 56(6):1371–1395.

Im, K. S., Pesaran, M., and Shin, Y. (2003). Testing for unit roots in heterogeneous panels. *Journal of Econometrics*, 115(1):53–74.

Ito, H. (2006). Financial development and financial liberalization in Asia: Thresholds, institutions and the sequence of liberalization. *The North American Journal of Economics and Finance*, 17(3):303–327.

Kaufmann, D., Kraay, A., and Mastruzzi, M. (2006). Governance matters V: aggregate and individual governance indicators for 1996 - 2005. Policy Research Working Paper Series 4012, The World Bank.

King, R. G. and Levine, R. (1995). Financial Intermediation and Economic Development. In Mayer, C. and Vives, X., editors, *Capital Markets and Financial Intermediation*, pages 156–189. Cambridge University Press, Cambridge/New York/Melbourne.

Knack, S. and Keefer, P. (1997). Does Social Capital Have an Economic Payoff? A Cross-Country Investigation. *The Quarterly Journal of Economics*, 112(4):1251–1288.

La Porta, R., de Silanes, F. L., Shleifer, A., and Vishny, R. W. (1997). Trust in Large Organizations. *The American Economic Review*, 87(2):333–338.

La Porta, R., de Silanes, F. L., Shleifer, A., and Vishny, R. W. (1998). Law and Finance. *Journal of Political Economy*, 106(6):1113–1155.

La Porta, R., Lopez-de Silane, F., Shleifer, A., and Vishny, R. W. (1996). Trust in Large Organizations. Working Paper 5864, National Bureau of Economic Research.

Levin, A. and Lin, C.-F. (1993). Unit Root Tests in Panel Data: New Results. *University of California at San Diego, Economics Working Paper Series.*

Levine, R. (1998). The Legal Environment, Banks, and Long-Run Economic Growth. *Journal of Money, Credit and Banking*, 30(3):596–613.

Levine, R., Loayza, N., and Beck, T. (2000). Financial intermediation and growth: Causality and causes. *Journal of Monetary Economics*, 46(1):31–77.

Love, I. (2003). Financial Development and Financing Constraints: International Evidence from the Structural Investment Model. *Review of Financial Studies*, 16(3):765–791.

Mama, T. (2006). Pour la mort de l'État en Afrique: de quel État faut-il souhaiter la mort? In Bekolo-Ebe, B., Mama, T., and Fouda, S. M., editors, *Mondialisation, Exclusion et Dveloppement Africain: Stratgies Des Acteurs Publics et Privs*, volume 2, pages 453–463. Maisonneuve & Larose.

McKinnon, R. I. (1973). *Money and Capital in Economic Development, 1973.* Washington, DC: The Brookings Institution.

Merton, R. C. (1992). Financial Innovation and Economic Performance. *Journal of Applied Corporate Finance*, 4(4):12–22.

Myrdal, G. (1963). *Challenge to Affluence: The Emergence of an Under-Class.* New York: Pantheon Books.

Putnam, R., Leonardi, R., and Nanetti, R. (1994). *Making Democracy Work: Civic Traditions in Modern Italy.* Princeton paperbacks. Princeton University Press.

Rajan, R. G. and Zingales, L. (1998). Financial Dependence and Growth. *American Economic Review*, 88(3):559–86.

Robinson, J. (1952). The Model of an Expanding Economy. *The Economic Journal*, 62(245):42–53.

Schumpeter, J. A. (1934). *The Theory of Economic Development: An Inquiry into Profits, Capital, Credit, Interest and the Business Cycle.* Cambridge, MA: Harvard University Press.

Shaw, E. (1973). *Financial Deepening in Economic Development.* Economic Development Report. Oxford University Press.

Stiglitz, J. E. and Weiss, A. (1981). Credit Rationing in Markets with Imperfect Information. *American Economic Review*, 71(3):393–410.

Wurgler, J. (2000). Financial markets and the allocation of capital. *Journal of Financial Economics*, 58(1–2):187–214.

Table 1: IPS Test

Variable	FD	FL	ID	GDP	INF
Model Without Trend	I(1)	I(1)	I(1)	I(1)	I(1)
Model With Trend	I(0)	I(0)	I(0)	I(0)	I(0)

Note: I(0) means that the series are stationary in a panel at the 5% significance level. I(1) means that series are not stationary in a panel.

Table 2: GMM Estimation

Variable	Coefficient	Standard Error	t_{cal}
FD_{lagged}	0.431*	0.08211	5.24
FL	0.00062*	0.00021	2.88
ID	-0.00311*	0.0002	-15.55
GDP	0.00061*	0.00021	3.11
INF	0.000001	0.000023	0.045
Constant	0.03251*	0.0053	6.2
Sargan test: 0.1324			
Arellano-Bond test for AR(2) in first differences: z = -3.4			
Arellano-Bond test for AR(1) in first differences: z = -2.72*			

Note: * coefficient significant at the 5% level, ** coefficient significant at the 10% level.

7

A Threshold Multivariate Model to Explain Fiscal Multipliers with Government Debt

Leonardo Augusto Tariffi*♣

♣University of Barcelona, Department of Economics

ABSTRACT: This paper shows fiscal multipliers, considering levels of public debt with multivariate threshold models. Non-linear behavior in sovereign debt-to-GDP ratio time series determine the relationship between output and government expenditure. The debt-to-GDP ratio has been selected optimally as an endogenous threshold variable to evaluate non-linearities; it has been useful for identifying estimators in a multivariate threshold autoregressive model; and it has been an important tool to observe how the multiplier changes during good times and bad. Expansionary fiscal policies seem to be counterproductive in this framework. This result highlights the link between real and financial variables.

Keywords: threshold models, non-linearity, public debt, fiscal multiplier

Introduction

Is expansionary government expenditure always the right economic policy in times of recession? Does the level of government debt have an impact on the relationship between public spending and economic growth? These two questions have long been at the core of several debates about public and financial economics. When production decreases and the output gap increases, counter-cyclical measures (such as a higher government expenditure)

*Corresponding Author. Email: ltariffi@ub.edu

can boost the demand for goods and services. If the fiscal policy is efficient, the aggregate supply returns to initial levels in order to match the increased demand and the output gap decreases. In this case, an expansionary fiscal policy has a positive effect over production. However, a higher government expenditure is sustainable only if government revenues (or the government debt) is also higher. At a certain point, increasing revenues or levels of public debt may have an impact on production. For instance, governments could charge households with new taxes in order to pay the accumulated debt, thereby diminishing consumption or savings. In both cases, production will shrink and the spread between production capacity and actual production will be bigger. This research finds that the government debt actually has an impact on the relationship between government expenditure and economic growth.

The impact of government expenditure on other macroeconomic variables has been long debated in the literature. According to Keynesians, government expenditure increases output because it boosts private consumption. Several authors with different models have presented evidence about a positive fiscal multiplier, a fiscal multiplier equal to 1 or higher than 1, or an underestimated expansionary fiscal effect. For instance, Blanchard and Perotti (2002), in a novel paper, show a positive effect of government spending on output with structural vector autoregressive regressions. Running a linear regression model, Blanchard and Leigh (2012) find that multipliers have been systematically too low since the start of the Great Recession. After studying the data from 28 economies they suggest that actual multipliers may be higher in environments of substantial economic slack and monetary policy constrained by the zero lower bound. Auerbach and Gorodnichenko (2012) estimate different measures of government spending multipliers during the business cycle. They develop a smooth transition autoregressive model to explain fiscal policy effects in both good times and bad. In their results, fiscal policies are considerably more effective in recessions than in expansions. Denes et al. (2012) analyze increases in demand via government spending when the nominal interest rate is bounded at the zero lower bound. In a standard New Keynesian dynamic stochastic general equilibrium (DSGE) model, they show that government spending increases output not only because of the current spending, but also through expectations about higher future government spending.

At the same time, other authors affirm that a fiscal stimulus could be diminished by high levels of government debt. If the debt-to-GDP ratio is "too high", expansionary fiscal policies cannot have any impact over other macroeconomic variables. This phenomenon is usually called the Ricardian equivalence or the spending reversal. For instance, Favero and Giavazzi (2007) show that, at some point, an increase in government spending might respond to the level of the public debt since the government intertemporal budget constraint will eventually have to be met. They include the debt-to-GDP ratio as a non-linear variable to augment a vector autoregressive model. Vansteenkiste and Nickel (2008) analyze the relationship between current accounts and government imbalances, considering also the debt-to-GDP ratio. In their opinion, households in very high debt countries tend to increase present savings to overcome a possible higher future expenditure. These authors estimate a dynamic panel threshold model for 22 countries in which the relationship between fiscal deficits and current accounts become statistically insignificant when public debts are relatively high.

Models explaining the impact of the debt-to-GDP ratio on fiscal multipliers can be improved by including other determinants. Reinhart and Rogoff (2010) study not only the relationship between economic growth fluctuations and government expenditure at different levels of public debt, but also the relationship between the inflation rate and the government expenditure at different levels of public debt. Their main finding is that the relationship between government debt and real GDP growth is weak below a threshold value of 90 and the growth rate falls 1% above 90. Although they do not find any link between inflation and public debt in industrialized countries, they find proportionally direct effects of public debt on inflation in emerging countries. Other variables considered in their analysis include political systems, institutions, exchange rate arrangements, and historical circumstances. Kim and Roubini (2008) and Ilzetzki et al. (2011) run vector autoregressive models to explain the link between fiscal indicators and international variables such as the current account. According to their empirical evidence, fiscal multipliers are lower in open economies than in closed economies and expansionary fiscal policies improve current accounts.

Another key factor which determines the effectiveness of government stimuli is the interest rate. Two seminal papers that analyze government spending multipliers in a New Keynesian DSGE framework when the nominal interest rate is bounded at the zero lower bound are those by Woodford (2010) and Christiano et al. (2011). In both papers, the multiplier effect is substantially plausible and large when monetary policies are constrained by the zero lower bound on nominal interest rates. The larger the fraction of government spending that occurs when the nominal interest rate is zero, the larger the value of the multiplier.

From a technical point of view, fiscal multipliers calculated with the dynamics of any linearized DSGE model or any standard VAR usually do not match with actual data because these methodologies do not allow for state dependence or do not take into account fiscal policies in different regimes. This mismeasure has encouraged the study of nonlinearities. "Our lack of knowledge stems significantly from the focus on linear dynamics: VARs and linearized (or close-to-linear) DSGEs" (Parker, 2011).

Non-linear relationships can be estimated using threshold models. Tsay (1998), using cointegration techniques to identify error correction mechanisms, generalizes the nonlinear autoregressive case in Tsay (1989) to a multivariate environment. He uses the resulting cointegrated series as a threshold variable and proposes a test statistic to detect nonlinearities in a multivariate regression, thereby evaluating whether there is more than one regime and finding their corresponding threshold values. He estimates the coefficients for all regimes with a least squares method, which includes the error correction mechanism and the number of lags. The threshold variable is chosen according to the Akaike information criterion.

Changing the order of the observations in the regression accordingly to an increasing threshold variable, the estimation of the threshold value corresponds to the estimation of a breakpoint. Therefore, estimation of the threshold regression and models with structural breaks are fundamentally equivalent. Bai and Perron (1998, 2003) address the issue of estimating structural break points and present an efficient algorithm to obtain global minimizers of the sum of squared residuals with least-squares operations. They estimate break dates with their threshold values and build tests to allow inference in the different regimes.

The relationship between GDP and government expenditure (GE) seems to be non-linear for some countries such as Belgium, Italy, and the United Kingdom. Scatter diagrams at Figures 1, 2, and 3 show a positive slope in the data when GDP is drawn in the horizontal axis (x) and GE in the vertical axis (y). This slope is relatively constant until a certain period of time, from which the government expenditure starts to grow faster than the GDP. Therefore, there is a change in the trend after both variables reach certain levels.

Figure 4 shows the debt-to-GDP ratio time series also for Belgium, Italy, and the UK. It can be seen that there is at least one structural break in the behavior of these variables around the year 2008 and a regime shift after this year. In this graph, a break point divides the data in high and low levels of the debt-to-GDP ratio for each country, changing the trend. These two regimes can be interpreted as good times and bad times, respectively; they are related to different GDP and GE growth rates (two separated fiscal multipliers), and they change the relationship between government expenditure and the GDP.

In the following sections, I first present a general multivariate threshold autoregressive model to explain non-lineal behaviors with two regimes. Second, I represent this model with a set of macroeconomic variables and several equations, taking into account the selection tools specified for the threshold variable. Data and results are shown for the above-mentioned three countries in Section 3. In order to improve robustness, I build a further multivariate threshold autoregressive model using a dynamic and interactive procedure in Section 4. Finally, I present some conclusions.

1 Econometric Technique and Estimation

The general multivariate threshold autoregressive model is the following:

$$y_{j,t} = \delta_j z_{j,t} + \theta_j q_{j,t-d} + u_{j,t}, \qquad \text{if} \quad \gamma_j \leq q_{t-d} < \gamma_{j+1} \tag{1}$$

where $y_{j,t}$ is the variable on the left hand side of the equation, $q_{j,t-d}$ are the threshold variables, u_t are the errors, and $z_{j,t}$ are the rest of the variables on the right hand side of the equations (including the constant).[1] The coefficients are δ_j and θ_j for the regressors $z_{j,t}$ and the threshold variables, respectively. Moreover, j is the number of regimes, t is the number of observations in each regime ($t = T_1, \ldots, T_j$), and d is the number of lags of the threshold variable. Note that $z_{j,t}$ could include lagged values of $y_{j,t}$. The non-linearity is modelled by structural changes in the threshold variable $q_{j,t-d}$ thereby shifting parameters in y_t and z_t for each regime. If there are strictly increasing threshold values $\gamma_1, \gamma_2, \ldots, \gamma_m$ (with m as the total number of breaks), the regime j is determined by those values of q_{t-d} (the m-partition) in between two threshold values γ_j and γ_{j+1}.

The general model (1) with two regimes ($j = 2$) is the following:

$$\begin{aligned} y_{1,t} &= \delta_1 z_{1,t} + \theta_1 q_{1,t-d} + u_{1,t}, \qquad &\text{if} \quad -\infty < q_{t-d} < \gamma_1 \\ y_{2,t} &= \delta_2 z_{2,t} + \theta_2 q_{2,t-d} + u_{2,t}, \qquad &\text{if} \quad \gamma_1 \leq q_{t-d} < \infty \end{aligned} \tag{2}$$

where d can be 1, 2, 3, or 4.

Parameter estimation is based on the least squares principle. Following Bai and Perron (1998, 2003) and assuming the existence of only two regimes, the associated least squares estimates of the coefficients δ_j and θ_j are obtained by minimizing the sum of squared residuals $\Sigma_{j=1}^{2}\Sigma_{t=1}^{T}\left[y_{j,t} - \delta_j z_{j,t} - \theta_j q_{j,t-d}\right]^2$ with respect to the coefficients. Given a specific threshold value γ_1, the minimization of the sum square residual is a simple least squares problem. Coefficients can be estimated by finding the threshold value and corresponding ordinary least square estimates that minimize the sum of squares across all possible sets of $m = 2$ threshold partitions.

Recalling (1) and (2), it is easy to see that models with two regimes will depend on values of the threshold variables q_{t-d} regarding the threshold value γ_1:

$$y_{j,t} = y_{1,t} + y_{2,t} = (\lambda)\left[\delta_1 z_{1,t} + \theta_1 q_{1,t-d} + u_{2,t}\right], \tag{3}$$

with $\lambda = 1$ when $-\infty < q_{t-d} < \gamma_1$ and $\lambda = 0$ when $\gamma_1 \leq q_{t-d} < \infty$.

Auerbach and Gorodnichenko (2012) specify a model without λ. In their model, variables

[1]In model (1), the multivariate threshold autoregressive model is represented by only one equation for several regimes j. For instance, $y_{j,t}$ is the gross domestic product. This equation corresponds to the first line of a vector autoregressive model (VAR). Substituting each endogenous variable in model (1) as variable $y_{j,t}$, the following rows of the VAR can be obtained. For instance, the gross domestic product can be substituted by the government expenditure as the variable on left hand side of the equation. The multivariate threshold autoregressive model can be treated as a threshold vector autoregressive model (TVAR) when there are no restrictions a priori in the TVAR.

are driven by a weighted average:

$$x_t = f(z_{t-1})\Pi_R x_{t-1} + (1 - f(z_{t-1}))\Pi_E x_{t-1} + u_t,$$

where weights are given by $f(z_t) = [(exp(-\varphi z_t))/(1 + exp(-\varphi z_t))]$, and $\varphi > 0$. This allows for a smooth transition and may give a better approximation of non-linearity. However, in short samples, the curvature parameter φ and the threshold value γ can be estimated only very imprecisely. Auerbach and Gorodnichenko (2012) overcome this problem by calibrating rather than estimating the curvature parameter using an exogenous source of information. This study uses specification (3) since λ is endogenous and depends on the threshold value γ of the threshold variable q_{t-d}.

2 Model Representation and Selection

Recalling model (1), it can be represented by the following equation:

$$GDP_{j,t} = c_j + \delta_{1,j}GE_{j,t} + \delta_{2,j}TO_{j,t} + \delta_{3,j}PI_{j,t} + \delta_{4,j}IR_{j,t} + \theta_j Debt_{j,t-d} + u_{j,t} \quad (4)$$

where $y_{j,t}$ is the gross domestic product (GDP), $z_{j,t}$ are the government expenditure (GE), trade openness (TO), consumer prices (PI), and interest rate (IR), and $q_{j,t-d}$ is the debt-to-GDP ratio (*Debt*). In equation (4), all variables have been included in differences (integrated of order 0) and augmented with lags of 1, 2, 3, and 4 periods. Therefore, time series have been transformed to $I(0)$ to run the model with only stationary variables.

The non-linearity is captured by the threshold variable $q_{j,t-d}$, which is the debt-to-GDP ratio. This variable (*Debt*) divides the model in two regimes ($j = 2$) after a structural break is found and allows a choice between 4 lags as in model (2).

There are 4 threshold candidates for each debt-to-GDP ratio variable in each country. Therefore, the multivariate threshold autoregressive model is selected through a dynamic and interactive procedure after the time series have been transformed to $I(0)$. Using least squares, this procedure excludes the less statistically significant variable in each interaction regarding the highest probability associated to the t statistic test of each coefficient. In order to improve the model's robustness, all variables are included in the regression in blocks[2].

Threshold variables are selected according to the Akaike selection criteria (AIC). As mentioned before, there are four lags ($d = 1, 2, 3,$ and 4) for each threshold variable debt-to-GDP

[2] The procedure can be seen as a general to specific methodology. This procedure can be used in the multivariate threshold's autoregressive model because, a priori, there are no restrictions in the parameters. In this model, the Akaike selection criteria (AIC) only chooses the best lag structure (delay) for the threshold variable. For further discussion on general to specific methodologies, see Campos et al. (2005)

ratio (*Debt*) in the multivariate threshold autoregressive model for all countries. This means that there are four candidates to determine the specification that minimizes the sum of squared residuals because the threshold variable will be lagged for 1, 2, 3, or 4 periods. AIC specifies a model asymptotically equivalent to a model that has the smallest generalized residual variance (Tsay, 1998).

3 Data and Results

There are six variables from 1996:q1 to 2015:q1 in three different countries: Belgium, Italy, and the United Kingdom. Regarding the time span, the maximum number of breaks is constrained to one. Primary sources are the World Bank, the National Bank of Belgium, the National Institute of Statistics of Italy (ISTAT), Eurostat, and the International Monetary Fund. Proxies are the following:

1) Variable GDP: The real gross domestic product at constant prices.
2) Variable GE: The government expenditure at constant prices.
3) Variable TO: The trade openness sums export of good and services plus import of goods and services in current prices divided by the real GDP.
4) Variable PI: The harmonized index of consumer prices.[3]
5) Variable IR: The three months reference rate of treasury certificates.
6) Variable *Debt*: The debt-to-GDP ratio of the central government.

The time series, such as prices in Italy, GDP in UK, and the debt-to-GDP ratio in Belgium, Italy, and UK, are integrated of order two. The rest of the variables show a one-unit root (see Table 1).

The time series have been transformed to $I(0)$ to build a multivariate threshold autoregressive model using the dynamic and interactive procedure. As mentioned before, this procedure excludes the less statistically significant variable in each interaction regarding the highest probability associated to the t statistic test of each coefficient. This procedure can be seen as a general to specific methodology and can be used in the multivariate threshold's autoregressive model because, a priori, there are no restrictions in the parameters. In this model, the Akaike selection criteria (AIC) only chooses the best lag structure (delay) for the threshold variable.

Table 2 shows results for the GDP differences in each country using the dynamic and interactive procedure described in Section 2. All variables have been transformed to $I(0)$ to be included in the multivariate threshold autoregressive model. Coefficients have been selected

[3]Prices proxies are the harmonized indices of consumer prices in Italy and England. This variable is more consistent with the GDP deflator used in the data of Belgium than inflation. They are all indices in levels.

excluding the less statistically significant variable in each interaction regarding the highest probability associated to the t statistic test of each coefficient. As mentioned before, all variables are included in the regression in blocks in order to improve the model's robustness.

Table 2 also shows the lags chosen, threshold values for all countries, and the number of observations in both regimes. The optimal delay is selected by determining the specification model that minimizes the sum of squared residuals from all candidates in the threshold variable. There are four threshold candidates for each debt-to-GDP ratio variable. Columns 2 and 3 in each country present estimations and p-values associated to the t statistics for the representation (4) of the multivariate threshold autoregressive model (1), augmented with variables lagged at 1, 2, 3, and 4 periods. In this table, D means 1st differences, $D2$ is 2nd differences, C is the constant, and the negative number in parenthesis is the lag of the variable.

The coefficients are all statistically significant at least at the 10% level in the first regime for each country, with the only exception being the value corresponding to the debt-to-GDP ratio in Italy. In Belgium, government expenditure with 3 lags is positive in the first regime and negative in the second regime. Trade openness and the GDP itself, both lagged at 1 period, are highly significant in both regimes. The debt-to-GDP ratio is only statistically significant in the first regime of this model. The threshold value is -1.28 and the R^2 is equal to 98%. In Italy, the debt-to-GDP ratio is only significant in the regime 2. Apart from the GDP lagged at 3 periods, all variables included in this model are significant in both regimes. Government expenditure is not only significant with 2 lags, but also with 4. The threshold value is 0.19 and the model explains the data well since the R^2 is higher than 70%. In the United Kingdom, government expenditure with 3 lags, prices with 4 lags, and the GDP with 1, 2, and 3 lags are significant in both regimes. The debt-to-GDP ratio is statistically significant only in the first period and the threshold value is 0.69. According to the R^2, which is equal to 95%, the threshold model fits the data very well.

Variables in the right-hand side of the equation are all significant. Coefficients of the government expenditure in differences (DGE) can be only interpreted as GDP variations with respect to government expenditure variations. Therefore, regarding the sum of all significant coefficients of the DGE (lags 1, 2, 3, and 4), fiscal multipliers in the very short term are 0.2 and -0.2 in Belgium, -0.8 and 0.5 in Italy, and 0.2 and -0.5 in the United Kingdom for regimes 1 and 2, respectively. According to the set of coefficients of the government expenditure in differences, an expansionary fiscal policy seems to be counterproductive in all countries.

The two main results are the following. First, government expenditure has an impact on the GDP in both regimes in all countries. In Belgium and the United Kingdom, an expansionary government expenditure effect is positive with low values of debt-to-GDP ratio, but it is negative when the debt-to-GDP ratio increases. In Italy, this result is not conclusive.

Second, the data shows at least two regimes in a nonlinear framework if the debt-to-GDP ratio is used as a threshold variable. However, following Tsay (1998), if the debt-to-GDP ratio is included in the least squares regression, this variable has an impact on the GDP only in regime 1 in Belgium and the United Kingdom, but it does in regime 2 in Italy.

4 Conclusion

Multivariate threshold models can be invoked in order to explain fiscal multipliers considering levels of public debt. Time series related to public finance such as government debt-to-GDP ratio usually show non-linear behaviors. The inclusion of these types of variables in models which explain fiscal multipliers requires non-linear methodologies.

When explaining the behavior of real variables such as the effect of government expenditure on output, the debt-to-GDP ratio plays an important role. The debt-to-GDP ratio ($Debt$) has been selected optimally as an endogenous threshold variable to evaluate non-linearities; it has been useful to identify estimators in a multivariate threshold autoregressive model (including the threshold value); and it has been a valuable tool to observe how fiscal multipliers change during good times (low levels of debt-to-GDP ratio) and bad times (high levels of debt-to-GDP ratio).

Expansionary fiscal policies seem to be counterproductive, and even negative, when other financial variables, such as levels of sovereign debt, are taken into account. Finding a relationship between government expenditure, output, and public debt, this research highlights the well-known link between real and financial macroeconomic variables. Recommendations for further research include cointegration issues under non-linear models.

Acknowledgements

Financial support is acknowledged from the European Commission under the programme FP7-SSH-2013-29 and the project MACFINROBODS.

References

Auerbach, A. and Gorodnichenko, Y. (2012). Measuring the Output Responses to Fiscal Policy. *American Economic Journal: Economic Policy*, 4(2):1–27.

Bai, J. and Perron, P. (1998). Estimating and Testing Linear Models with Multiple Structural Changes. *Econometrica*, 66(1):47–78.

Bai, J. and Perron, P. (2003). Computation and analysis of multiple structural change models. *Journal of Applied Econometrics*, 18(1):1–22.

Blanchard, O. and Leigh, D. (2012). Are We Underestimating Short-Term Fiscal Multipliers? In *World Economic Outlook of the International Monetary Fund*, pages 41–43.

Blanchard, O. and Perotti, R. (2002). An Empirical Characterization of the Dynamic Effects of Changes in Government Spending and Taxes on Output. *The Quarterly Journal of Economics*, 117(4):1329–1368.

Campos, J., Ericsson, N., and Hendry, D. (2005). General-to-specific modeling: an overview and selected bibliography. International Finance Discussion Papers 838, Board of Governors of the Federal Reserve System (U.S.).

Christiano, L., Eichenbaum, M., and Rebelo, S. (2011). When Is the Government Spending Multiplier Large? *Journal of Political Economy*, 119(1):78–121.

Denes, M., Eggertsson, G., and Gilbukh, S. (2012). Deficits, Public Debt Dynamics and Tax and Spending Multipliers. *The Economic Journal*, pages 133–163.

Favero, C. and Giavazzi, F. (2007). Debt and the Effects of Fiscal Policy. NBER Working Papers 12822, National Bureau of Economic Research, Inc.

Ilzetzki, E., Mendoza, E., and Végh, C. A. (2011). How Big (Small?) are Fiscal Multipliers? IMF Working Papers 11/52, International Monetary Fund.

Kim, S. and Roubini, N. (2008). Twin deficit or twin divergence? Fiscal policy, current account, and real exchange rate in the U.S. *Journal of International Economics*, 74(2):362–383.

Parker, J. (2011). On Measuring the Effects of Fiscal Policy in Recessions. NBER Working Papers 17240, National Bureau of Economic Research, Inc.

Reinhart, C. M. and Rogoff, K. S. (2010). Growth in a Time of Debt. Working Paper 15639, National Bureau of Economic Research.

Tsay, R. S. (1989). Testing and Modeling Threshold Autoregressive Processes. *Journal of the American Statistical Association*, 84(405):231–240.

Tsay, R. S. (1998). Testing and Modeling Multivariate Threshold Models. *Journal of the American Statistical Association*, 93(443):1188–1202.

Vansteenkiste, I. and Nickel, C. (2008). Fiscal policies, the current account and Ricardian equivalence. Working Paper Series 935, European Central Bank.

Woodford, M. (2010). Simple Analytics of the Government Expenditure Multiplier. Working Paper 15714, National Bureau of Economic Research.

Figure 1: Belgium. Government Expenditure with respect to Gross Domestic Product (millions of euros at constant prices)

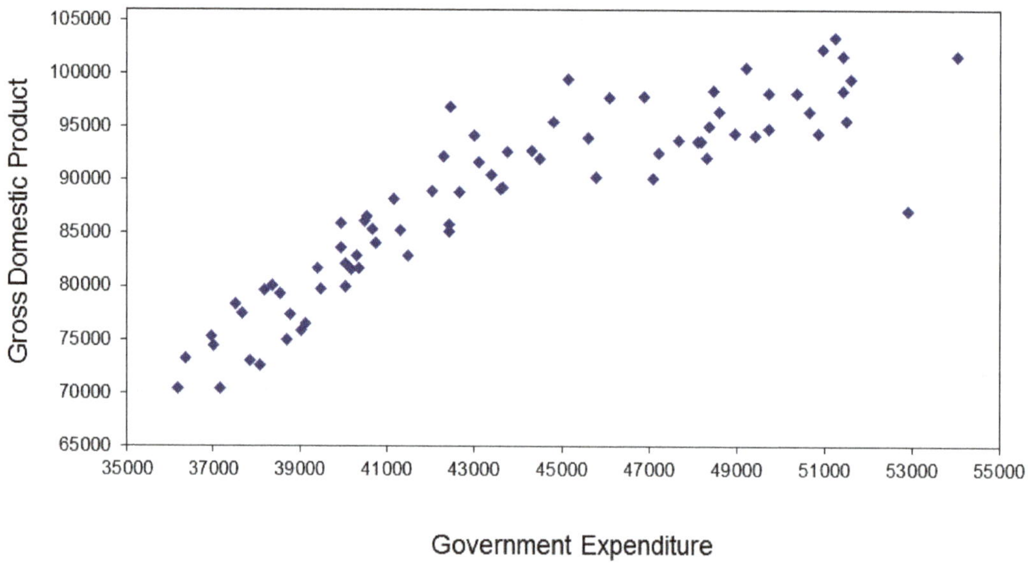

Figure 2: : Italy. Government Expenditure with respect to Gross Domestic Product (millions of euros at constant prices)

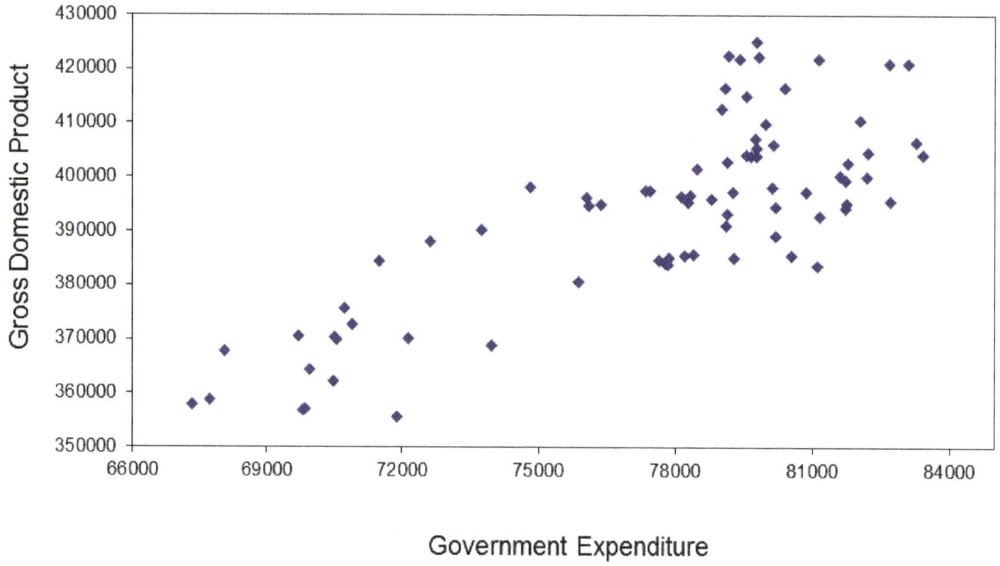

Figure 3: The United Kingdom. Government Expenditure with respect to Gross Domestic Product (millions of euros at constant prices)

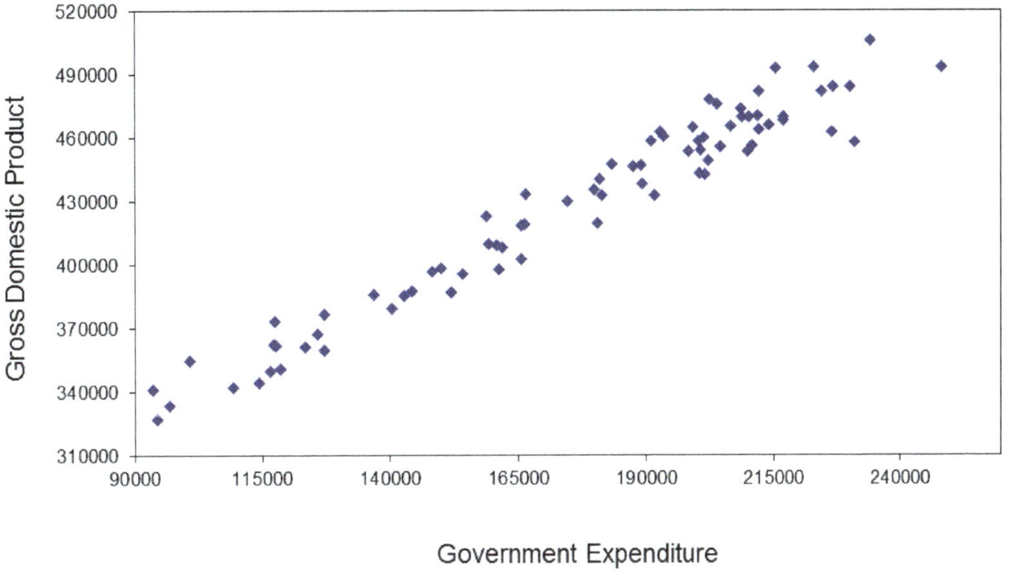

Figure 4: Debt to GDP ratio

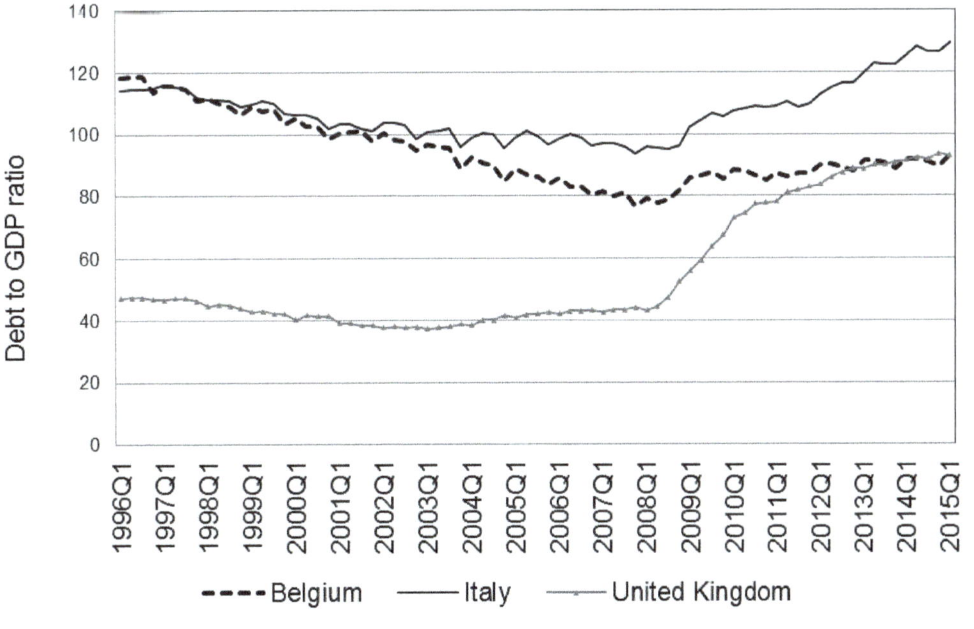

Table 1: Testing unit roots (augmented Dickey-Fuller) Order of integration

	GDP	GE	TO	PI	IR	DEBT
Belgium	$I(1)$	$I(1)$	$I(1)$	$I(1)$	$I(1)$	$I(2)$
Italy	$I(1)$	$I(1)$	$I(1)$	$I(2)$	$I(1)$	$I(2)$
UK	$I(2)$	$I(1)$	$I(1)$	$I(1)$	$I(1)$	$I(2)$

Table 2: Multivariate Threshold Model for the GDP
Least Squares Regression

Belgium		
Delay chosen: $D2DEBT(-2)$		
Threshold value: -1.2830201		
Period: 1997Q2 - 2015Q1		
Regime 1 : 32 obs		
Variable	Coefficient	t: Prob.
C	43330.993	0.00
$DGE(-3)$	o.180264	0.03
$DTO(-1)$	-23840.32	0.00
$DTO(-4)$	-32070.61	0.00
$DPI(-4)$	-905.9993	0.01
$DIR(-1)$	3624.398	0.00
$DIR(-4)$	1333.666	0.02
$DGDP(-1)$	-0.638202	0.00
$D2DEBT(-1)$	-259.6987	0.00
Regime 2 : 40 obs		
Variable	Coefficient	t: Prob.
C	-1134.611	0.00
$DGE(-3)$	0.162341	0.06
$DTO(-1)$	8727.018	0.02
$DTO(-4)$	4141.552	0.56
$DPI(-4)$	-368.4489	0.37
$DIR(-1)$	109.5743	0.81
$DIR(-4)$	-374.3632	0.57
$DGDP(-1)$	-0.618922	0.00
$D2DEBT(-1)$	-103.6821	0.32
R-squared: 0.977344		

Italy		
Delay chosen: $D2DEBT(-2)$		
Threshold value: 0.18700999		
Period: 1997Q2 - 2015Q1		
Regime 1 : 43 obs		
Variable	Coefficient	t: Prob.
C	2065.355	0.00
$DGE(-2)$	-1.132098	0.00
$DGE(-4)$	0.347494	0.07
$DTO(-3)$	-94723.89	0.00
$D2PI(-1)$	2931.710	0.00
$DGDP(-1)$	0.672861	0.00
$DGDP(-3)$	0.587665	0.00
$D2DEBT(-1)$	53.56649	0.62
Regime 2 : 29 obs		
Variable	Coefficient	t: Prob.
C	-563.0763	0.19
$DGE(-2)$	-0.380822	0.03
$DGE(-4)$	0.893265	0.00
$DTO(-3)$	-77830.24	0.02
$D2PI(-1)$	1109.942	0.09
$DGDP(-1)$	0.640372	0.00
$DGDP(-3)$	-0.016035	0.93
$D2DEBT(-1)$	448.6241	0.02
R-squared: 0.730388		

United Kingdom		
Delay chosen: $D2DEBT(-4)$		
Threshold value: 0.69364999		
Period: 1997Q3 - 2015Q1		
Regime 1 : 46 obs		
Variable	Coefficient	t: Prob.
C	3535.921	0.01
$DGE(-3)$	0.151158	0.05
$DPI(-1)$	-1878.823	0.09
$DPI(-3)$	-2448.939	0.05
$DPI(-4)$	2434.786	0.05
$D2GDP(-1)$	-1.248711	0.00
$D2GDP(-2)$	-0.976543	0.00
$D2GDP(-3)$	-0.851123	0.00
$D2DEBT(-1)$	-2307.837	0.00
Regime 2 : 25 obs		
Variable	Coefficient	t: Prob.
C	-1306.832	0.46
$DGE(-3)$	-0.476401	0.00
$DPI(-1)$	-55.93476	0.98
$DPI(-3)$	-776.5352	0.66
$DPI(-4)$	3627.101	0.07
$D2GDP(-1)$	-0.763402	0.00
$D2GDP(-2)$	-1.005545	0.00
$D2GDP(-3)$	-0.934715	0.00
$D2DEBT(-1)$	-477.4724	0.50
R-squared: 0.954197		

Note: Time series have been transformed to $I(0)$

8

The U.S. Shale Oil Revolution and the Behavior of Commodity Prices

Afees A. Salisu[*♣♠] and **Idris A. Adediran** [♣]

[♣]Centre for Econometric and Allied Research, University of Ibadan, Nigeria

[♠]Department of Economics, Obafemi Awolowo University, Nigeria

---

ABSTRACT: The United States is committed to technological improvements in horizontal drilling and hydraulic fracturing in its drive of toppling the world's leading oil producers by the mid-2020s and evolving into a net oil exporter by 2030. Consequently, these technological innovations revolutionized the U.S. oil sector and the international oil market with increasing relevance of the shale oil and attendant shock spillovers to financial and commodity markets. Upon these attractions and consistent with evidence in the literature, we trace the oil price and commodity price dynamics to the shale oil revolution using a recursive structural VAR model of the shale supply shocks. In line with the standard practice of ensuring sensitivity of results, we conduct analyses such as impulse responses, forecast-error variance decomposition, and historical decompositions to accommodate energy and nonenergy commodity components. We show, in addition to the popular view in the extant literature, that the shale oil revolution is not only associated with the recent oil price plunge, but also responsible for the tumble in the total energy-based commodity prices with crude oil price being just a component.

Keywords: U.S. shale oil revolution, oil shocks, commodity prices, SVAR

[*]Corresponding Author. Email: aa.salisu@cear.org.ng

Introduction

Due to unabated reliance of the world's economy on fossil fuels in the face of sustained energy demand worldwide, the shale oil revolution came about through advances in horizontal drilling and hydraulic fracturing, a technological leap heralding improvement in exploration, extraction, processing, and drilling oil and gas from previously nonrecoverable sources (shales) (Wakamatsu and Aruga, 2013; Melikoglu, 2014; Bilgili et al., 2016; Zendehboudi and Bahadori, 2017a,b). The technological developments use these techniques to facilitate the extraction of oil and gas from shales in economically viable quantities. The process of hydraulic fracturing involves pumping water, sand, and chemicals at high pressure to fracture the shale formation and create artificial permeability to release the oil and gas from shale erstwhile trapped in tight formations (Ansari, 2017; Zendehboudi and Bahadori, 2017a,b). Interestingly, the process allows for long-term production given opportunity for large-scale exploitation of existing shale wells (Middleton et al., 2017).

In addition, the shale oil revolution represents a giant step in the goal of making the United States the world's leading crude oil producer, ahead of the top OPEC producer, Saudi Arabia, by the mid-2020s and evolving into a net oil exporter by 2030 (see the International Energy Agency projection of 2012). In this vein, the technological change in the oil and gas extractive industry has sped-up the rate of production in the United States; has seen the U.S. domestic oil production surge from 5 million barrels per day in 2008 to more than 9 million barrels per day in recent months; is responsible for about half of U.S. total crude oil production in 2015, and reduced the U.S. oil imports from OPEC to a 28-year low (Bataa and Park, 2017; Khan, 2017). It has also engendered cheaper energy prices for residential, commercial, and industrial consumers (due to relative lower cost of shale oil production in the United States relative to most of the world) and improved targets to meet domestic consumption. Thus, with the United States hedging closer to energy independence coupled with its ability to wrestle power from OPEC, the shale oil revolution could represent an additional win in its global hegemony. These came with consequences for oil-dependent economies such as Yemen, Egypt, Qatar, Saudi Arabia, Nigeria, and Algeria who once enjoyed heavy patronage from the United States energy supply needs, but now grapple with lower prices (see Khan, 2017, for more).

In the literature, studies on the shale oil revolution, as well as the possible spillover effects, are gradually emerging. The few related empirical papers are those conducted by Mănescu and Nuño (2015); Bilgili et al. (2016); Ansari (2017); Bataa and Park (2017) and Paris (2017) and Monge et al. (2017) and their findings offer some insightful motivations for further empirical inquiry. For instance, Bataa and Park (2017) and Monge et al. (2017) find that the shale oil revolution has a greater potential to influence global oil prices. On the other hand, Mănescu and Nuño (2015) reveal that the impact of the shale oil revolution on the GDP of oil importers is more likely to be minimal given that the consequences of the expected increases in U.S. oil supply due to the shale oil revolution filter through (consumer) prices. These evidences point to the possible connection of the shale oil revolution with oil and consumer markets and their price evolution. We therefore extend the literature further to capture the probable response of the commodity market to shocks due to the U.S. shale oil revolution. This exercise is borne out of the established nexus between the international crude oil and commodity markets in the extant literature.

Theoretically, the connection between oil price changes and the commodity markets stems from, one, the increasing evidence of swings in international oil prices and global commodity prices; two, the evidence of volatility spillover from the oil market to nonenergy commodity markets in recent times; three, the liberalization of capital flows stimulating increased integration between commodity markets so that commodity prices tend to respond to the same shock; and four, the financialization and integration of commodity markets exposing it to potential contagion risks (Ji and Fan, 2012; Hegerty, 2016; Bastianin et al., 2016; Algieri and Leccadito, 2017). Empirically, the nexus has been largely limited to the interaction between energy and agricultural commodity markets. Studies such as Liu (2014); Wang et al. (2014); Chen (2015); Fernandez-Perez et al. (2016); Lucotte (2016); Pal and Mitra (2018) report either a direct impact of crude oil or comovements with the commodities. Also, there are corroborative evidences suggesting that some economic policies or energy developments can buffer the interdependence between oil prices and world commodity prices (e.g., Natanelov et al., 2011; Paris, 2017).

The foregoing discussions are insightful for the present study. Although further empirical motivations for the present study are bared in the succeeding section, we argue here on the basis of the previous claims that the U.S. energy development policy resulting in the shale oil revolution could influence the oil-commodities dynamics. The focus of the present paper, therefore, is to trace the shale oil shocks through oil price and commodity price indices. There are notable attractions for this intellectual exercise. First, the shale oil revolution represents a significant leap especially for the United States in its quest to improve crude oil production capacity to overtake Saudi Arabia as the leading global oil producer (see the International Energy Agency projection of 2012). Second, the shale oil revolution has been linked to the recent oil market imbalances and oil price fluctuations even as it affords the United States considerable advantage in the international oil scene (Hamilton, 2014; Mănescu and Nuño, 2015; Arezki and Blanchard, 2014; Bilgili et al., 2016; Baumeister and Kilian, 2016; Ansari, 2017; Bataa and Park, 2017).

The motivation to direct our research focus on the shale oil revolution is further enhanced when we stress the distinction between shale and conventional crude oil. Shale oil, by definition is a member in the family of crude oil, although it is formed in tight formations and explored with unconventional methods of fracturing and hydraulic drilling (Wakamatsu and Aruga, 2013; Aguilera, 2014; Melikoglu, 2014; Mănescu and Nuño, 2015; Bilgili et al., 2016; Monge et al., 2017; Zendehboudi and Bahadori, 2017a,b; Tan and Barton, 2017). It is therefore safe to refer to shale oil as an unconventional crude oil (Zendehboudi and Bahadori, 2017a). There are evidences in recent times that the United States has been able to significantly increase its total crude oil supply chiefly due to the shale oil revolution and this oil sector revolution in the Unites States has not only evoked oil price responses, but also induced reactions from OPEC regarding production quotas (Khan, 2017; Bataa and Park, 2017; Genc, 2017; Kim, 2018). These arguments point to the particular relevance of unconventional crude oil, hence, by implication, our research focus on the oil-commodities dynamics must necessarily emanate from unconventional oil and trace the transmission of shocks via the conventional crude oil.

Remarkably, with these motivations forming the backbone of the research methodology, we are able to establish responses for conventional oil output and oil price, particularly due to the shale oil supply shocks, and trace the transmission of such shocks to energy-containing and nonenergy commodity prices. The rest of the paper is structured as follows. The next section provides further motivation of the study. Section 2 describes the research methodology. Section 3 presents the preliminary analysis of results before the main discussion of results in Section 4. Section 5 concludes the paper.

1 Motivations for Studying the Shale Oil-Commodity Prices Volatility Nexus

The empirical analysis of the shale oil-commodity prices contagion has remained unexplored in the extant literature despite arguments of contagion spillovers from the conventional oil market to other nonenergy markets. There are, however, evidences to show that the impact of the shale oil revolution can be felt in the real economy (e.g., Mănescu and Nuño, 2015; Bilgili et al., 2016).

Mănescu and Nuño (2015) analyze the impact of the shale oil revolution on oil prices and economic growth with a general equilibrium model of the world oil market. Results suggest that most of the expected increase in U.S. oil supply due to the shale oil revolution has already been incorporated into prices and that it will produce an additional increase of 0.2% in the GDP of oil importers in the period 2010-2018.

Further, Bilgili et al. (2016) examine the impacts of the shale oil revolution on industrial production in the United States. The dynamic ordinary least squares estimator explores that shale oil production has a positive effect on industrial production. Besides that, evidence from the Granger causality test show that shale gas production causes industrial production in the United States.

Other empirical evidences in the extant literature address the impact of conventional oil markets to other financial and commodity markets. In terms of volatility spillover to financial markets, considerable works have been done in the past to connect oil price changes with stock price/returns (e.g., Hamilton, 1996; Sadorsky, 1999; Kilian, 2009; Nandha and Faff, 2008; Miller and Ratti, 2009; Chen, 2010; Aloui et al., 2013; Salisu and Oloko, 2015). More recently, Bastianin et al. (2016) study the effects of oil price shocks on the stock market volatility of the G7 countries. Findings show that stock market volatility does not respond to oil supply shocks, but rather to demand shocks.

Mohaddes and Pesaran (2017) confirm an unstable relationship between oil and equity prices during the 1946-2016 period. Further, Nadal et al. (2017) investigate the time-varying impacts of demand and supply oil shocks on correlations between changes in oil prices and stock market returns. The findings indicate that demand shocks positively affect the correlations between oil prices and stock market returns during and after the 2007/08 financial markets volatility and at the height of uncertainties about Chinese economic growth in 2015.

Away from oil price volatility spillover to financial markets, considerable studies have been done on contagion effects of conventional oil markets to nonfinancial commodities markets. One of these is Nazlioglu et al. (2013) who examine volatility spillover between oil prices and the prices of agricultural commodities (prices of corn, soybeans, wheat, and sugar), conducting analysis for the pre-crisis period (01 January 1986 to 31 December 2005) and the post-crisis period (01 January 2006 – 21 March 2011). The findings show evidence of no volatility spillover between the oil market and agricultural commodities markets in the pre-crisis period, but establish interdependence between the markets afterward. With structural breaks cointegration and nonlinear causality tests, Fowowe (2016) also shows that agricultural commodity prices in South Africa are neutral to global oil prices.

Like Nazlioglu et al. (2013); Wang et al. (2014) also find that oil shocks explain marginal variations in agricultural commodity prices before the food crisis in 2006-2008, whereas in the post-crisis period their explanatory abilities become much higher.

In light of the present study, Ji and Fan (2012) examine the influence of the oil market on nonenergy commodity markets before and after the 2008 financial crisis. The results reveal that the oil market exerts significant volatility spillover effects on nonenergy commodity markets, which demonstrates its core position among commodity markets. This position is also in tune with Algieri and Leccadito (2017) who show that commodity markets generate contagion risks, which are mainly triggered by financial factors for the energy market and that there are spillovers from energy to food markets.

2 Methodology

Essentially, this study considers the strength of the U.S. economy as a major player that exogenously influences the world oil price with its large crude oil production, be it conventional crude oil or shale oil from unconventional sources. On the one hand, this is corroborated by evidences showing that the impact of the shale oil revolution can be felt in the real economy (e.g., Mănescu and Nuño, 2015; Bilgili et al., 2016). On the other hand, it reflects the influence of the conventional oil market fundamentals on real variables, such as commodity prices as argued from the evidence of volatility spillover from the oil market to energy commodity markets (Ji and Fan, 2012; Hegerty, 2016; Bastianin et al., 2016; Algieri and Leccadito, 2017).

Thus, the modelling highlights the role of U.S. shale oil supply and studies the linkage with crude oil output, oil price (measured with the West Texas Intermediate), and commodity prices. In line with the theoretical specification consistent with Kilian (2009), Wang et al. (2014), Baumeister and Kilian (2016), Mohaddes and Raissi (2015), Mohaddes and Pesaran (2016), Khan (2017), Algieri and Leccadito (2017), and Bataa and Park (2017) we adopt a structural VAR model consisting of four endogenous variables, namely, U.S. shale oil production, U.S. crude oil supply, international oil price, and the all-commodity prices of the form:[1]

$$\Pi_0 y_t = \alpha + \sum_{j=1}^{p} \Pi_j y_{t-1} + \varepsilon_t \tag{1}$$

where y_t is a 4×1 column vector of endogenous variables, y_{t-1} is the vector of lagged values of endogenous variables up to lag order p, and ε_t is a vector of serially and mutually uncorrelated structural shocks containing variances of U.S. shale oil supply, U.S. crude oil production, oil price, and the all-commodity prices such that:

$$\begin{aligned} y_t &= (USshale_t, UScrude_t, oilp_t, comm_t)' \\ \varepsilon_t &= \left(\varepsilon_{USshale,t}, \varepsilon_{UScrude,t}, \varepsilon_{oilp,t}, \varepsilon_{comm,t}\right)' \\ E(\varepsilon_t \varepsilon_t') &= \Sigma \end{aligned} \tag{2}$$

where Π_j is a 4×4 matrix of the SVAR parameters and Π_0 is a lower triangular matrix of recursive short run impulse responses. Inheriting the characteristics of Π_0, Π_0^{-1} also possesses a recursive structure, hence, the reduced form of the errors designated as ξ_t can be decomposed thus:

[1]For robustness, we substitute nonfuel commodity prices for the all-commodity prices because the energy component in the latter may influence the outcome of the analysis due to possible correlation with the WTI oil price in the specification.

$$\xi_t = \Pi_0^{-1}\varepsilon_t = \begin{bmatrix} \xi_t^{USshale} \\ \xi_t^{UScrude} \\ \xi_t^{oilp} \\ \xi_t^{comm} \end{bmatrix} = \begin{bmatrix} a_{11} & 0 & 0 & 0 \\ a_{21} & a_{22} & 0 & 0 \\ a_{31} & a_{32} & a_{33} & 0 \\ a_{41} & a_{42} & a_{43} & a_{44} \end{bmatrix} \begin{bmatrix} \xi_t^{USshalesupplyshock} \\ \xi_t^{UScrudesupplyshock} \\ \xi_t^{oilpriceshock} \\ \xi_t^{commoditypriceshock} \end{bmatrix} \tag{3}$$

This specification is based on a recursive model that allows us to trace the transmission of shocks emanating from the U.S. shale oil revolution across crude oil supply, oil price, and commodity prices. The structural VAR model is analyzed with the tools of impulse response functions and historical decompositions. In our specification, the shock responses could be derived through the representation in (4) and the historical decomposition in (5):

$$y_t - \left(\sum_{j=0}^{p} \Pi_j^* L^j\right)^{-1} \varepsilon_t = \left(\sum_{k=0}^{\infty} \varphi_k L^k\right)\varepsilon_t = \left(\sum_{k=0}^{\infty} \varphi_k \varepsilon_{t-k}\right) \tag{4}$$

$$y_t = \sum_i \sum_{k=0}^{\infty} \varphi_{i,k}^{(k)} \varepsilon_{i,t-k} \tag{5}$$

3 Data and Preliminary Analyses

The shale oil revolution being the centrepiece of this paper necessitates need for data on U.S. shale oil production. We utilize monthly data set on shale oil production across the seven U.S. oil-rich regions: Anadarko region, Appalachia region, Bakken region, Eagle Ford region, Haynesville region, Niobrara region, and Permian region. This data allows us to explore the probable effects of shocks due to (shale) oil supply following the revolution in the energy sector. We trace the effect of these shocks first to the total U.S. crude oil supply, then to oil and commodity prices, given the prior hints in the literature that the shocks have perceptible influence on energy and nonenergy prices. Consequently, we sought data on total crude oil production in the United States, oil price (Western Texas Intermediate), and commodity price indices (all components and nonfuel, excluding the energy fuel component). The data scope spans from 1st January 2007 to 31st December 2017, yielding exactly 132 observations for each series (Table 1). The intuition behind this scope is that it captures the start date of shale oil production in commercial quantities as one of the institutional responses to the global financial crisis at that time.

It is customary in empirical studies of this nature to explore the historical information of the series from statistical and graphical perspectives to provide insights into the nature and distribution of the series individually, as well as understand the likely comovements or divergence among the variables of interest. In essence, we assess the descriptive statistics of the series of interest, including the mean, standard deviation, skewness, and kurtosis (Table 2), and also provide the graphical analyses (Figures 1 to 4) as a foundation to build our study. Based on the descriptive statistics, all the series are widely spread given the standard deviation values with respect to the mean values. Commonplace, also, is that the series deviate from normal distribution, with the exception of the nonfuel commodity price index. A salient observation here, however, is the observed difference in the distributions between the all-commodities price index and the nonfuel commodities price index. This indicates that the analysis based on the two series may differ given that the price index, excluding energy components, is positively skewed and almost normally distributed, whereas the all-commodities price index behaves otherwise.[2]

In Figures 1 to 4, we plot the U.S. shale oil production series against each of the variables expected to respond to the shock: total crude oil production, the oil price, and commodity price indices (all- and nonfuel commodity price index respectively). The shale and crude oil outputs appear to move together and experience convergence, especially starting around 2014. This phenomenon is also noted for the relationship between the shale series and the oil, general, and nonfuel commodity prices. It is also noteworthy that the three commodity prices mirror one another and, as such, share some common characteristics. As common with inflation measures, the commodity prices witness spikes whereas, on the other hand, oil productions appear to soar with time to converge with shale oil production series around 2014. This observation agrees with positions in the literature that the oil supply shocks may actually have a hand in the oil price plunge of that period (Hamilton, 2014; Arezki and Blanchard, 2014; Mănescu and Nuño, 2015; Baumeister and Kilian, 2016; Bataa and Park, 2017; Ansari, 2017; Kilian, 2017; Khan, 2017).

To be properly guided in the estimation process, we examine the time series properties of the series using a battery of stationarity and nonstationarity tests. These tests are conducted on the transformed series of the variables; they are transformed as growth rates in line with the seminal paper from which this study draws inspiration (Kilian, 2009). The analysis entails testing for nonstationarity; that is, the presence of a unit root in the series employing the Augmented Dickey-Fuller (ADF) and Phillips-Perron (PP) tests (Table 3). These are confirmed with the Kwiatkowski-Phillips-Schmidt-Shin (KPSS) test, which specifically tests for stationarity in the series (Table 4). Taken together, results from the analyses reveal that the Augmented Dickey-Fuller (ADF) and the Phillips-Perron (PP) tests indicate a rejection of the nonstationarity null hypotheses at a level showing that the series are integrated of the order of zero. For confirmation, we also rely on the Kwiatkowski-Phillips-Schmidt-Shin stationarity test. In the same vein, with results from the KPSS tests, we could not reject

[2]This is found to be true at the estimation stage where the Impulse Response graphs produce dissimilar results for the all-commodity prices containing energy components and the nonfuel prices devoid of same.

the null of stationarity for the series at level. Hence, the ADF, PP, and KPSS tests point to the stationarity of the series at level. Thus, by intuition, these results taken together with submissions in the graphical analysis indicate evidence of cointegration among the variables.

4 Discussion of Results

In this study, we are concerned with the analysis of the U.S. energy and international commodity markets dynamics where we subject the ensuing multivariate model to oil production shocks, namely, shocks from U.S. shale oil production. We adopt the structural VAR (SVAR hereinafter) framework to trace the shock transmission mechanism from the shale oil revolution as the source of oil supply shocks through the total U.S. crude production to the different commodity prices: energy price (oil price), nonenergy (nonfuel) price, and the composite commodity prices (the all-commodity prices comprising fuel, nonfuel, and other prices). As instructed in Breitung (1998), we are guided by relevant theoretical constructs in our specification of the SVAR model dynamics. In essence, we dealt with a recursive SVAR where we impose relevant restrictions on the system of equations to trace the impacts of the shock in the VAR system coming from the shale oil supply shocks. Based on the instanta-neous impacts associated with the interrelationship between oil supply and oil price and the direct spillover to commodity prices, we work with a short SVAR, where current values of the variables affect each other to show contemporaneous effects of the shock pass-through.

Our VAR model is, therefore, a recursive dynamic structural model where commodity prices respond to oil price changes and oil supply shocks (conventional and unconventional oil supply), in that order. In line with the extant literature in this area (e.g., Kilian, 2009, and others), we apply the SVAR methodology to achieve three major feats. First, we produce the graphical representations of the impulse response functions (hereafter, IRFs) to show the average responses of the target variables (all-commodity prices and oil and nonfuel prices) to structural shocks from the shale oil revolution. Second, we construct forecast error variance decompositions (hereafter, FEVDs) to measure the average contribution of the structural shock across the system. Third, we generate historical decompositions (hereafter, HDs) to determine the cumulative contribution of the structural shocks to the evolution of the target variables through time. We focus on shale oil supply shocks (LSHALE) through responses from crude oil output (LCRUDE), oil price (LOILP), and all-commodity prices (LCOMM) and follow it up by replacing all-commodity prices with nonfuel prices (LNONFUEL) for robustness. We attend to the foregoing in the listed order in subsequent sections.

4.1 The Impulse Response Functions

We begin the analysis by assessing the tools that tell us how the shale oil supply shocks reverberate through the SVAR system. The IRFs partly assist in this regard (Figures 5 to 8). In simple language, the IRFs measure the effects of these oil supply shocks on the other endogenous (target) variables. More technically, the IRFs show the effects of the shale oil production shocks on the adjustment path of the target variables (arranged on one hand as crude oil supply, oil price, and all-commodity prices, and on the other hand arranged as crude oil supply, oil price, and nonfuel prices). The IRFs capturing the shale oil supply revolution shock transmission are contained in Figures 5 to 8. The impacts of the supply shocks on the target variables differ; the effects of the shale supply shocks stayed longer on crude oil supply and nonfuel prices before dying out, in comparison with oil price and the commodity price with an energy component (all-commodity prices). The shale oil revolution evokes instant positive responses from the total crude oil output before dying out around the 10th period. However, the U.S. shale oil production shock induces negative responses from the three prices, although the response of nonfuel commodity prices appears to be more lasting. Thus, we cannot ignore the glaring semblance where the responses of oil price to the shale oil revolution mirror that of all-commodity prices to the same shock. The graphical view appears like a plunge in those prices (oil and all-commodity prices) as a result of the shale oil supply shock. The foregoing reveals the strength of the U.S. energy sector in transmitting shocks that could alter the world energy prices given that the shale oil revolution appears to alter the energy prices. We seek further insights from the forecast error variance decompositions in the next section.

4.2 The Forecast Error Variance and Historical Decompositions (FEVDs)

To further shed light on the shale oil supply shocks transmission, we turn to the FEVDs (Tables 5 and 6). Like the IRFs, the FEVDs serve as a supporting tool to assess the shock transmission through the VAR system. In our specific case, the FEVDs measure the contribution of the orthogonal (uncorrelated) forecast error variance of the shale oil supply shocks attributable to itself or to the other (target) variables (crude oil supply, oil price, and commodity prices). Tables 5 and 6 represent the FEVDs results for the transmission of shocks emanating from U.S. shale oil supply shock through total crude oil supply to either oil price and all-commodity prices or to oil price and nonfuel commodity prices, respectively. As expected, the results in Table 5 show that shale oil accounts for predominant variation of own shock with significant shock spillover to conventional oil, but infinitesimal shock spillover to either oil price or commodity prices. Results from Table 6 also show overwhelming prevalence of own shock in the variance decomposition of shale oil supply shock with major shock spillover to conventional crude oil supply. The implication of these results is that the impacts of the shale oil revolution are more pronounced on the supply side of the energy market and are, therefore, slightly transmitted to the international oil price and commodity prices.

Building on the previous discussions, which situate the shale oil revolution, an unconventional crude oil, as a relevant shock in the evolutionary path of conventional crude oil, the price of oil, and commodity prices (both energy related and nonenergy related), we extend our analysis to cover information provided by the historical decompositions (as obtained in Figures 9 to 12). By definition, the historical decompositions show the extent to which the structural shocks (from the shale oil revolution) explains the historical fluctuations in the endogenous variables (conventional oil, oil price, and the all- and nonfuel- commodity prices). In other words, we use the HD to trace the genesis of the shock impacts on the endogenous variables and, therefore, provide information on the cumulative effect of the shale oil supply shock on each of the endogenous variables. These are apparent in Figures 9 to 12. In these figures, the lines representing shale oil shock are significantly visible; hence, the shale oil revolution appears to explain significant portions of the fluctuations in the crude oil output, the international oil price, and the commodity prices.

5 Conclusion

The United States has committed to technological improvements in its drive to topple the world's leading crude oil producer by the mid-2020s and evolving into a net oil exporter by 2030. The resulting technological change in the oil and gas extractive industry aimed at furthering this goal has, among others, sped up the rate of crude production in the United States; has seen a surge in the U.S. domestic oil production; is responsible for all-time low U.S. oil imports from OPEC; and has enhanced employment and income generation in resource-rich communities. These feats have been attributed to the shale oil revolution. Based on these attractions around the shale oil revolution, we extend discussion from a body of literature (e.g., Kilian, 2009; Hamilton, 2014; Arezki and Blanchard, 2014; Mănescu and Nuño, 2015; Baumeister and Kilian, 2016; Ansari, 2017; Kilian, 2017; Bataa and Park, 2017), linking the recent oil price tumble to the U.S. shale oil revolution by capturing the possible spillover of such disturbances to commodity prices. Hence, we work with a structural VAR model that traces the recursive transmission dynamics from the oil supply shocks through oil price linkage with fundamentals in the commodity market. In this exercise, we explore the impulse response, forecast-error variance decomposition and historical decomposition functions for the total and U.S. shale oil production shocks. We provide robust empirical evidences to show that the shale oil revolution has indeed enhanced the U.S. oil supply capabilities and is in reality associated with the recent plunge in not only oil price, but all-commodity prices, i.e., commodity prices with energy components.

References

Aguilera, R. F. (2014). Production costs of global conventional and unconventional petroleum. *Energy Policy*, 64:134 – 140.

Algieri, B. and Leccadito, A. (2017). Assessing contagion risk from energy and non-energy commodity markets. *Energy Economics*, 62:312 – 322.

Aloui, R., Hammoudeh, S., and Nguyen, D. K. (2013). A time-varying copula approach to oil and stock market dependence: The case of transition economies. *Energy Economics*, 39:208 – 221.

Ansari, D. (2017). OPEC, Saudi Arabia, and the shale revolution: Insights from equilibrium modelling and oil politics. *Energy Policy*, 111:166 – 178.

Arezki, R. and Blanchard, O. (2014). Seven questions about the recent oil price slump. *IMFdirect-The IMF Blog*, 22.

Bastianin, A., Conti, F., and Manera, M. (2016). The impacts of oil price shocks on stock market volatility: Evidence from the G7 countries. *Energy Policy*, 98:160 – 169.

Bataa, E. and Park, C. (2017). Is the recent low oil price attributable to the shale revolution? *Energy Economics*, 67:72 – 82.

Baumeister, C. and Kilian, L. (2016). Understanding the Decline in the Price of Oil since June 2014. *Journal of the Association of Environmental and Resource Economists*, 3(1):131–158.

Bilgili, F., Koçak, E., Bulut, U., and Sualp, M. N. (2016). How did the US economy react to shale gas production revolution? An advanced time series approach. *Energy*, 116:963–977.

Breitung, J. (1998). Neuere Entwicklungen auf dem Gebiet ökonometrischer Strukturmodelle: Strukturelle Vektorautoregressionen. Technical report, Discussion Papers, Interdisciplinary Research Project 373: Quantification and Simulation of Economic Processes.

Chen, P. (2015). Global oil prices, macroeconomic fundamentals and China's commodity sector comovements. *Energy Policy*, 87:284 – 294.

Chen, S.-S. (2010). Do higher oil prices push the stock market into bear territory? *Energy Economics*, 32(2):490 – 495.

Fernandez-Perez, A., Frijns, B., and Tourani-Rad, A. (2016). Contemporaneous interactions among fuel, biofuel and agricultural commodities. *Energy Economics*, 58:1 – 10.

Fowowe, B. (2016). Do oil prices drive agricultural commodity prices? Evidence from South Africa. *Energy*, 104:149 – 157.

Genc, T. S. (2017). OPEC and demand response to crude oil prices. *Energy Economics*, 66:238 – 246.

Hamilton, J. (2014). Oil prices as an indicator of global economic conditions. *Econbrowser*.

Hamilton, J. D. (1996). This is what happened to the oil price-macroeconomy relationship. *Journal of Monetary Economics*, 38(2):215 – 220.

Hegerty, S. W. (2016). Commodity-price volatility and macroeconomic spillovers: Evidence from nine emerging markets. *The North American Journal of Economics and Finance*, 35:23 – 37.

Ji, Q. and Fan, Y. (2012). How does oil price volatility affect non-energy commodity markets? *Applied Energy*, 89(1):273 – 280. Special issue on Thermal Energy Management in the Process Industries.

Khan, M. I. (2017). Falling oil prices: Causes, consequences and policy implications. *Journal of Petroleum Science and Engineering*, 149:409 – 427.

Kilian, L. (2009). Not All Oil Price Shocks Are Alike: Disentangling Demand and Supply Shocks in the Crude Oil Market. *American Economic Review*, 99(3):1053–69.

Kilian, L. (2017). The Impact of the fracking boom on Arab oil producers. *Energy Journal*, 38(6):137–160.

Kim, M. S. (2018). Impacts of supply and demand factors on declining oil prices. *Energy*, 155:1059 – 1065.

Liu, L. (2014). Cross-correlations between crude oil and agricultural commodity markets. *Physica A: Statistical Mechanics and its Applications*, 395:293 – 302.

Lucotte, Y. (2016). Co-movements between crude oil and food prices: A post-commodity boom perspective. *Economics Letters*, 147:142 – 147.

Melikoglu, M. (2014). Shale gas: Analysis of its role in the global energy market. *Renewable and Sustainable Energy Reviews*, 37:460 – 468.

Middleton, R. S., Gupta, R., Hyman, J. D., and Viswanathan, H. S. (2017). The shale gas revolution: Barriers, sustainability, and emerging opportunities. *Applied Energy*, 199:88 – 95.

Miller, J. I. and Ratti, R. A. (2009). Crude oil and stock markets: Stability, instability, and bubbles. *Energy Economics*, 31(4):559 – 568.

Mohaddes, K. and Pesaran, M. H. (2016). Country-specific oil supply shocks and the global economy: A counterfactual analysis. *Energy Economics*, 59:382 – 399.

Mohaddes, K. and Pesaran, M. H. (2017). Oil prices and the global economy: Is it different this time around? *Energy Economics*, 65:315 – 325.

Mohaddes, K. and Raissi, M. (2015). The U.S. oil supply revolution and the global economy. *IMF Working Paper WP/15/259.*

Monge, M., Gil-Alana, L. A., and de Gracia, F. P. (2017). U.S. shale oil production and WTI prices behaviour. *Energy*, 141:12 – 19.

Mănescu, C. B. and Nuño, G. (2015). Quantitative effects of the shale oil revolution. *Energy Policy*, 86:855 – 866.

Nadal, R., Szklo, A., and Lucena, A. (2017). Time-varying impacts of demand and supply oil shocks on correlations between crude oil prices and stock markets indices. *Research in International Business and Finance*, 42:1011 – 1020.

Nandha, M. and Faff, R. (2008). Does oil move equity prices? A global view. *Energy Economics*, 30(3):986 – 997.

Natanelov, V., Alam, M. J., McKenzie, A. M., and Huylenbroeck, G. V. (2011). Is there co-movement of agricultural commodities futures prices and crude oil? *Energy Policy*, 39(9):4971 – 4984.

Nazlioglu, S., Erdem, C., and Soytas, U. (2013). Volatility spillover between oil and agricultural commodity markets. *Energy Economics*, 36:658 – 665.

Pal, D. and Mitra, S. K. (2018). Interdependence between crude oil and world food prices: A detrended cross correlation analysis. *Physica A: Statistical Mechanics and its Applications*, 492:1032 – 1044.

Paris, A. (2017). On the link between oil and agricultural commodity prices: Do biofuels matter? *International Economics*.

Sadorsky, P. (1999). Oil price shocks and stock market activity. *Energy Economics*, 21(5):449 – 469.

Salisu, A. A. and Oloko, T. F. (2015). Modeling oil price-US stock nexus: A VARMA-BEKK-AGARCH approach. *Energy Economics*, 50:1–12.

Tan, S. H. and Barton, P. I. (2017). Optimal shale oil and gas investments in the United States. *Energy*, 141:398 – 422.

Wakamatsu, H. and Aruga, K. (2013). The impact of the shale gas revolution on the U.S. and Japanese natural gas markets. *Energy Policy*, 62:1002 – 1009.

Wang, Y., Wu, C., and Yang, L. (2014). Oil price shocks and agricultural commodity prices. *Energy Economics*, 44:22 – 35.

Zendehboudi, S. and Bahadori, A. (2017a). Chapter Seven - Properties of Shale Oil. In Zendehboudi, S. and Bahadori, A., editors, *Shale Oil and Gas Handbook*, pages 231 – 283. Gulf Professional Publishing.

Zendehboudi, S. and Bahadori, A. (2017b). Chapter Ten - Shale Oil and Gas: Current Status, Future, and Challenges. In Zendehboudi, S. and Bahadori, A., editors, *Shale Oil and Gas Handbook*, pages 357 – 404. Gulf Professional Publishing.

Figure 1: Trends in US Shale and US Crude Oil Production

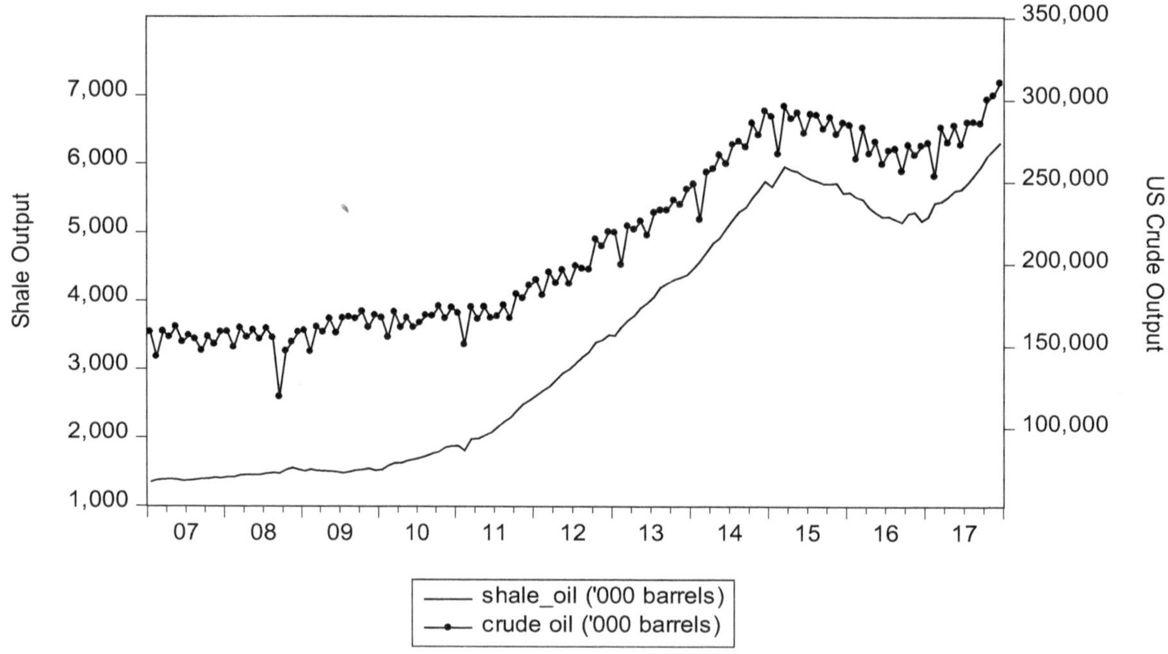

Figure 2: Trends in US Shale Production and Oil Price

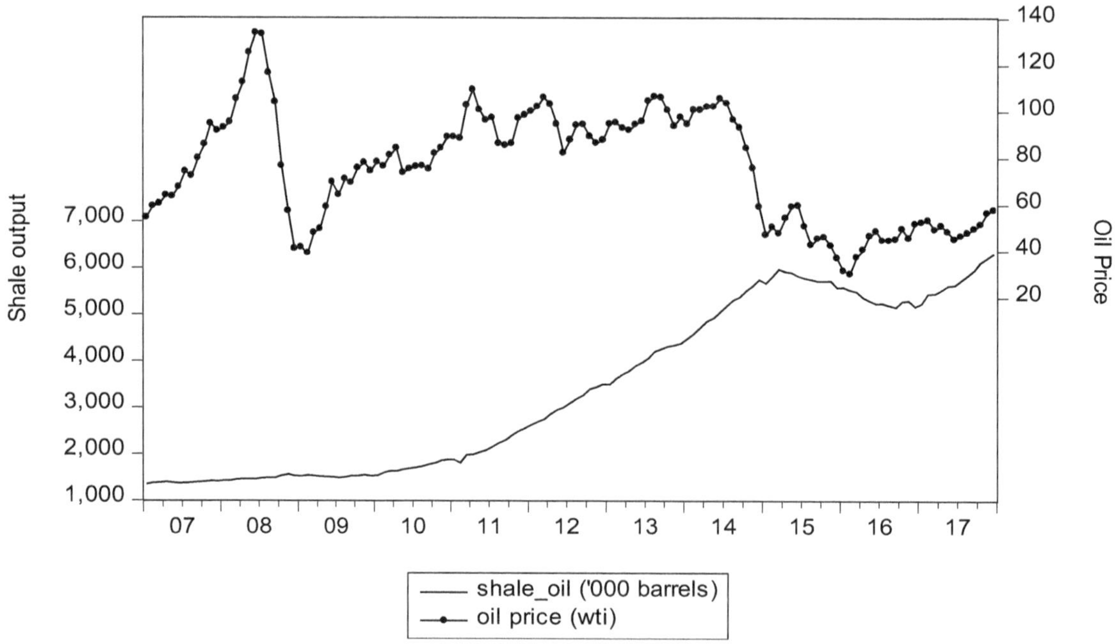

Figure 3: Trends in US Shale Production and Commodity Price Index

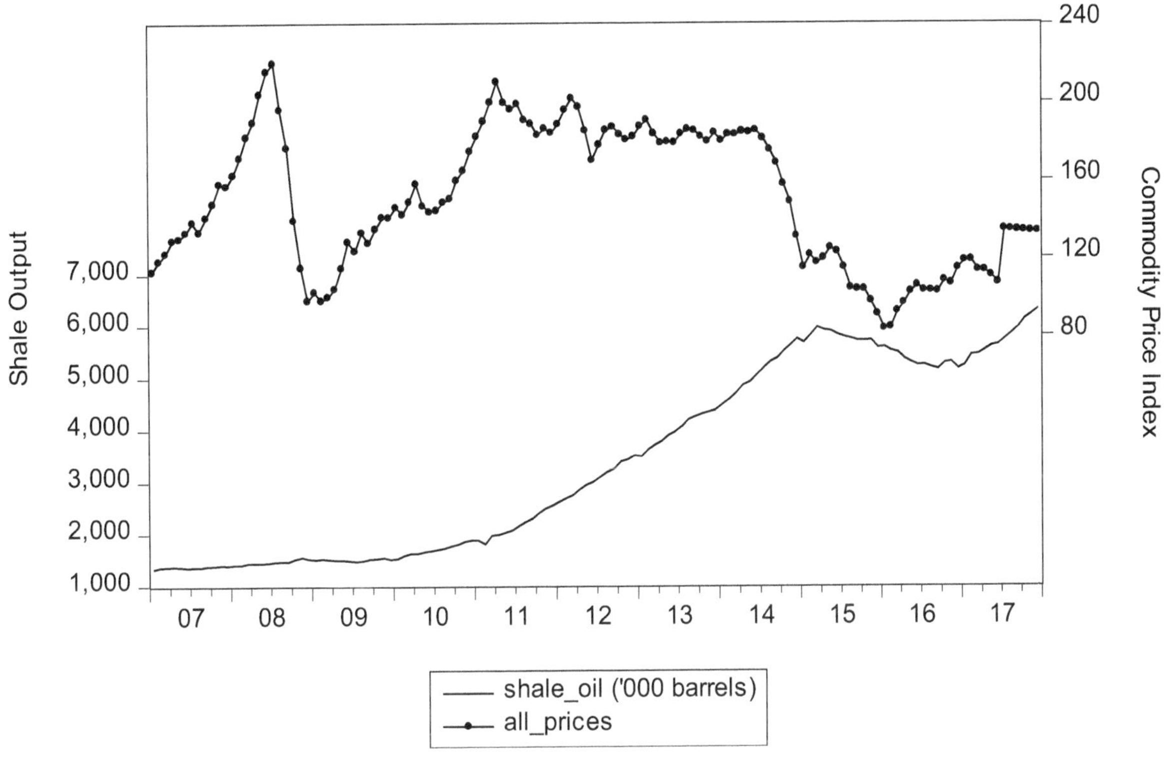

Figure 4: Trends in US Shale Production and Nonfuel Price Index

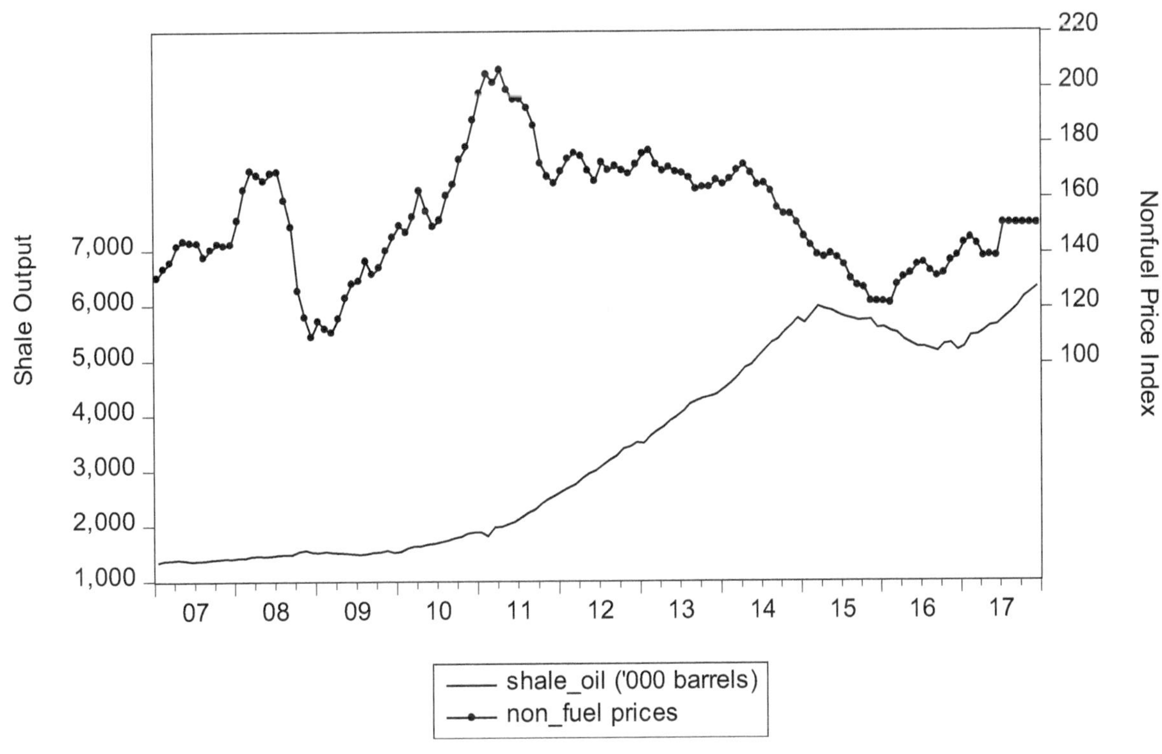

Figure 5: Impulse Response of US Crude from US Shale Production

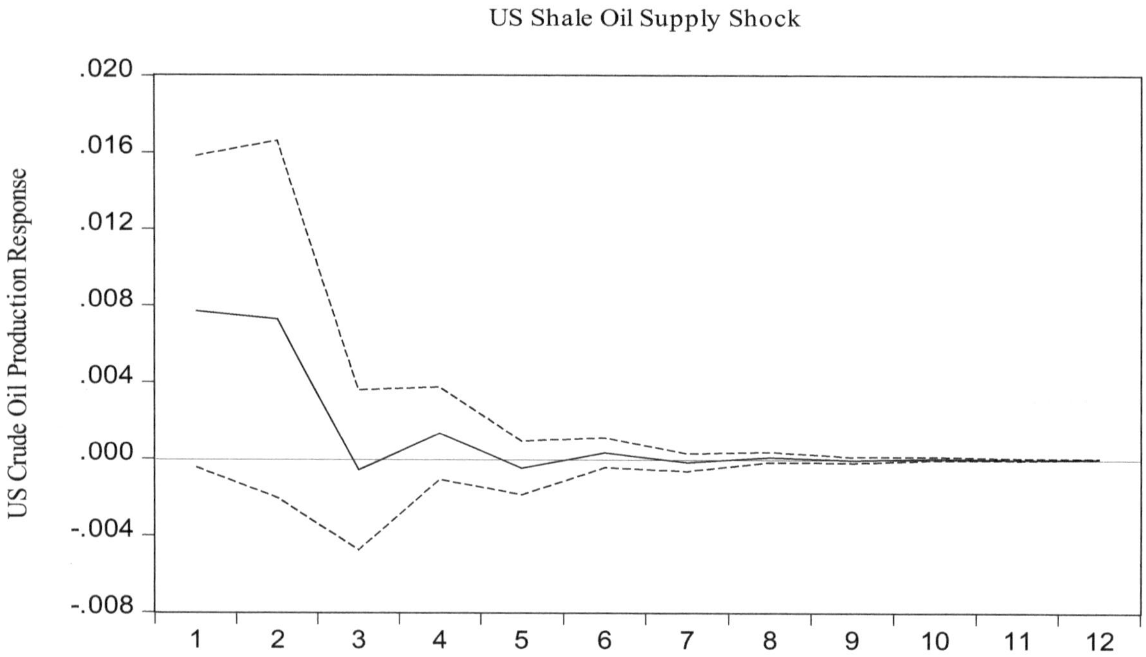

Figure 6: Impulse Response of Oil Price from US Shale Production

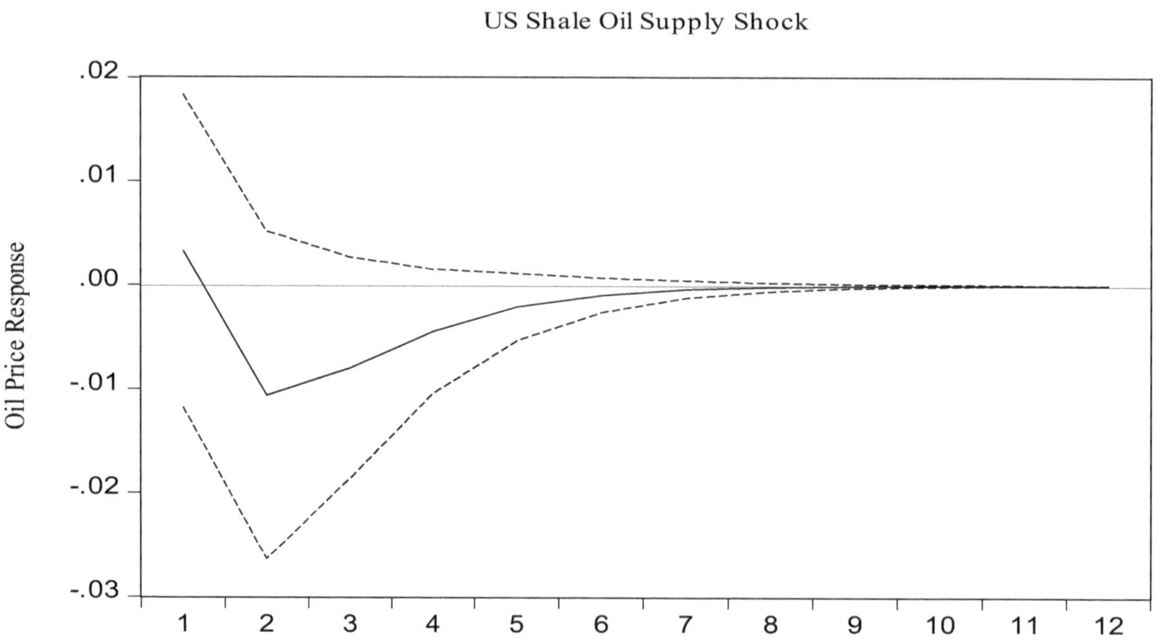

Figure 7: Impulse Response of Commodity Prices from US Shale Production

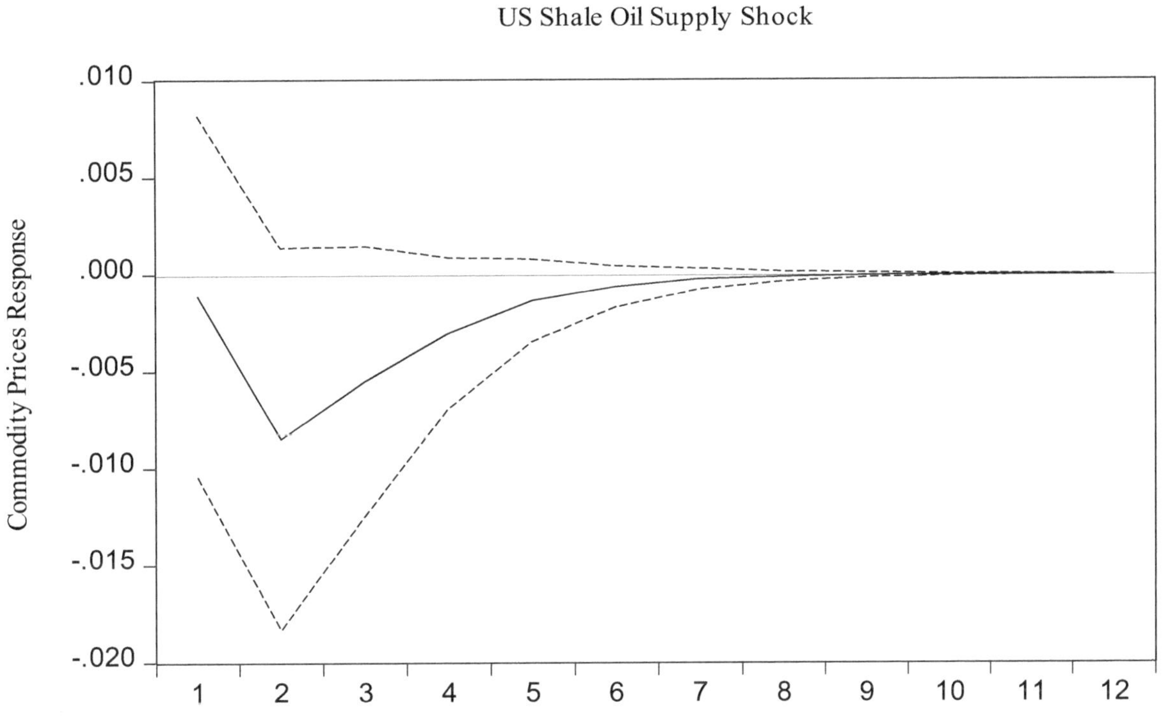

Figure 8: : Impulse Response of Nonfuel Prices from US Shale Production

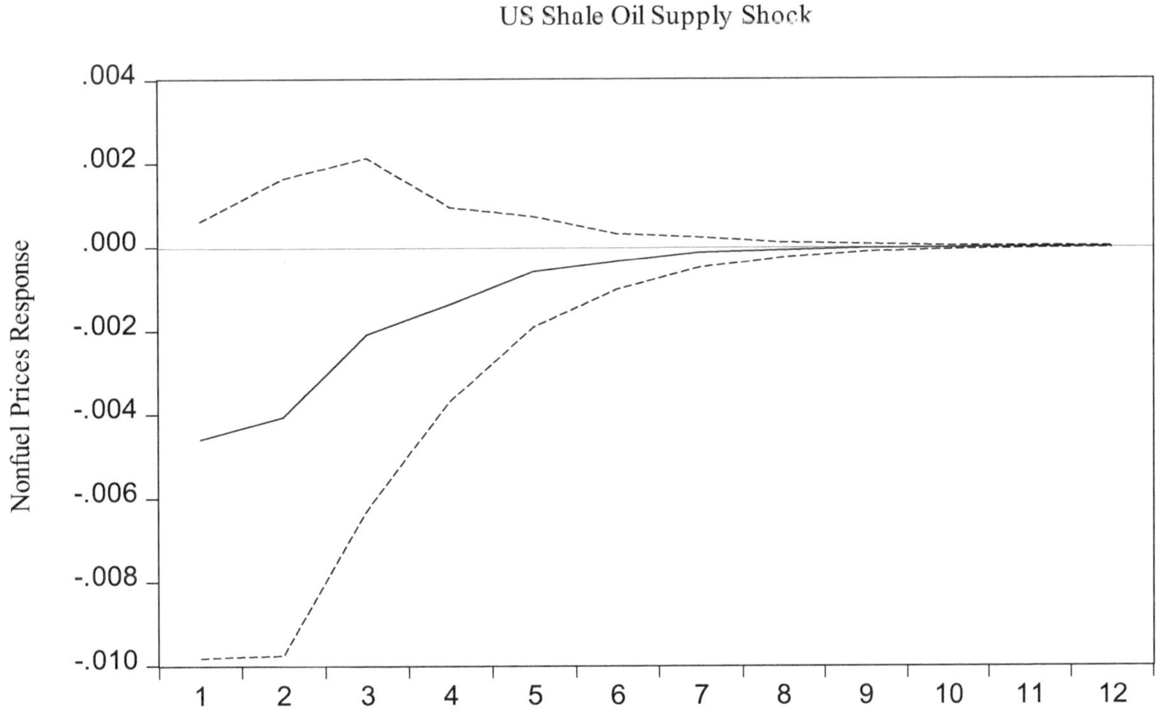

Figure 9: Historical Decomposition of Crude Oil from Shale Oil

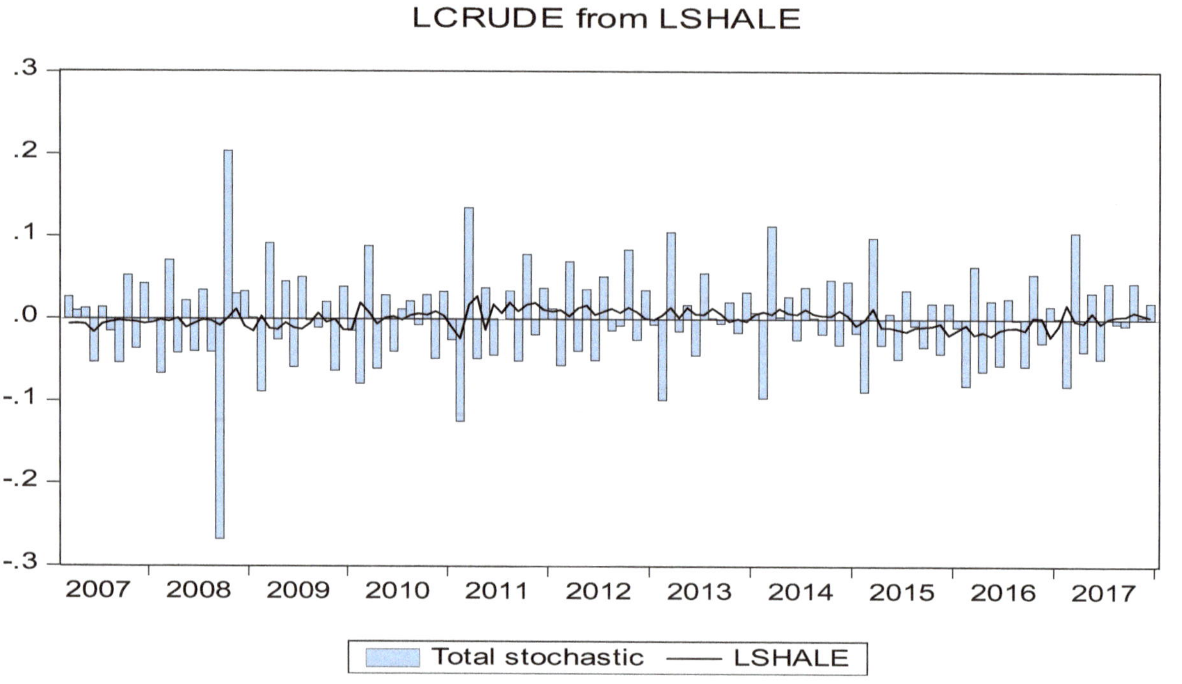

Figure 10: Historical Decomposition of Oil Price from Shale Oil

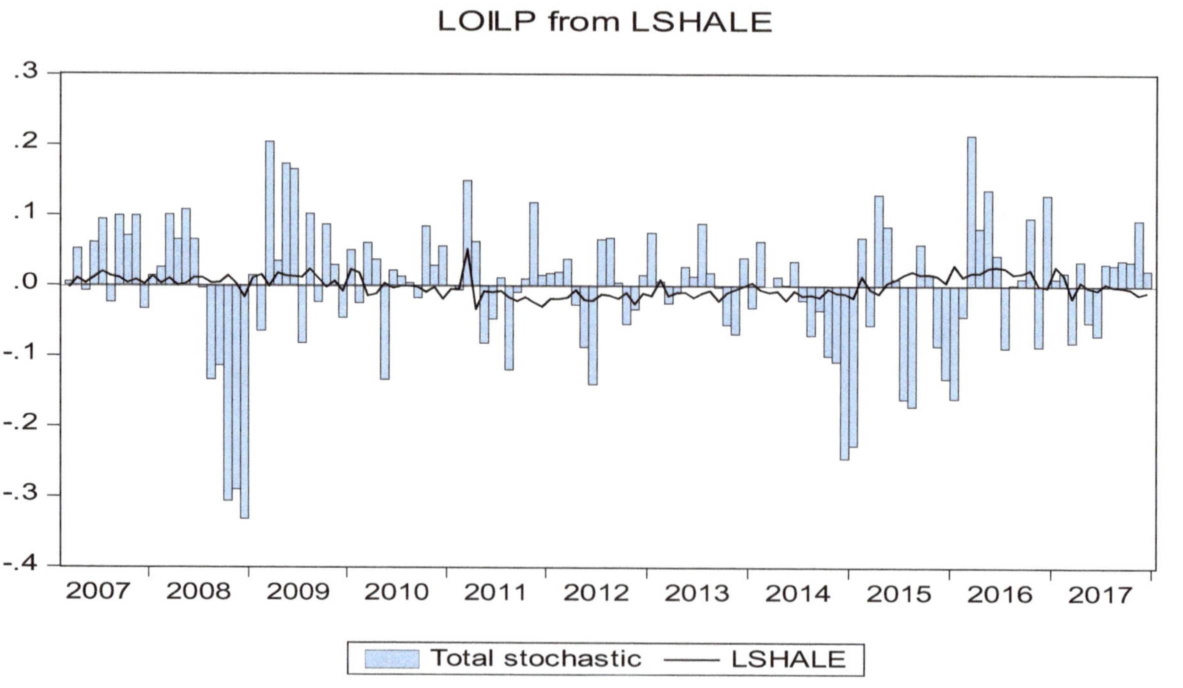

Figure 11: Historical Decomposition of All-Commodity Prices from Shale Oil

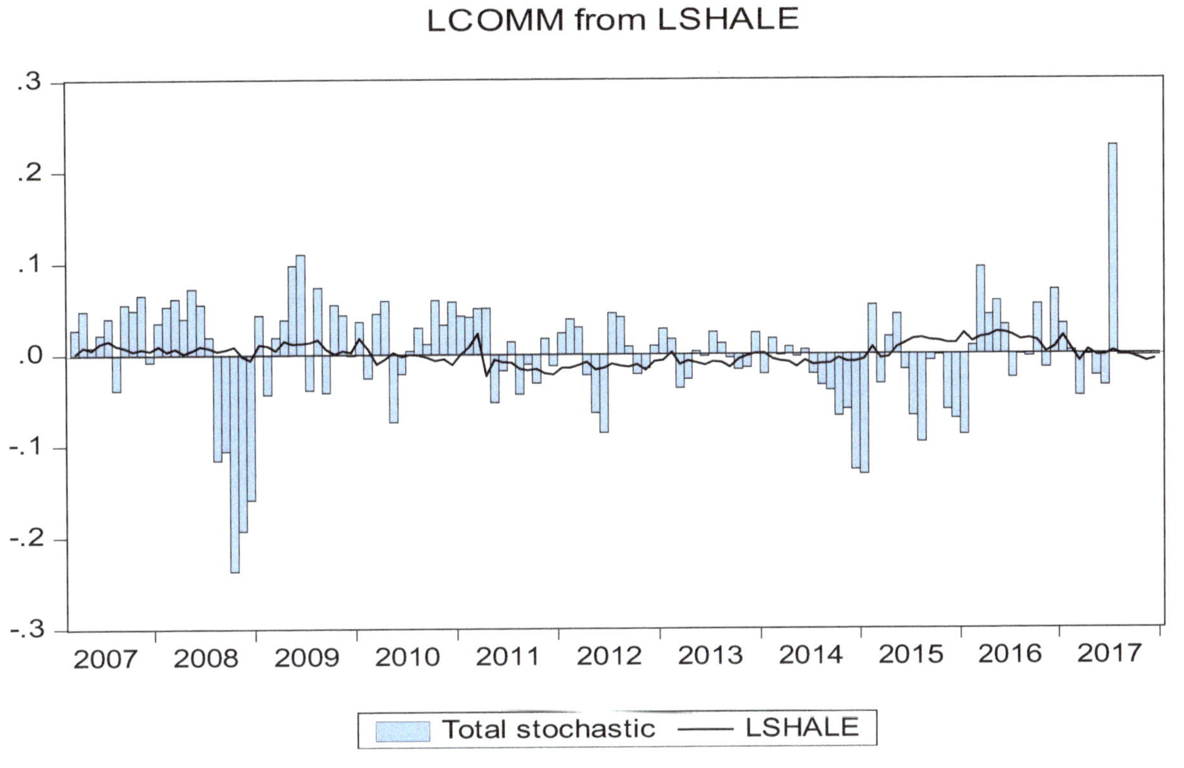

Figure 12: Historical Decomposition of Nonfuel Prices from Shale Oil

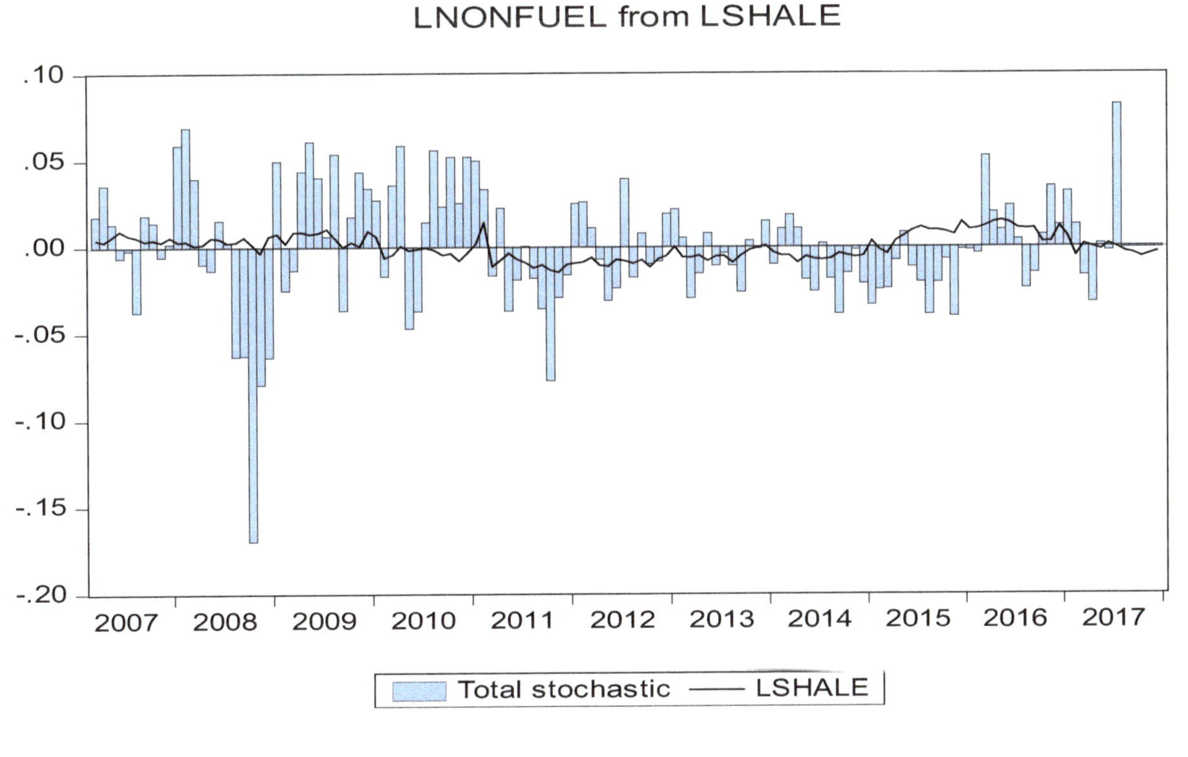

Table 1: Data Scope

Variables	Start Date	End Date	No.
US Shale Oil Production	01/1/2007	31/12/2017	132
US Crude Oil Production	01/1/2007	31/12/2017	132
WTI	01/1/2007	31/12/2017	132
Commodity Price Index (all)	01/1/2007	31/12/2017	132
Commodity Price Index (non-fuel)	01/1/2007	31/12/2017	132

Table 2: Summary Statistics

Variables	Mean	Std. Dev.	Skewness	Kurtosis	Jarque-Bera
US Shale Oil Production	3386.923	1779.642	0.209151	1.357023	15.8089*** (0.00036)
US Crude Oil Production	212722.8	53863.95	0.271639	1.467636	14.5381*** (0.00069)
WTI	75.98227	23.90436	0.014113	2.020951	5.2763* (0.07149)
Commodity Prices (all)	149.9644	35.29284	-0.039890	1.702526	9.2939*** (0.00959)
Commodity Prices (non-fuel)	153.1948	21.26639	0.249284	2.636638	2.09331 (0.35110)

Note: values in "()" parenthesis are probability values associated with the respective statistics. The symbol *** indicates 1% level of significance.

Table 3: Unit Root Tests (ADF and PP)

Series	ADF					
	Level			1st Difference		
	None	Intercept	Intercept & trend	None	Intercept	Intercept & trend
US shale oil	-1.5630	-2.41915	-2.40942	-13.251***	-13.204***	-13.147***
	(0.1107)	(0.1385)	(0.3730)	(0.0000)	(0.0000)	(0.0000)
US crude oil	-4.60***	-5.265***	-5.291***	-10.046***	-10.009***	-9.9659***
	(0.0000)	(0.0000)	(0.0001)	(0.0000)	(0.0000)	(0.0000)
Oil price	-7.62***	-7.597***	-7.579***	-17.220***	-17.153***	-17.087***
	(0.0000)	(0.0000)	(0.0000)	(0.0000)	(0.0000)	(0.0000)
comm_all	-7.29***	-7.266***	-7.256***	-16.965***	-16.899***	-16.834***
	(0.0000)	(0.0000)	(0.0000)	(0.0000)	(0.0000)	(0.0000)
nonfuel	-7.03***	-7.003***	-6.985***	-9.9268***	-9.8876***	-9.8499***
	(0.0000)	(0.0000)	(0.0000)	(0.0000)	(0.0000)	(0.0000)

Continued on the next page

Table 3: Unit Root Tests (ADF and PP) (Continued)

Series	PP						I(d)
	Level			**1st Difference**			
	None	Intercept	Intercept & trend	None	Intercept	Intercept & trend	
US shale oil	-8.07***	-9.9931***	-9.974***	-34.322***	-34.1733***	-34.001***	I(0)
	(0.0000)	(0.0000)	(0.0000)	(0.0000)	(0.0001)	(0.0001)	
US crude oil	-23.4***	-25.325***	-25.26***	-124.72***	-124.210***	-123.59***	I(0)
	(0.0000)	(0.0000)	(0.0000)	(0.0000)	(0.0001)	(0.0001)	
oil price	-7.70***	-7.672***	-7.656***	-41.730***	-41.503***	-42.216***	I(0)
	(0.0000)	(0.0000)	(0.0000)	(0.0000)	(0.0000)	(0.0000)	
comm_all	-7.29***	-7.266***	-7.256***	-32.187***	-32.0287***	-33.254***	I(0)
	(0.0000)	(0.0000)	(0.3807)	(0.0000)	(0.0000)	(0.0000)	
nonfuel	-7.04***	-7.021***	-7.005***	-30.570***	-30.3844***	-30.364***	I(0)
	(0.0000)	(0.0000)	(0.0000)	(0.0000)	(0.0001)	(0.0000)	

Table 4: Stationarity Test (KPSS)

	KPSS				
	Level		**1st Difference**		**Decision**
	Intercept	Intercept & trend	Intercept	Intercept & trend	
US shale oil	0.188896	0.189239	–	–	I(0)
	[0.739000]	[0.216000]			
US crude oil	0.173979	0.112779	–	–	I(0)
	[0.739000]	[0.216000]			
Oil price	0.096420	0.047026	–	–	I(0)
	[0.739000]	[0.216000]			
Comm all	0.099114	0.055571	–	–	I(0)
	[0.739000]	[0.216000]			
Nonfuel	0.079137	0.050910	–	–	I(0)
	[0.739000]	[0.216000]			

Table 5: Variance decomposition from shale oil supply up to commodity prices

Period	S.E.	Shock1 (Shale Oil)	Shock2 (Crude Oil)	Shock3 (Oil Price)	Shock3 (Comm Price)
1	0.016744	100.0000	0.000000	0.000000	0.000000
2	0.017786	97.12061	2.721146	0.014104	0.144136
3	0.017855	96.83088	2.721146	0.034232	0.204710
4	0.017873	96.68458	3.066039	0.040340	0.209043
5	0.017877	96.64657	3.100263	0.042317	0.210849
6	0.017878	96.63503	3.111451	0.042645	0.210872
7	0.017878	96.63126	3.115087	0.042731	0.210926
8	0.017878	96.63018	3.116153	0.042741	0.210924
9	0.017878	96.62982	3.116509	0.042744	0.210926
10	0.017878	96.62972	3.116614	0.042744	0.210925
11	0.017878	96.62968	3.116649	0.042744	0.210926
12	0.017878	96.62967	3.116659	0.042744	0.210926

Table 6: Variance decomposition from shale oil supply up to nonfuel prices

Period	S.E.	Shock1 (Shale Oil)	Shock2 (Crude Oil)	Shock3 (Oil Price)	Shock3 (Comm Price)
1	0.016754	100.0000	0.000000	0.000000	0.000000
2	0.017793	97.12178	2.814805	0.027369	0.036042
3	0.017857	96.92635	2.994879	0.037070	0.041700
4	0.017875	96.79445	3.123130	0.040145	0.042270
5	0.017878	96.76415	3.151815	0.040728	0.043304
6	0.017878	96.75453	3.161254	0.040882	0.043331
7	0.017879	96.75155	3.164116	0.040906	0.043425
8	0.017879	96.75073	3.164924	0.040913	0.043428
9	0.017879	96.75047	3.165184	0.040913	0.043436
10	0.017879	96.75039	3.165257	0.040914	0.043436
11	0.017879	96.75037	3.165280	0.040914	0.043437
12	0.017879	96.75036	3.165287	0.040914	0.043437

9

Adjusted Evaluation Measures for Asymmetrically Important Data

George-Jason Siouris♣, Despoina Skilogianni♣, Alex Karagrigoriou*♣

♣Lab of Statistics and Data Analysis, Department of Statistics and Actuarial-Financial Mathematics, University of the Aegean

---

ABSTRACT: In this paper we introduce adjustments for standard evaluation measures appropriate for the analysis of data with asymmetrical importance. In risk analysis, it is understood that the returns of an asset do not all provide the same amount of information. This asymmetry of information is crucial for choosing the most appropriate model and evaluating its forecasting ability. In risk analysis, measures like value at risk (VaR) and expected shortfall (ES) concentrate on the left tail of the distribution of returns so that failures in fitting a model on the right tail are not important. Therefore, when we estimate the VaR of an asset, the days of violations are more important than the days of non-violations. The proposed adjustments take into consideration the asymmetry in importance and are filling the gap in the theory of evaluation of percentiles measures. The measures are divided into *fixed partition*, based on prior information or the goal of forecasting, and *non fixed partition*, based on the time proximity of the model failure. The performance of the proposed measures is illustrated with the use of a stock from the industrial metals and minerals index of the American Stock Exchange (NYSE MKT), as well as a warrant, from the Athens Exchange (ATHEX).

Keywords: PVaR, violation ratios, low price effect, low price correction, back-testing, evaluation measures

*Corresponding Author. Email: alex.karagrigoriou@aegean.gr

Introduction

Risk measures have been proposed and used, over the years, to quantify overall risk exposure for the purpose of financial supervision, including internal control and banking supervision. Value at risk (VaR) and expected shortfall (ES) are the most popular of such measures, primarily due to their simplicity. Furthermore, VaR has also been popular due to its easy validation and backtesting. The introduction of ES as a new risk measure that possesses the sub-additivity property and measures the loss in the tail, came naturally as a response to the limitations of VaR, specifically its failure to fulfill the sub-additivity property in non-normal cases, and its inability to capture tail risk (Artzner et al., 1997, 1999; Acerbi and Tasche, 2002).

In order to judge the forecasting quality of typical methodologies such as the above, one may rely on a number of popular evaluation measures, such as the mean square error (MSE), the mean absolute error (MAE), and the mean absolute percent error (MAPE). The problem with these measures is that they fail to evaluate the risk measure estimators such as VaR, because these are percentiles. Indeed, the distance between the realization and the percentile does not provide any information about the accuracy of the percentile estimation and as such it must be adjusted. Even though, many evaluation measures and their adjustments have been proposed over the year (see Wang and Bovik, 2009; Singh et al., 2014; Imbens et al., 2005), no one has introduced any appropriate adjustment for percentile evaluation. Therefore, the problem is an open scientific problem with many applications to a variety of fields. Moreover, our proposed adjustments provide a framework for a far greater family of problems as we will show later. For comparison purposes, backtesting methods, such as the violation ratio (VR) for VaR and normalised shortfall (NS) for ES, are commonly used (see for example Broda and Paolella, 2011).

Recently, two published papers (Siouris and Karagrigoriou, 2017; Siouris et al., 2019), have shown that improvement in forecasting based on the price of a stock is possible. The improvement is made in a subset of the dataset with a specific property (e.g., a very low price). For the same subset of very low-priced stocks, in this paper, adjusted evaluation measures are proposed and implemented in order to evaluate forecasting ability and demonstrate the advantages of the method at hand.

The motivation for the present paper, lies in the fact that in risk analysis, it is often understood that the returns of an asset do not all contain the same amount of information, and do not have the same degree of significance (Sokolova and Lapalme, 2009; Asadabadi et al., 2018; Al-Hawamdeh, 2008; Aladag et al., 2010). This is also apparent in other scientific areas, related to medical, climatological, geophysical or meteorological phenomena. The "asymmetry in the importance" of information is crucial both in choosing the most appropriate model and in evaluating its forecasting ability. In the case of risk analysis, risk measures like

VaR and ES, concentrate on the left tail of the distribution of returns. Hence, failures in fitting a model to the right tail are not considered important. When the VaR of an asset at time t is evaluated, the days of violations are more important than the days of non-violations; the same happens with ES. Similar behavior is also found in other situations, such as health sciences and geosciences. Indeed, in biosurveillance systems for instance, the same phenomenon occurs for epidemic and non epidemic periods, the former being the important ones although it is the latter that are frequently modelled. Based on the above, evaluation measures should take into account this "asymmetry in the importance" of information borne in the data.

The concept of "asymmetry in the importance" of information is not rare in science. For example, great earthquakes provide much more information for the estimation of seismic magnitude than smaller ones. Days of extreme losses on the financial markets bear greater information compared to the "normal" days, as correlations are non-linear within each financial market in the day-by-day returns as well as between financial markets. Epidemic days carry disproportionate information compared to non-epidemic days. This is true in general, whenever the cost function for the difference between the estimation and the realized value is not constant. This non-constant cost function depends on the distance between the two values as in the case of a risk measure when a violation occurs, on the value of the realization and the range that it belongs to as in the case of seismology and epidemiology, or on a pre-specified partition of the dataset.

In this paper, we introduce for the first time, to the best of our knowledge, adjustments of standard evaluation measures appropriate for asymmetrically important data. The proposed adjustments fill a gap in the literature of percentile evaluation both for situations where the cost of error is not equal for all cases and for situations where a clear partition of the dataset exists. The proposed measures will be divided into two general categories based on the method of partitioning the dataset; fixed partition, based on prior information or the goal of the forecasting, and non fixed partition, based on the time proximity of the model failure. The two categories of measures are presented in Section 1 and an evaluation of their performance is given in Section 2. Concluding remarks are provided in Section 3.

1 Methodology

Let Ω be the available dataset, and A_i be a partition of Ω based on our criteria. Any family of non-empty sets is a partition of Ω, if and only if the following conditions hold.

1. $\Omega = \bigcup_{i \in I} A_i$ where A_i are non-empty subsets of Ω, $\forall i \in I \in \mathcal{N}$
2. $A_i \cap A_j = \emptyset$ for $i \neq j$.

The partitioning of the dataset will be done in two main ways, which we will call Type 1 and Type 2. Type 1 is a fixed partition, based on prior information for the dataset or the goal of the forecasting procedure. Type 2 is a dynamically adjusted partition of unit sets, based on their time proximity to the present. Both types, with respective examples, are presented below.

For the purpose of this work, we concentrate on a risk measure for estimating possible losses, and below we introduce the Type 1 adjusted evaluation measure.

The percentage VaR (PVaR), which is a risk measure for estimating the possible percentage losses from trading assets, within a set time period, is defined as follows:

Definition 1: (a) PVaR(p) is the 100pth percentile of the distribution of returns.

(b) PVaR$_t$(p) is the PVaR(p) at time t, where the distribution of standardized returns with standard deviation σ, (R_t/σ), is denoted by $F(\cdot)$. Observe that the PVaR of an asset takes the form:

$$PVaR_t(p) = -\sigma F^{-1}(p).$$

where $F^{-1}(p)$ is the $100p^{th}$ percentile of the inverse of the distribution of (R_t/σ), namely the standardized returns with standard deviation σ.

(c) Let p_t be the asset value at time t and $c(p_t)$ be the minimum price variation (market accuracy) associated with the value of the asset at time t. Then, the minimum possible return of an asset at time t (mpr_t) is the logarithmic return that the asset will produce if its value changes by $c(p_t)$ and is given by:

$$mpr_t = log\left(\frac{p_t + c(p_t)}{p_t}\right)$$

(d) The low price effect area is the range of prices for which the mpr is greater than a pre-specified threshold Θ.

As a simple example consider the case where a stock market operates with a fixed accuracy $c(p_t) = 0.001$. If the threshold is chosen to be $\Theta = 0.001$, then according to Definition 1(c), it is easy to see that for a stock price p_t less than 0.999001 the minimum possible return mpr_t is greater than Θ. Thus, the low price effect area is the set $\{p_t : p_t < 0.999001\}$.

Siouris et al. (2019) proposed the low price correction by rounding the PVaR$_t$(p) estimate to a legitimate value, namely the next integer multiple of the mpr_t. In particular, the low price correction of the estimation denoted by $\widetilde{PVaR_t}(p)$ is given by:

$$\widetilde{PVaR_t}(p) = \begin{cases} \left(\left\lfloor \frac{PVaR_t(p)}{mpr_t} \right\rfloor + 1 \right) \cdot mpr_t, & \text{if} \quad mpr_t \geq \Theta \\ PVaR_t(p), & \text{if} \quad mpr_t < \Theta \end{cases} \tag{1}$$

where $\lfloor w \rfloor$ is the floor function (integer part) of w.

Observe that under the above low price correction, the market accuracy is passed on to the evaluation of the PVaR, resulting in reasonable estimations and as a result fewer violations. Let $\{y_t\}_{t=1}^{T}$ be a sample of daily logarithmic losses on a trading portfolio, and define the indicator η_t that takes the value 1 if $y_t > PVaR_t(p)$ (or $\widetilde{PVaR_t}(p)$ if the above correction has been enforced) and 0 otherwise. A PVaR violation is said to have occurred if $\eta_t = 1$. Observe that the low price correction is associated with the rationalization of the estimated asset returns as it is the next integer multiplier of the minimum possible return.

In order to measure the accuracy of the above procedure, one cannot rely on popular evaluation measures, such as the MSE, MAE, MAPE, or the heteroskedasticity mean square error (HMSE), because VaR estimations are percentile estimations. The fact that the proximity of the realzsed returns to the estimated percentile does not provide any information creates the need for introducing appropriately adjusted accuracy measures. Note though that this is not the case for backtesting procedures; by concentrating on the underlining risk, only the proximity in days of violation provides information on the quality and accuracy of the proposed methodology. The decrease in the values of the adjusted evaluation measures will show and verify the improved forecasting quality of the low price correction. It is easily seen, that the MSE in the above setting, is defined as follows:

$$MSE = \frac{1}{\sum_{t \leq T} \eta_t} \sum_{t \leq T \& \eta_t = 1} (y_t - PVaR_t(p))^2. \tag{2}$$

Observe that the above is a special weighted MSE expression and can be written as

$$MSE = \sum_{t \leq T} \frac{\eta_t}{v(T)} \cdot (y_t - PVaR_t(p))^2$$

where

$$v(T) = \sum_{t \leq T} \eta_t.$$

All popular evaluation measures used in the literature can be adjusted to fit our proposed methodology by generalizing the special weights used above. The adjusted MSE is defined below.

1.1 Type 1 Evaluation Measures

Definition 2: Adjusted MSE (AMSE) is given by

$$AMSE = \frac{1}{w}\sum_{i=1}^{n} w_i(y_i - \hat{y}_i)^2,$$

where w_i is a pre-specified weight given to the i-th observation based on its importance, y_i is a sample observation, $\hat{y}_i$ is the observation forecast, n is the sample size, and $w = \sum_{i=1}^{n} w_i$.

We also provide the respective formulas for the adjusted mean absolute error (MAE), the adjusted mean absolute error (AMAE), the adjusted mean absolute percent error (AMAPE), and the adjusted heteroskedasticity mean square error (AHMSE):

$$AMAE = \frac{1}{w}\sum_{i=1}^{n} w_i|y_i - \hat{y}_i|,$$

$$AMAPE = \frac{1}{w}\sum_{i=1}^{n} w_i\left|\frac{100(y_i - \hat{y}_i)}{y_i}\right|,$$

$$AHMSE = \frac{1}{w}\sum_{i=1}^{n} w_i\left[\frac{y_i}{\hat{y}_i} - 1\right]^2.$$

The adjusted measures presented in this work, provide a more general and flexible framework, for addressing "asymmetry in importance data".

As shown in (3), examples of the applicability of these measures can be found in risk analysis; other examples are found in biosurveillance, among other settings. In the case of risk analysis, and specifically in the case of VaR estimations, days in which a violation occurred, are obviously more important than others. The same logic holds for ES estimations. Also, we may want to give different weights to days with positive returns than to days with negative returns, because days with positive returns are not so important from the risk analyst's point of view. In this case, the partition can be done as follows:

$$A_1 = \{i \in I | y_i \le 0\},$$

$$A_2 = \{i \in I | 0 < y_i \le PVaR_i(p)\},$$

$$A_3 = \{i \in I | y_i > PVaR_i(p)\},$$

where y_i are the daily logarithmic losses of a stock, and $PVaR_i(p)$ is the Percentage Value at Risk, as defined in Siouris et al. (2019).

Under this partition, weights can be given as follows

$$w_i = \begin{cases} g_1, & i \in A_1 \\ g_2, & i \in A_2 \\ g_3, & i \in A_3. \end{cases} \tag{3}$$

As it is clear these weights are chosen arbitrarily, which is the main weakness of Type 1 adjustment of evaluation measures. One possible choice for the weights is $g_1 = 0$, $g_2 = 1$ and $g_3 = 10$, assuming that days of PVaR violation are 10 times more important than days of positive losses that did not violate PVaR and days of negative losses (days of positive returns) are not taken into account.

Analogously, in biosurveillance we have epidemic and non epidemic periods, and the failures of the model should not be evaluated as the same in these two periods.

Remark 1: When equal weights are assigned to all observations, we obtain the standard evaluation measures. As a result, a standard evaluation measure constitutes a special case of the adjusted measures defined above.

Remark 2: Additional functions like the one proposed by Gónzalez-Rivera et al. (2004) could also be used for exploring the robust capabilities of the proposed methodology. Such explorations will be the main theme of a future study.

1.2 Type 2 Evaluation Measures

In the second type of partition, the weights applied are time dependent and exponentially decreasing as we go further back in time. In this case, models that are generally good but fail in the latter part of the time series, should be replaced by more appropriate ones. Weights can be assigned in the same fashion as in the exponentially weighted moving average (EWMA) model, a well-known and widely used model in risk analysis and financial time series:

$$w_{t+1} = \lambda w_t = \lambda^2 w_{t-1} = \ldots = \lambda^{n+1} w_{t-n},$$

where λ is the EWMA constant. Under the assumption that the weights sum to one, namely

$$\sum_{t=1}^{\infty} w_t = w_1 \sum_{t=1}^{\infty} \lambda^t = 1$$

and for $|\lambda| < 1$, we have that $w_1 = 1 - \lambda$. For a finite dataset, which is usually the case, $w_1 = \frac{1-\lambda}{\lambda - \lambda^{n+1}}$, where n is the sample size. In contrast to Type 1 adjustment, the weights in the Type 2 case, are not chosen arbitrarily.

2 Applications

To apply the proposed methodology, in this section we use, for illustrative purposes, the Northern Dynasty Minerals, Ltd. (NAK) stock from the industrial metals and minerals index of the Americal stock exchange, NYSE MKT, as well as, the National Bank of Greece (NBG) warrant from the Athens stock exchange, ATHEX. These assets, the basic statistical characteristics of which are furnished in Table 1, were chosen for their low prices which will help fully explore the capabilities of the proposed methodology.

2.1 The NBG warrant

Warrants are in many ways similar to options, but with a few key differences distinguishing them. Warrants are generally issued by the company itself, not by a third party and they are traded over-the-counter more often than on an exchange market. Unlike options, warrants cannot be written by investors and they tend to have much longer periods between issue and expiration. They do not pay dividends or come with voting rights. Investors are attracted to warrants as a means of leveraging their positions in a security, hedging against downside risk, or exploiting arbitrage opportunities. The warrants of the National Bank of Greece (NBG) were issued in 2013 as part of the first recapitalization of the Greek banking system, and they were traded on the Athens Exchange (ATHEX). The expiration date of the warrants was 4.5 years from the issue date. They had 9 exercise dates, one every six months. On each exercise date, the owner can buy stocks at a specific price, which in the case of the NBG was 4.6761 euros per stock. Later, when the NBG stock price collapsed, the warrants' price also collapsed.

Below, we first implement the low price correction (lpc) on the PVaR methodology given in (1). Then, the backtesting results for various models considered (EWMA, Normal, historic simulations [HS] and generalized autoregressive conditional heteroskedasticity [GARCH] model with skewed t-student innovations and estimated degrees of freedom) are considered; these appear in Table 2. Note that the primary tool for backtesting is the violation ratio

(VR) which is obtained by comparing observed frequencies and expected number of violations. The predictive ability of all models used is presented in Tables 3-7: the standard evaluation measures (Table 3); the special case of adjusted measures given in (2) (Table 4); Type 1 evaluation measures only in the final days of violations (the days of violations of the corrected model) (Table 5); Type 1 measures given in (3) with $g_1 = 0$, $g_2 = 1$, $g_3 = 10$ (Table 6); and Type 2 evaluation measures, with a typical choice for the parameter λ equal to 0.94 (Table 7).

We must point out the differences in the results from the various evaluation methods in the following tables. Table 2 shows that in all 4 models, the low price correction methodology produces estimations with fewer violations, a result that by itself proves the usefulness of this correction. In contrast, in Table 3 the standard evaluation measures completely fail to demonstrate any improvement of estimations. On the contrary, most of the times the estimations were far worse than previously. This is due to the aforementioned inability of standard evaluation measures to evaluate percentiles. Due to this inconsistency between Tables 2 and 3, we are motivated to provides appropriate adjustments of the standard evaluation measures.

Table 2 gives the VRs for the PVaR estimations for four different models, with and without low price correction implemented, as well as, the PVaR volatilities. Based on the results of the PVaR estimations shown in Table 2 and the fact that an acceptable range of VR (according to the Basel III accords) is 0.8-1.2, the HS and GARCH(1,1) fail the most among all the models considered. The estimations of all the models systematically underestimate the underlying risk. We observe that the proposed low price correction methodology significantly improves the VR in all models. In fact, Table 2 clearly shows that in all 4 models, the low price correction methodology produces PVaR estimations with fewer violations. As a result, in all cases examined, VaR estimations have been improved in the sense that their VR is considerably reduced with the low price correction. Indeed, the VR (2nd vs. 1st column in Table 2) is always improved, in the sense that the frequency of violations is reduced which is associated with a more defensive approach in accordance with Basel III. This is a result that by itself clearly proves the usefulness of the low price methodology methodology. The same conclusions are also evident from Figures 1 and 2. These figures show the improvement arising from the use of the proposed methodology and are provided for a visual understanding of the contribution of this work.

The first adjustment is presented in Table 4, where only the violations are taken into consideration. Even though this table is closer to the truth, it still fails to capture the improvement shown by the VR. This is due to the different denominator in the adjusted evaluation measures for the estimations with and without the low price correction. By far the best adjusted evaluation measure, one, that completely captures the genuine improvement in our estimations with the help of the low price correction, is that in Table 5. In this table, the improvement is genuine for all models and for all measures, as was expected from the definition of the low price correction. The adjusted evaluation measure results shown in Table 5 completely agree with the VR results of Table 2 and also quantify something that was clear from the definition of low price correction, specifically, that the improvement from the risk analysis point of view is genuine. Tables 6 and 7 present the results from other variations of adjusted evaluation models and have to do with the needs of the researchers. Last but not least, Table 5 in almost all cases selects a different model as the best, compared to Table 2.

As we see in Tables 3-7, the chosen model depends on the evaluation measure used and the adjustment chosen. For example, HS is the best model according to the standard MSE evaluation measure, whereas EWMA appears to be superior based on the Type 1 adjustments presented in Tables 4 and 6. GARCH(1,1) is the model selected according to the Type 2 adjusted evaluation measure of Table 7. The most important result, is that, although the standard evaluation measures fail to capture the obvious improvement of the low price correction, the Type 1 adjustment completely succeeds in illustrating this improvement. This is clear from the results for all measures in Table 5 which contains the evaluation measures results for PVaR with and without low price correction in the final days of violations (the days of the violations of the corrected model). Finally, the decrease of HMSE for the lpc GARCH(1,1), in all adjusted cases, is more extreme than before. Note that, various measures based on both quadratic and absolute errors were used for completeness. The investigator is free to choose the most appropriate measure for his/hers purposes. However, caution is needed when AMAE and AMAPE measures are used because both are scale sensitive.

Remark 3: It should be mentioned that any distribution can be used, as in Siouris and Karagrigoriou (2017) where Gaussian and non-Gaussian innovations were examined. In the present work, the best among a series of candidate models was chosen to be presented, namely the one with skewed t-Student innovations. Furthermore, note that alternative models that have recently attracted considerable attention such as the generalized autoregressive score (GAS) models (Creal et al., 2013; Harvey, 2013), will be left for future work.

Remark 4: Note that in addition to the VR, which is equivalent to the well-known Kupiec's test (Kupiec, 1995) other backtesting procedures (see e.g., Christoffersen, 1998) could also be applied.

2.2 The NAK stock

The NAK data (2500 observations) extend from January 8, 2008 until December 12, 2017. Details about the behavior of the NAK stock can be found in Siouris et al. (2019). The low price correction methodology is again implemented. Backtesting is done with the same models as before with the addition of the asymmetric power autoregressive conditional heteroskedasticity (APARCH) model with skewed t-student innovations model and degrees of freedom estimated. The results of the backtesting are presented in Table 8 and Figures 1 and 2. Furthermore, the performance of the low price correction methodology according to the accuracy measures, is presented in Tables 9-13: the standard evaluation measures (Table 9); the special case of adjusted measures given in (2) (Table 10); Type 1 evaluation measures only in the final days of violations (the days of violations of the corrected model) (Table 11); Type 1 measures given in (3) with $g_1 = 0$, $g_2 = 1$, $g_3 = 10$ (Table 12); and Type 2 evaluation measures, with a typical choice for the parameter λ equal to 0.94 (Table 13).

Tables 8 and 9 present a comparison of the results of the evaluation methods identical to the ones presented in Tables 4 and 5 and discussed above. These results confirm the necessity of adjusted evaluation measures and provide the motivation for their definition and their implementation.

Table 8, gives the VRs for the PVaR estimations for six different models, with and without low price correction implemented, as well as, the PVaR volatilities. Based on the results shown in Table 8, and the fact that an acceptable range of VR is 0.8-1.2, we have that the PVaR estimation under normality, GARCH(1,1) and GARCH(2,2), are the three models that fail the most. The estimation under normality systematically overestimates the underlying risk, as it misinterprets big positive returns as risk factors, whereas GARCH(1,1) and GARCH(2,2) systematically underestimate it, and EWMA seems to fail. Acceptable models are the ones based on historical simulation and APARCH(1,1). It can be observed that the proposed methodology of the low price correction improves or leaves unchanged the VR in all models.

The first adjustment is presented in Table 10, where only the violations are taken into consideration. Even though this table is closer to the truth, it still fails to capture the improvement shown by the violation ratio. This is due to the different denominator in the adjusted evaluation measures for the estimations with and without the low price corrction. By far the best adjusted evaluation measure, one that completely captures the genuine improvement in our estimations with the help of low price correction, is that in Table 11. In this table the improvement is genuine for all models and all measures, as was expected from the definition of low price correction. The adjusted evaluation measure results shown in Table 11 agree completely with the VR results of Table 8 and also quantify something that was clear from the definition of low price correction, specifically, that the improvement from the risk analysis point of view is genuine. Tables 12 and 13 present results of other variations of the adjusted evaluation models and have to do with the needs of the researchers. Last, but not least, Table 11 in almost all cases selects a different best model as compared to Table 8.

Based on MSE, we observe that for the standard case (Table 9), GARCH(1,1) is the best model for the PVaR estimation. The same is also the case according to Type 1 (Table 12) and Type 2 adjusted measures (Table 13). On the other hand, this is not the case for the results shown in Table 10 which are based on the special Type 1 measure given in (2)) and clearly pick EWMA as the best model. However, such a conclusion is expected if one takes into consideration the fact that EWMA is the most "nervous" among the competing models, and, additionally, that the focus of the study is solely on violations. It must be noted, that even though GARCH(1,1) was not acceptable based on the VR, it is the one that behaves the best, according to the results in Tables 9, 11 and 13, and is among the best performing models based on the results in Table 10.

Comparing the results of Tables 9 and 13, which are both based on the entire set of observations, we clearly verify the effectiveness and significance of the EWMA weights (i.e., of type 2 measures), as compared to the standard evaluation measures. On the other hand, whereas the standard evaluation measures fail to reveal the failure level of the Normal model, the adjusted evaluation measures do not. Also, the low price correction is evaluated more accurately with the techniques presented in Tables 10-12, which concentrate on the violations and the negative returns, respectively. This is paticularly the case for the Type 1 adjustment, as shown in Table 11 which contains the evaluation measures results for PVaR with and without low price correction in the final days of violations (the days of the violations of the corrected model). Lastly, it must be noted that HMSE is not an appropriate measure for testing normality, and should not be taken into consideration.

3 Conclusions

In this paper, we have presented adjusted evaluation measures, applicable to situations in which not all observations are equally important. The phenomenon is quite common in finance as, for instance, in the case of asset returns which do not all contain the same amount of information. The proposed adjusted evaluation measures are categorized in two general classes, according to the method of partition of the data. Type 1 is a fixed partition, based on prior information or the goal of the forecasting procedure whereas Type 2 is a dynamically adjusted partition of unit sets, based on the model failures, and their time proximity to the present.

For equal weights, Type 1 adjusted evaluation measures are simplified to standard measures. In other words, a standard evaluation measure constitutes a special case of the class of Type 1 adjusted measures. As shown in the application section, adjusted evaluation measures of Type 1, are quite useful, offering additional information about the forecasting ability of models. On the other hand, their main weakness is associated with the fact that weights are arbitrarily chosen. However, if the main goal is to narrow the evaluation to a subset of the available values, as is needed for the correct evaluation of the low price correction, then the choice of weights is straight forward and the results quite clear as it is shown on Tables 4 and 10.

In contrast, the weights in the Type 2 case, are given according to the EWMA models' weights. Such weights typically decrease at an exponential rate as time goes back, which resembles the autocorrelation behavior of assets returns. These time dependent weights provide a framework within which the most appropriate model in the latter part of the time series is chosen. Note that the applicability of the proposed measures is not limited to finance; it can easily be extended to other scientific areas where data do not necessarily carry the same amount of information, such as in physical (earthquakes, floods etc.) or climatological (heat or cold waves) phenomena.

Acknowledgements: This work was completed as part of the research activities of the *Laboratory of Statistics and Data Analysis* of the University of the Aegean. The authors wish to express their appreciation to the Editor and an anonymous reviewer whose comments and suggestions have greatly improved the quality as well as the presentation of the manuscript.

References

Acerbi, C. and Tasche, D. (2002). Expected shortfall: a natural coherent alternative to value at risk. *Economic Notes by Banca Monte dei Paschi di Siena SpA*, 31(2):379–388.

Al-Hawamdeh, S. (2008). *Knowledge Management: Competencies and Professionalism*, volume 7. World Scientific, Singapore.

Aladag, C. H., Egrioglu, E., Gunay, S., and Basaran, M. A. (2010). Improving weighted information criterion by using optimization. *Journal of computational and applied mathematics*, 233(10):2683–2687.

Artzner, P., Heath, D., Delbaen, F., and Eber, J.-M. (1997). Thinking coherentlyg. *Risk*, 10:68–71.

Artzner, P., Heath, D., Delbaen, F., and Eber, J.-M. (1999). Coherent measures of risk. *Mathematical Finance*, 9(3):203–228.

Asadabadi, M. R., Saberi, M., and Chang, E. (2018). Targets of Unequal Importance Using the Concept of Stratification in a Big Data Environment. *International Journal of Fuzzy Systems*, pages 1–12.

Broda, S. A. and Paolella, M. S. (2011). Expected shortfall for distributions in finance. In *Statistical tools for finance and insurance*, pages 57–99. Springer, London.

Christoffersen, P. (1998). Evaluating interval forecasts. *International Economic Review*, 39:841–862.

Creal, D., Koopman, S. J., and André, L. (2013). Generalized autoregressive score models with applications. *Journal of Applied Econometrics*, 28:777–795.

Das, K., Jiang, J., and Rao, J. (2004). Mean squared error of empirical predictor. *Annals of Statistics*, 32(2):818–840.

Gónzalez-Rivera, G., Lee, T.-H., and Mishra, S. (2004). Forecasting volatility: A reality check based on option pricing, utility function, value-at-risk, and predictive likelihood. *International Journal of Forecasting*, 20:629–645.

Harvey, A. (2013). Generalized autoregressive score models with applications. *Dynamic models for volatility and heavy tails: with applications to financial and economic time series*, 52.

Imbens, G. W., Newey, W. K., and Ridder, G. (2005). Mean-square-error calculations for average treatment effects. https://dx.doi.org/10.2139/ssrn.954748.

Kupiec, P. (1995). Techniques for verifying the accuracy of risk measurement models. *Journal of Derivatives*, 3:73–84.

Singh, S., Singh, D. S., and Kumar, S. (2014). Modified Mean Square Error Algorithm with Reduced Cost of Training and Simulation Time for Character Recognition in Backpropagation Neural Network. In *Proceedings of the International Conference on Frontiers of Intelligent Computing: Theory and Applications (FICTA) 2013*, pages 137–145. Springer, London.

Siouris, G.-J. and Karagrigoriou, A. (2017). A low price correction for improved volatility estimation and forecasting. *Risks*, 5(3):45.

Siouris, G.-J., Skilogianni, D., and Karagrigoriou, A. (2019). Post model correction in value at risk and expected shortfall. *International Journal of Mathematics, Engineering and Management Sciences*, 4(3):542–566.

Sokolova, M. and Lapalme, G. (2009). A systematic analysis of performance measures for classification tasks. *Information Processing & Management*, 45(4):427–437.

Wang, Z. and Bovik, A. C. (2009). Mean squared error: Love it or leave it? A new look at signal fidelity measures. *IEEE Signal Processing Magazine*, 26(1):98–117.

Figure 1: Backtesting PVaR without low price correction (NBG warrants)

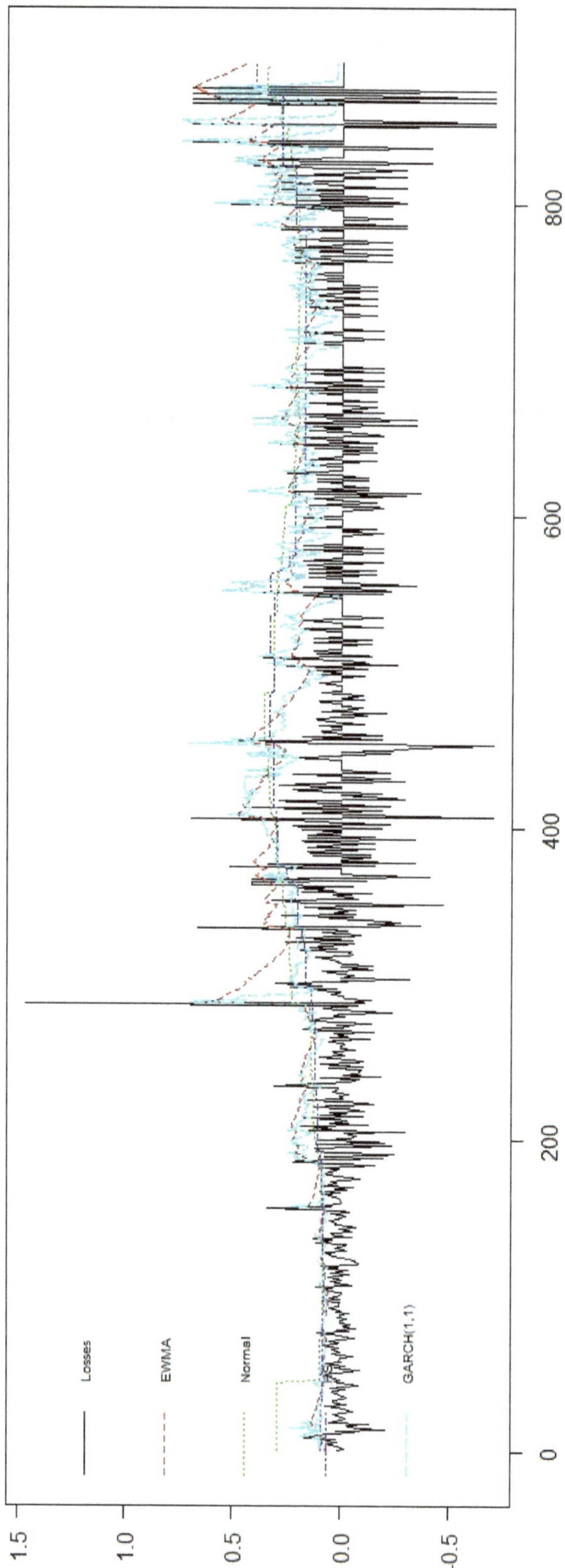

Figure 2: Backtesting PVaR with low price correction (NBG warrants)

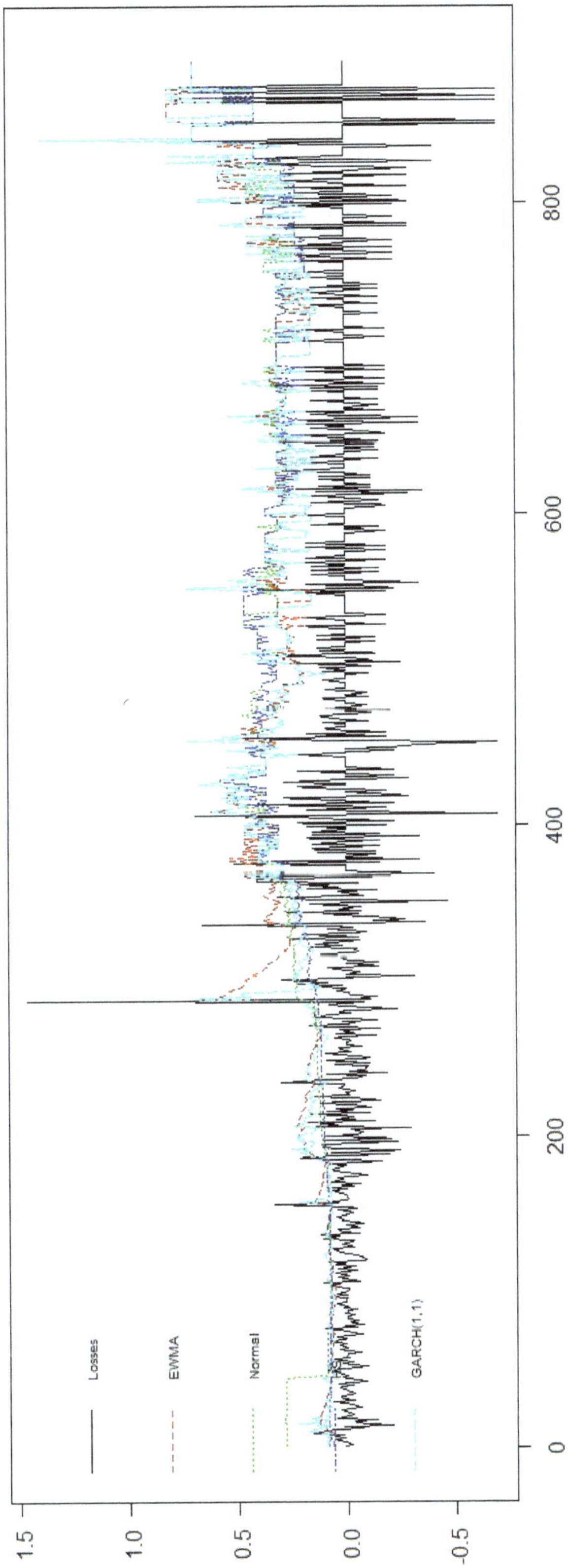

Figure 3: Backtesting PVaR without low price correction (NAK stock)

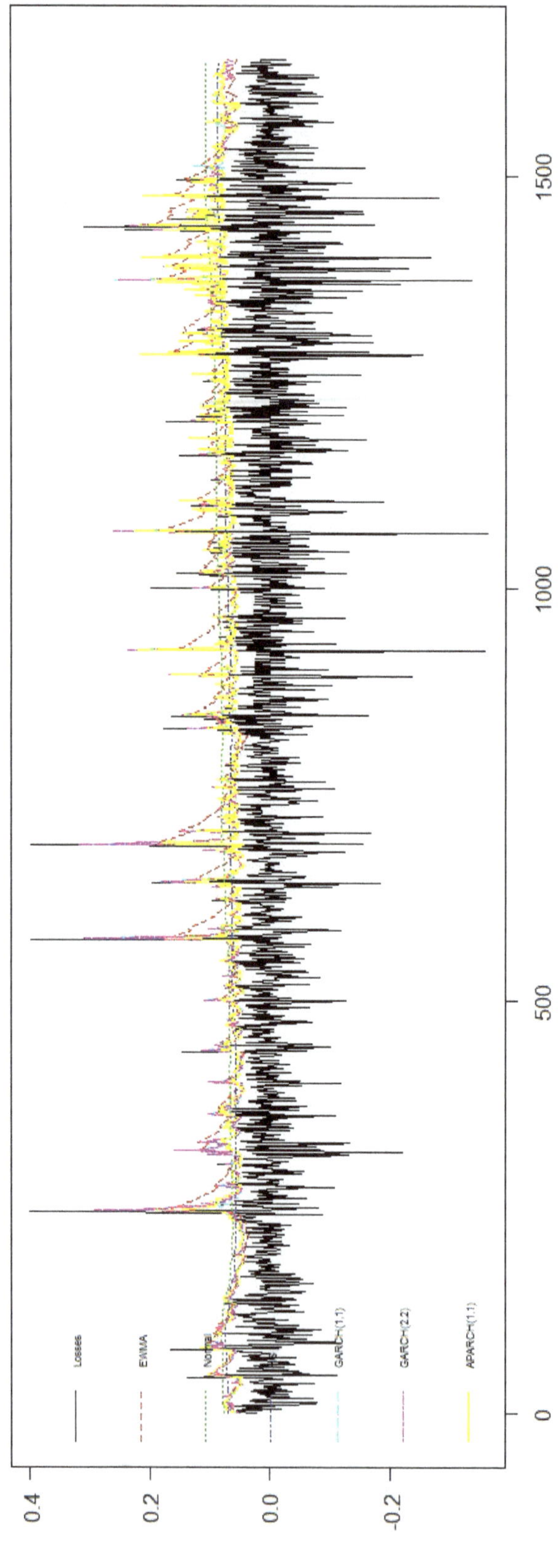

Figure 4: Backtesting PVaR with low price correction (NAK stock)

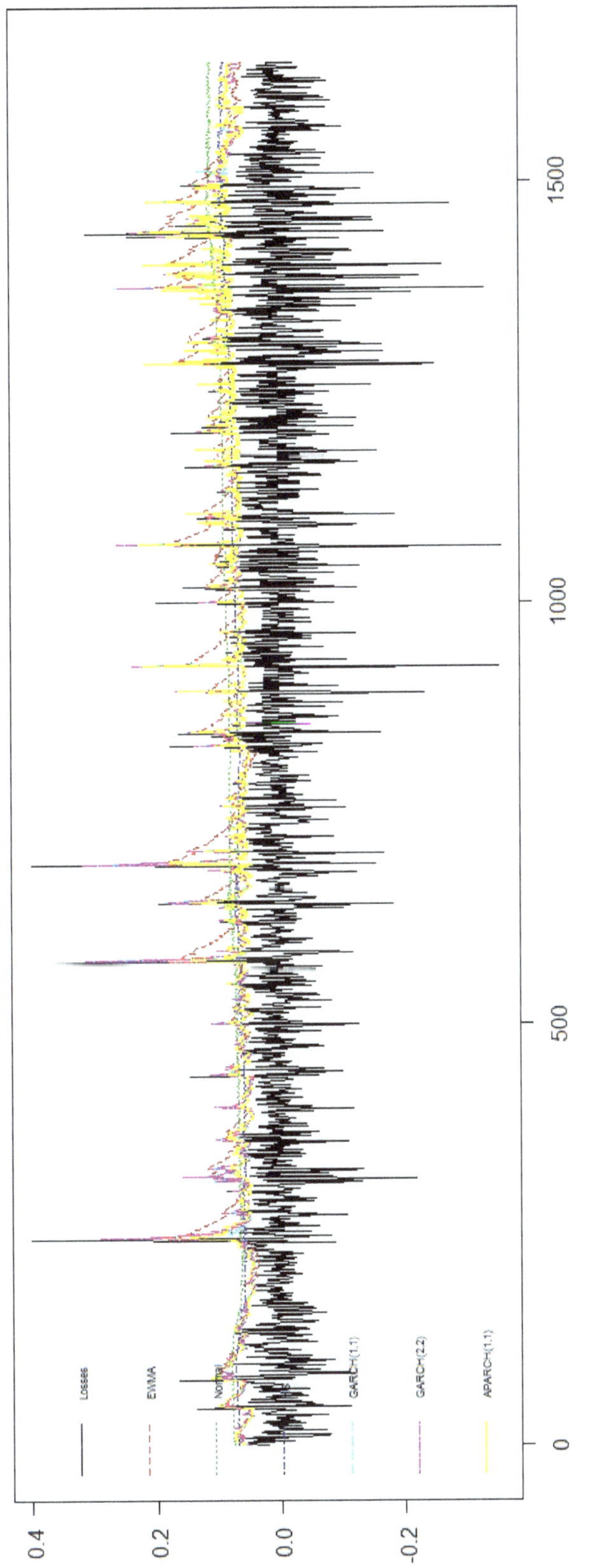

Table 1: Descriptive Statistics for Prices, First Differences of Prices and Logarithmic Returns

	NBG Prices	NBG 1st Dif.	NBG Log(Returns)	NAK Prices	NAK 1st Dif.	NAK Log(Returns)
MEAN	0.3269217	-0.00125592	-0.006584553	4.419676	-0.004597839	-0.0007760009
MEDIAN	0.031	0	0	2.69	0	0
VAR	0.2107202	0.002277542	0.02655832	17.0206	0.0561949	0.002804873
SD	0.4590427	0.0477236	0.1629672	4.125603	0.2370546	0.05296105
MIN	0.001	-0.759	-1.608385	0.21	-2.96	-0.4002432
MAX	1.84	0.82	1.670682	21.08	2.22	0.3566749
SKEWNESS	1.25837	1.214182	-0.5977321	1.083448	-0.3358244	0.1930199
KURTOSIS	3.264962	143.9865	30.42116	3.835573	25.34604	11.83174

Note: Descriptives of Prices, First Differences of Prices and Logarithmic Returns for NBG warrant and NAK.

Table 2: Backtesting With and Without Low Price Correction (lpc) for PVaR - NBG Warrants

	VR without lpc	VR with lpc	PVaR vol without lpc	PVaR vol with lpc
EWMA	1.414141	0.8754209	0.1224841	0.1701248
Normal	1.436588	0.9876543	0.08374533	0.1390613
HS	1.885522	1.234568	0.08965133	0.1495181
GARCH(1,1)	1.818182	1.257015	0.1204021	0.1731923

Note: Violation Ratio (VR) and % Value at Risk (PVaR) volatility are provided with and without lpc for the National Bank of Greece (NBG) warrants for the models EWMA, Normal, Historic Simulations (HS) and GARCH with skewed t-Student errors.

Table 3: Standard Evaluation Measures Results for PVaR With and Without Low Price Correction (lpc) of NBG Warrants

	MSE	MAE	MAPE	HMSE	Number of Violations
EWMA	0.08959510	0.2345721	283.0198	1.414714	891
EWMA (lpc)	0.13321386	0.2882063	296.3516	1.312602	891
Normal	0.07842356	0.2313674	335.4894	1.499397	891
Normal (lpc)	0.11700468	0.2815343	348.1618	1.366298	891
HS	0.06918058	0.2083804	233.1994	1.627136	891
HS (lpc)	0.10728055	0.2591924	245.8914	1.476536	891
GARCH(1,1)	0.07873061	0.2113150	256.1190	2.746523	891
GARCH(1,1) (lpc)	0.12377995	0.2687740	268.0334	1.373017	891

Note: MSE, MAE, MAPE and HMSE *standard* measures are provided with and without lpc for the National Bank of Greece (NBG) warrants for the models EWMA, Normal, Historic Simulations (HS) and GARCH with skewed t-Student errors.

Table 4: Adjusted Type 1 Evaluation Measures Results for PVaR With and Without Low Price Correction (lpc) of NBG Warrants

	MSE	MAE	MAPE	HMSE	Number of Violations
EWMA	0.04454162	0.10670786	27.19767	1.679775	63
EWMA (lpc)	0.05632466	0.09550818	24.05620	2.408766	39
Normal	0.05569806	0.13136742	29.03018	1.924203	64
Normal (lpc)	0.05046753	0.08729689	19.76906	2.075661	44
HS	0.04582400	0.11644768	29.33722	1.929689	84
HS (lpc)	0.04486931	0.09170765	25.06878	2.299259	55
GARCH(1,1)	0.05232076	0.12790622	35.75844	9.692231	81
GARCH(1,1) (lpc)	0.04195689	0.08042647	21.16355	1.881913	56

Note: MSE, MAE, MAPE and HMSE *adjusted* measures given in (2) are provided with and without lpc for the National Bank of Greece (NBG) warrants for the models EWMA, Normal, Historic Simulations (HS) and GARCH with skewed t-Student errors.

Table 5: Adjusted Type 1 Evaluation Measures Results for PVaR With and Without Low Price Correction (lpc) of NBG Warrants

	MSE	MAE	MAPE	HMSE	Number of Violations
EWMA	0.06993500	0.14457923	33.78901	2.658553	39
EWMA (lpc)	0.05632466	0.09550818	24.05620	2.408766	39
Normal	0.07788985	0.16334422	34.04885	2.742979	44
Normal (lpc)	0.05046753	0.08729689	19.76906	2.075661	44
HS	0.06790716	0.15499175	37.27808	2.908765	55
HS (lpc)	0.04486931	0.09170765	25.06878	2.299259	55
GARCH(1,1)	0.07232273	0.15283203	37.89425	10.886520	56
GARCH(1,1) (lpc)	0.04195689	0.08042647	21.16355	1.881913	56

Note: MSE, MAE, MAPE and HMSE *Type 1* measures for the final days of violations are provided with and without lpc for the National Bank of Greece (NBG) warrants for the models EWMA, Normal, Historic Simulations (HS) and GARCH with skewed t-Student errors.

Table 6: Adjusted Type 1 Evaluation Measures Results for PVaR With and Without Low Price Correction (lpc) of NBG Warrants

	MSE	MAE	MAPE	HMSE	Number of Violations	
	MSE	MAE	MAPE	HMSE	Number of Violations	M(*)
EWMA	0.03656765	0.10480884	133.24073	1.302309	63	254
EWMA (lpc)	0.04329688	0.10755786	174.29886	1.564897	39	278
Normal	0.04488074	0.12469699	172.85350	1.488760	64	253
Normal (lpc)	0.04054776	0.10345640	211.37578	1.434692	44	273
HS	0.03782291	0.10781418	97.02337	1.586415	84	233
HS (lpc)	0.03547745	0.09325940	122.11400	1.671224	55	262
GARCH(1,1)	0.04341466	0.11944931	110.73903	7.589229	81	236
GARCH(1,1) (lpc)	0.03491252	0.08956792	127.48493	1.403276	56	261

Note: MSE, MAE, MAPE and HMSE *Type 1* measures given in (3) are provided with and without lpc for the National Bank of Greece (NBG) warrants for the models EWMA, Normal, Historic Simulations (HS) and GARCH with skewed t-Student errors.

Table 7: Adjusted Type 2 Evaluation Measures Results for PVaR With and Without Low Price Correction (lpc) of NBG Warrants

	MSE	MAE	MAPE	HMSE	Number of Violations
EWMA	0.3535559	0.5649415	14.27348	1.295894	891
EWMA (lpc)	0.5957803	0.7379845	15.31295	1.163027	891
Normal	0.1762310	0.3972225	14.83337	1.755109	891
Normal (lpc)	0.4567260	0.6492885	11.36114	1.397210	891
HS	0.2024337	0.4331419	14.92063	1.793435	891
HS (lpc)	0.4558232	0.6481503	11.20965	1.400882	891
GARCH(1,1)	0.1512406	0.2297988	17.07272	10.058642	891
GARCH(1,1) (lpc)	0.5364373	0.6970300	13.72804	1.253154	891

Note: MSE, MAE, MAPE and HMSE *Type 2* measures are provided with and without lpc for the National Bank of Greece (NBG) warrants for the models EWMA, Normal, Historic Simulations (HS) and GARCH with skewed t-Student errors.

Table 8: Backtesting With and Without Low Price Correction (lpc) for PVaR - NAK

	VR without lpc	VR with lpc	PVaR vol without lpc	PVaR vol with lpc
EWMA	0.8038977	0.7917174	0.03178796	0.03203627
Normal	0.7551766	0.7308161	0.01371889	0.01399949
HS	1.242387	1.205847	0.009581244	0.009917231
GARCH(1,1)	1.144945	1.084044	0.02573922	0.02595559
GARCH(2,2)	1.096224	1.010962	0.02578427	0.02595401
APARCH(1,1)	1.181486	1.010962	0.02228844	0.02245804

Note: Violation Ratio (VR) and % Value at Risk (PVaR) volatility are provided with and without lpc for Northern Dynasty Minerals, Ltd. (NAK) for the models EWMA, Normal, Historic Simulations (HS), GARCH with skewed t-Student errors and APARCH with skewed t-Student errors.

Table 9: Standard Evaluation Measures Results for PVaR With and Without Low Price Correction (lpc) of NAK

	MSE	MAE	MAPE	HMSE	Number of Violations
EWMA	0.011649290	0.08958197	377.9544	1.437325	1642
EWMA (lpc)	0.011871865	0.09067956	384.4612	1.422141	1642
Normal	0.009965702	0.08464938	371.0182	1.437617	1642
Normal (lpc)	0.010171222	0.08578432	378.1745	1.422154	1642
HS	0.007967333	0.07329502	318.6766	1.611337	1642
HS (lpc)	0.008140035	0.07439704	325.7300	1.589516	1642
GARCH(1,1)	0.008671210	0.07447498	318.9933	1.619391	1642
GARCH(1,1) (lpc)	0.008847690	0.07557095	325.9550	1.595655	1642
GARCH(2,2)	0.008645398	0.07438822	317.6607	1.620310	1642
GARCH(2,2) (lpc)	0.008821949	0.07549002	324.6830	1.596413	1642
APARCH(1,1)	0.008435548	0.07389520	315.4472	1.640718	1642
APARCH(1,1) (lpc)	0.008608753	0.07496037	322.5007	1.615285	1642

Note: MSE, MAE, MAPE and HMSE *standard* measures are provided with and without lpc for Northern Dynasty Minerals, Ltd. (NAK) for the models EWMA, Normal, Historic Simulations (HS), GARCH with skewed t-Student errors and APARCH with skewed t-Student errors.

Table 10: Adjusted Type 1 Evaluation Measures Results for PVaR With and Without Low Price Correction (lpc) of NAK

	MSE	MAE	MAPE	HMSE	Number of Violations
EWMA	0.007639176	0.04453162	26.02664	1.935885	66
EWMA (lpc)	0.007639877	0.04418522	25.19443	1.837000	65
Normal	0.008402171	0.05068587	26.36000	1.625744	62
Normal (lpc)	0.008505468	0.05119064	26.16090	1.530473	60
HS	0.005996688	0.04143981	26.46755	1.428645	102
HS (lpc)	0.006074069	0.04175005	26.25985	1.363650	99
GARCH(1,1)	0.006066455	0.04011085	26.98915	1.832928	94
GARCH(1,1) (lpc)	0.006277397	0.04128416	27.30712	1.779717	89
GARCH(2,2)	0.006327416	0.04170298	28.05656	1.902314	90
GARCH(2,2) (lpc)	0.006719502	0.04402593	29.09760	1.900888	83
APARCH(1,1)	0.006006253	0.04017759	26.93264	1.952717	97
APARCH(1,1) (lpc)	0.006370651	0.04217833	27.69914	1.958707	90

Note: MSE, MAE, MAPE and HMSE *adjusted* measures given in (2) are provided with and without lpc for Northern Dynasty Minerals, Ltd. (NAK) for the models EWMA, Normal, Historic Simulations (HS), GARCH with skewed t-Student errors and APARCH with skewed t-Student errors.

Table 11: Adjusted Type 1 Evaluation Measures Results for PVaR With and Without Low Price Correction (lpc) of NAK

	MSE	MAE	MAPE	HMSE	Number of Violations
EWMA	0.007756672	0.04519538	26.38935	1.965658	65
EWMA (lpc)	0.007639877	0.04418522	25.19443	1.837000	65
Normal	0.008682149	0.05233320	27.17981	1.679915	60
Normal (lpc)	0.008505468	0.05119064	26.16090	1.530473	60
HS	0.006178286	0.04263564	27.17236	1.471903	99
HS (lpc)	0.006074069	0.04175005	26.25985	1.363650	99
GARCH(1,1)	0.006406549	0.04219355	28.24221	1.935671	89
GARCH(1,1) (lpc)	0.006277397	0.04128416	27.30712	1.779717	89
GARCH(2,2)	0.006860086	0.04500551	30.09218	2.062461	83
GARCH(2,2) (lpc)	0.006719502	0.04402593	29.09760	1.900888	83
APARCH(1,1)	0.006472701	0.04313437	28.76565	2.104373	90
APARCH(1,1) (lpc)	0.006370651	0.04217833	27.69914	1.958707	90

Note: MSE, MAE, MAPE and HMSE *Type 1* measures for the final days of violations are provided with and without lpc for Northern Dynasty Minerals, Ltd. (NAK) for the models EWMA, Normal, Historic Simulations (HS), GARCH with skewed t-Student errors and APARCH with skewed t-Student errors.

Table 12: Adjusted Type 1 Evaluation Measures Results for PVaR With and Without Low Price Correction (lpc) of NAK

	MSE	MAE	MAPE	HMSE	Number of Violations	M (*)
EWMA	0.005783502	0.05026074	203.1109	1.1478504	66	732
EWMA (lpc)	0.005855648	0.05078779	208.2615	1.0977242	65	733
Normal	0.005466878	0.05030973	204.9854	0.9769964	62	736
Normal (lpc)	0.005546999	0.05119376	212.3019	0.9261190	60	738
HS	0.004351346	0.04089672	140.4530	1.0091305	102	696
HS (lpc)	0.004413035	0.04156739	145.8659	0.9645801	99	699
GARCH(1,1)	0.004474295	0.04057048	143.7540	1.2120823	94	704
GARCH(1,1) (lpc)	0.004587856	0.04173164	151.1883	1.1624685	89	709
GARCH(2,2)	0.004567731	0.04135123	145.4559	1.2322970	90	708
GARCH(2,2) (lpc)	0.004738480	0.04304300	154.9257	1.1989760	83	715
APARCH(1,1)	0.004407723	0.04039633	140.5289	1.2949761	97	701
APARCH(1,1) (lpc)	0.004577134	0.04194031	149.2077	1.2671618	90	708

Note: MSE, MAE, MAPE and HMSE *Type 1* measures given in (3) are provided with and without lpc for Northern Dynasty Minerals, Ltd. (NAK) for the models EWMA, Normal, Historic Simulations (HS), GARCH with skewed t-Student errors and APARCH with skewed t-Student errors. (*) M is the number of losses that did not violate the PVaR.

Table 13: Adjusted Type 2 Evaluation Measures Results for PVaR With and Without Low Price Correction (lpc) of NAK

	MSE	MAE	MAPE	HMSE	Number of Violations
EWMA	0.004548872	0.06121097	437.8729	1.305457	1642
EWMA (lpc)	0.004881161	0.06386919	456.6321	1.276753	1642
Normal	0.012498704	0.11032323	787.3810	1.117259	1642
Normal (lpc)	0.013002047	0.11266620	803.0433	1.112968	1642
HS	0.008485877	0.08887018	632.3044	1.156358	1642
HS (lpc)	0.008890938	0.09126820	650.0581	1.151683	1642
GARCH(1,1)	0.006948708	0.07920440	564.2632	1.192386	1642
GARCH(1,1) (lpc)	0.007330618	0.08192787	582.4148	1.187543	1642
GARCH(2,2)	0.006356866	0.07447842	529.4152	1.211453	1642
GARCH(2,2) (lpc)	0.006767026	0.07746784	551.9782	1.203366	1642
APARCH(1,1)	0.006909158	0.07894514	562.4500	1.196158	1642
APARCH(1,1) (lpc)	0.007282727	0.08161779	580.4357	1.190488	1642

Note: MSE, MAE, MAPE and HMSE *Type 2* measures are provided with and without lpc for Northern Dynasty Minerals, Ltd. (NAK) for the models EWMA, Normal, Historic Simulations (HS), GARCH with skewed t-Student errors and APARCH with skewed t-Student errors.

10

Modelling Nonlinear Dynamics of Oil Futures Market

Ayben Koy *♣

♣Istanbul Ticaret University, Department of Banking and Finance

ABSTRACT: Due to the fact that oil prices had a falling outlook after the global crisis, modeling oil market prices has been a topic of interest among researchers. The goals of this study are to investigate the recession or growth periods of oil futures markets using Markov switching autoregressive models, and to analyze the models' durations and probabilities to provide information to the investors who invest in these markets. The study findings indicate that oil prices have a nonlinear pattern with three regimes. The model that best describes the oil futures markets is MSIH(3)-AR(0) with three regimes.

Keywords: oil futures, Markov switching, regime switching, regime dependence

Introduction

The study of oil prices has been growing in importance in recent years because of the falling outlook. The extreme movements of both oil and oil futures prices as well as oil prices beginning in 2008 sparked the interest. 2009 was keenly watched after the oil prices exceeded \$145 and then sharply decreased below \$50 in 2008. The oil futures prices never reached \$100 USD after July 2014, and the following year prices fell. According to the Organization of the

*Corresponding Author. Email: Akoy@ticaret.edu.tr

Petroleum Exporting Countries' (OPEC) Annual Report 2015, crude prices fell by around 50%, The OPEC Reference Basket averaged just under $50 per barrel in 2015, and as a result many investments were deferred and some were cancelled, with exploration and production spending falling by around 20% compared to 2014.

This research aims to analyze oil futures prices following the global crisis by using Markov switching autoregressive models (MS-AR) and to bring to light the oil futures market. The models examine the futures prices from a nonlinear perspective. Additionally, the information about the duration and probabilities of the regimes in the nonlinear switching models is important for investors in these markets. Taking a look at the literature, it can be seen that many studies related to the price dynamics of futures markets exist. What makes this study different from those others is that it examines the prices using Markov regime switching models which also provide detailed information about market performance for international investors.

1 Literature

The theoretical basis for the observed price behavior of futures was examined by Working (1949), with a particular focus on *inter-temporal price relations,* "defined as relations *at a given time* between prices applicable to different times" (Working, 1949, p.1254). Working found that the inter-temporal price relation was explained by the commodity's carrying cost because participants in the futures market try to make profit, the arbitrage possibilities eliminate any bias in the futures prices. In another early study, Rockwell et al. (1967), examined 25 commodity markets for the period 1947–1965 and found that futures prices rose by about 4% annually. Breeden and Litzenberger (1978), and Breeden (1979, 1980) modeled expected returns in commodity futures by using *intertemporal capital arbitrage pricing model* (CAPM). They found that changes in the expected returns were associated with real consumption and the consumption betas. In addition, Dusak (1973) and Breeden (1980) also related futures prices to the expected risk premium.

One recent study examines price discovery in the prominent market price benchmarks crude oil West Texas Intermediate (WTI) and crude oil Brent (Elder et al., 2014). The authors find no evidence that the dominant role of crude oil WTI in price discovery was diminished by the price spread between WTI crude oil and Brent crude oil that emerged in 2008. In another study, the volatility of crude oil price futures returns were analyzed by Baum and Zerilli (2016) for the period from October 2001 to December 2012. The results of the model applied to the intraday data indicate that stochastic volatility models are effective in fitting the volatility of oil price futures returns. Bernard et al. (2015) modeled oil futures prices using weekly and monthly data and maturities of one to four months. Their results show that forecast performances improve with longer date-to-maturity futures, suggesting that the role of the convenience yield is greater when physical oil inventories are held for longer durations. In addition, forecast accuracy is highest at the one year horizon, though the time-varying convenience models (the mean-reverting class of models from Schwartz and Smith (2000) and Schwartz (1997)) have a much higher accuracy than the autoregressive conditional heteroskedasticity (ARCH) and generalized autoregressive conditional heteroskedasticity (GARCH) models over the three and five-year horizons.

Even though there is not a wide literature on the nonlinear approach, there have been some studies examining spot oil prices by Vo (2009), Kordnoori et al. (2013), and Zlatcu et al. (2015). Vo (2009) used the Markov switching stochastic volatility (MSSV) model to explain the behavior of crude oil prices in order to forecast their volatility. Zlatcu et al. (2015) studied the fuel markets of Romanian, Germany, France, Poland and the Czech Republic, examining the price volatility and the response of retail fuel prices to changes in international crude oil prices by estimating univariate and multivariate GARCH models, as well as applying a momentum threshold autoregressive (MTAR) co-integration model. Kordnoori et al. (2013) modelled the fluctuations of Brent oil prices by integrating the limit probability distribution of a Markov chain and Gumbel Max distribution.

One of the previous studies examining the nonlinear behavior of oil futures considers the daily returns of the second nearest crude oil futures based on WTI: Fong and See (2002) examine the effect of volatility in daily returns on crude oil futures using GARCH, RS, RSARCH-t and RSGARCH-t models. They find that RS models are useful both to financial historians interested in studying the factors behind the evolution of volatility and to oil futures traders interested in using the model to extract short-term forecasts of conditional volatility. Similarly, Chevallier (2013) used the Markov regime switching vector autoregression (MS-VAR) model to explore the influence of different economic variables on the 2008 oil price swing. Zhang and Zhang (2015) singled out a Markov switching model (MS(3)-AR(2)) with three regimes for the samples of Brent and WTI crude oil prices before and after the 2008 financial crisis. They found three regimes for both crude oil markets before and after the crisis.

2 Data and Model

2.1 Data

The data used includes daily crude oil WTI futures (1539 days) and crude oil Brent futures (1592 days) from January 4, 2010 to December 31, 2015 (Figure 1). For the futures oil prices, we used the nearest contracts' prices of WTI. The data is obtained from investing.com, which is a global financial portal that offers 27 localized editions in 20 languages. We used the differential natural logarithmic prices (logarithmic returns).

One crude oil WTI futures or crude oil Brent futures contract is equivalent to 1000 US barrels (42 000 gallons) of light, sweet crude oil. These contracts are some of the world's most liquid oil commodities and are important benchmark for oil markets.

Table 1 shows that the skewness is negative for both WTI and Brent. This negative skew indicates that the tail on the left side of the probability density function is fatter than that on the right side, which has already been seen in Figure 1. Similarly, the kurtosis is less than 3 for both series – these series are said to be *platykurtic*. These distributions produce fewer and less extreme outliers than do normal distributions.

2.2 Markov Switching Autoregressive Model

The Markov Regime Switching model is used to describe a situation or stochastic process that determines the change from one regime to another via a Markov chain. In Markov switching models, the Markov chain is used to model the behavior of a state variable that cannot be directly observed and determines the regime of the market. The regime of the state variable should be strongly related to the regime of the economy or market. The economy might be in a recession regime or a growth regime. In a Markov Regime Switching model, the state (regime) of the economy (s_t) cannot be directly observed, although the time series variable y_t can be observed. The state of the market can only be identified with some probability. At the same time those observations are supposed to be dependent on the properties of the regime. When the state of the economy in the Markov regime is determined, the next regime can be expressed as a probability.

The general idea behind this class of RS models is that there is a time series process y_t dependent on an unobservable regime variable s_t that represents the probability of being in a particular state of the world (Krolzig, 2000). This can be written as follows:

$$p(y_t|Y_{t-1};X_t;s_t) = \begin{cases} f(y_t|Y_{t-1};X_t;\theta_1) & \text{if } s_t = 1 \\ \vdots & \\ f(y_t|Y_{t-1};X_t;\theta_m) & \text{if } s_t = m \end{cases} \tag{1}$$

where X_t are exogenous variables; and θ_m is the parameter vector associated with regime m.

In Markov switching models, the regime-generating process is an ergodic Markov chain with a finite number of states defined by the transition probabilities (Krolzig, 2000).

$$p_{i,j} = Pr(s_{t+1} = j|s_t = i); \qquad \sum_{j=1}^{m} p_{i,j} = 1 \text{ and } i, j = \{1, \ldots, m\} \tag{2}$$

s_t follows an ergodic M-state Markov process with an irreducible transition matrix:

$$\mathbf{P} = \begin{bmatrix} p_{1,1} & \cdots & p_{1,m} \\ \vdots & \ddots & \vdots \\ p_{m,1} & \cdots & p_{m,m} \end{bmatrix} \tag{3}$$

In a two-state model, the transition probabilities of moving from one state to the other are denoted as:

$$\begin{aligned} Pr(s_{t+1} = 1|s_t = 1) &= p_{1,1} \\ Pr(s_{t+1} = 2|s_t = 1) &= p_{1,2} \\ Pr(s_{t+1} = 1|s_t = 2) &= p_{2,1} \\ Pr(s_{t+1} = 2|s_t = 2) &= p_{2,2} \end{aligned} \tag{4}$$

Note that for each $p_{i,j}$ to define a proper probability, it must be nonnegative, and it should also hold that $p_{11} + p_{12} = 1$ and $p_{21} + p_{22} = 1$ (Franses and van Dijk, 2000).

The probability of which regime is in operation at time t conditional on the information at time $t - 1$ only depends only on the statistical inference on s_{t-1}:

$$Pr(s_t|Y_{t-1}; X_t; S_{t-1}) = Pr(s_t|s_{t-1}) \tag{5}$$

If the probabilities of switching between regimes are known, the ergodic probability of any state can be calculated. The probability of any observation being in any state is called the ergodic probability. The ergodic probabilities for a two-state model are given as (Bildirici et al., 2010):

$$Pr(s_t = 1) = \frac{1 - p_{2,2}}{1 - p_{1,1} - p_{2,2}}, \qquad Pr(s_t = 2) = \frac{1 - p_{1,1}}{1 - p_{1,1} - p_{2,2}} \tag{6}$$

The Markov switching time series analysis was first implemented by Hamilton (1989) to analyze business cycles. Hamilton investigated the possibility that macroeconomic variables fluctuate on a cyclical time scale between calendar time (e.g., month, quarter or another unit of time) and economic time. The time transformations between economic and calendar time depend on the economic history of the process such as whether the economy has been in a cyclical recession or growth phase. The two main types of Markov switching models are the Markov switching model of conditional mean (MSM) and the Markov switching intercept (MSI) model. In the MSM model, the regime switches according to the conditional mean (μ_{s_t}), while in the MSI model, the regime switches according to the constant (c_{s_t}). In addition, the Markov switching intercept and heteroskedasticity (MSIH) Model is a third type of Markov switching model that has proven to be strong in explaining financial time series. These three models are denoted as follows:

$$\text{MSM model}: \quad y_t - \mu_{s_t} = \Phi(y_{t-1} - \mu_{s_{t-1}}) + u_t \tag{7}$$

$$\text{MSI model}: \quad y_t - c_{s_t} = \Phi \cdot y_{t-1} + u_t \tag{8}$$

$$\text{MSIH model}: \quad y_t - c_{s_t} = \Phi \cdot y_{t-1} + u_t \cdot \sigma_{s_t} \tag{9}$$

where Φ is an autoregressive coefficeint; u_t is an unobservable zero-mean white noise vector process; y_{t-1} is the lagged value of the dependent variable; and σ_{s_t} is the standard deviation of the error term conditional on the state variable s_t.

The regime in MS-AR models is defined as an unobserved state variable affecting the levels or volatility of the distributions of financial asset returns (Perez-Quiros and Timmermann, 2001; Guidolin and Timmermann, 2006). These models also explain the fat tails, periods of turbulence followed by periods of low volatility, and skewness of many financial series. Moreover, these models can capture nonlinear stylized dynamics of asset returns in a framework based on linear specifications, or conditionally normal or log-normal distributions, within a regime (Ang and Timmermann, 2011).

3 Empirical Analysis

We applied autoregressive models with different numbers of regimes (2 or 3) and different lags (0–4) to the time series of the oil futures logarithmic returns. Taking linearity as our null hypothesis, and following Davies (1987), we considered a p-value less than 0.05 a statistically significant rejection of the null hypothesis. We estimated 15 models for crude oil WTI and 14 models for crude oil Brent that show non-linear characteristics.

3.1 Markov Switching Autoregressive Model for Crude Oil WTI

The model that best explains the nonlinearity of crude oil WTI is MSIH(3)-AR(0), which has the minimum Hannan-Quinnn criterion (HQ) (−5.2666) and Schwarz criterion (SIC) (−5.2404) from among the models tested. This model has a large log-likelihood ratio statistic (4063.3734) that signifies the maximum likelihood estimate of the transition possibilities for the Markov model. Additionally, the MSIH(3)-AR(0) model has the largest value of the likelihood ratio (LR) statistics (370.1262) which indicates how much more the nonlinear model explains the relation than does the linear model. Of the 15 models that shows statistically significant nonlinearity, the MSIH(3)-AR(0) is the most powerful one. The regime switching mechanism in the MSIH model is specified by the intercept (I) and volatility/heteroskedasticity (H).

Coefficients of the MSIH(3)-AR(0) model for crude oil WTI are shown in Table 3. The estimation procedure implemented in the "Ox Metrics program" identifies regime 1 (slightly downward), regime 2 (slightly upward) and regime 3 (sharply downward) of the model. In many studies, regime 3 is identified as an expansion period with positive coefficients appropriate to the business cycle (Krolzig, 2000; Markov, 2010; Medhioub, 2015; Koy, 2017). Due to the falling trend across the whole observation period, we have negative coefficients in regime 1 and regime 3. With negative returns and high volatility, regime 1 is called *slightly downward* by Zhang and Zhang (2015), while regime 3 with the highest volatility and absolutely negative returns, is called *sharply downward.* Regime 2, which has the only positive coefficient, is called *slightly upward.*

Transition probability represents the likelihood that the crude oil WTI price return will stay in the original regime or switch to another regime. According to the matrix of transition probabilities for crude oil WTI (Table 4), if an observation is in regime 1, the following observation has a probability of 97.33% of being in regime 1, a probability of 0.85% of being in regime 2 and a probability of 1.82% of being in regime 3. In other words, if the oil futures market has been observed to have a slightly downward regime a given day, a low negative return is expected to be observed on the following day with a probability of 97.33%. Similarly, the probabilities for regimes 2 and 3 are shown in Table 4. For example, if the market is observed to be in regime 2, the following day is expected to be in regime 2 with a probability of 98.75%. There is also a probability of 1.25% that it will be in regime 1 and essentially 0% probability that it will be in regime 3.

In the six year period studied, the greatest number of observations (728) and the highest probability (0.47) belong to the slightly downward regime (regime 1). The longest duration (80 days) is seen in the slightly upward regime (regime 2); if the returns are positive, the market is expected to stay in the slightly upward regime for 80 days. The smallest number of observations (306), the lowest probability (0.21), and the shortest duration (24) all belong to the sharply downward regime (regime 3). In addition, according to the ergodic probabilities (Table 5), being in regime 1 has the highest probability for any observation at any moment (0.4709).

3.2 Markov Switching Autoregressive Model for Crude Oil Brent

The model that best explains the nonlinearity of crude oil Brent is the MSIH(3)-AR(0) which has the smallest values of the HQ (-5.4687) and SIC (-5.4432), and the largest value of the LR statistic (400.2764). According to the LR statistic, the model with the most descriptive power is the MSIH(3)-AR(0) with three regimes.

Coefficients of the MSIH(3)-AR(0) model for crude oil Brent are shown in Table 7. As for the crude oil WTI futures, regime 1 is the slightly downward regime, regime 2 is the slightly upward regime, and regime 3 is the sharply downward regime.

As was the case with the transition possibilities for crude oil WTI, the matrix of transition probabilities for crude oil Brent (Table 8) shows that there is a strong probability that any given observation will be in the same regime as the observation that immediately preceded it. For the models of crude oil Brent futures, the greatest number of observations (782) belong to the slightly downward regime (regime 1). Thus, the probability of the slightly downward regime (0.49) is the highest. The durations of all regimes are very similar, ranging from 25 to 30 days. The smallest number of observations (291) and, the lowest probability (0.20) belong to the sharply downward regime (regime 3) that also has the longest duration (30 days). The ergodic probability of regime 1 (0.4873) is the highest among the three states, a result that is similar to crude oil WTI futures model.

3.3 Regime Probabilities and Business Cycle Dates

The regime probabilities of the MSIH(3)-AR(0) model for crude oil futures are shown in Figures 2 and 3. The cycle dates of the models are shown in the tables that follow (Tables 10 and 11). Both the figures and tables indicate that Brent switches more between regime 1 and regime 2 than does WTI. These switching mechanisms cause the difference in the durations noted in Tables 4 and 8. In contrast to regime 1 and regime 2, the regime 3 cycle dates are nearly the same for both the models.

While economic events affect oil market prices, they also affect global demand and supply. Despite the difficulties in specifying the RS dates in detail, we tried to relate the RS mechanism to business cycles on the basis of the Markov Switching time series analysis first applied. If the cycle dates of crude oil futures are considered in relation to the business cycle, the slightly upward regime (regime 2) of our models is associated with the minimum world GDP growth which occurred in 2012 and 2013 (2.5%, and 2.48%, respectively).

Following the steady prices between \$70 and \$80 in the first 11 months of 2010, the last month of 2010 was a growing period which was observed to be in regime 2. The oil futures prices in both the second period of 2014 and the whole of 2015 have followed a falling trend and never reached \$100 USD after July 2014. This period of high volatility has been seen in regime 1 and regime 3.

4 Conclusion

As extreme price movements have recently been recorded, the interest in predicting oil futures prices has been renewed. In this study, we found evidence that the behavior of oil futures prices changes conditional on the state of other related economic variables. The findings indicate that oil prices have a nonlinear pattern involving three regimes. The model which best describes the oil futures logarithmic returns is the MSIH(3)-AR(0). The regime switching mechanism in the MSIH model is specified by the intercept (I) and volatility/heteroskedasticity (H).

The three regimes that the models identify are the same for the two analyzed time series. They are: regime 1, slightly downward (with high volatility); regime 2, slightly upward (with low volatility); and regime 3 sharply downward (with high volatility).

The slightly downward period has the greatest number of observations for both crude oil WTI futures (728 days) and crude oil Brent futures (782 days). On the other hand, the sharply downward period has the smallest number of observations for both crude oil WTI futures (306) and crude oil Brent futures (291). Additionally, the difference in the durations of the periods is important. In particular, the duration of the slightly upward period is significantly different between the crude oil WTI and the crude oil Brent futures, 80 days for crude oil WTI futures and 25 days for crude oil Brent futures. The nonlinear structure of oil futures prices and the probabilities and durations of the regime switching mechanisms in this model are important for international investors who invest in oil futures. For instance, if the market is not too volatile and returns are positive, an investor should expect these returns for 80 days for crude oil WTI futures, and 20 days for crude oil Brent futures. We need to specify that there are many economic events and other reasons which are causes of switching mechanisms, and there is a wide potential study area on this subject. While we consider that volatility or heteroskedasticity (H) is important in specifying the regime switching mechanism in modelling returns, modelling the volatility of oil futures markets with the Markov regime switching GARCH models would be another potential area for study.

References

Ang, A. and Timmermann, A. (2011). Regime Changes and Financial Markets. Working paper 17182, National Bureau of Economic Research.

Baum, C. and Zerilli, P. (2016). Jumps and stochastic volatility in crude oil futures prices using conditional moments of integrated volatility. *Energy Economics*, 53(C):175–181.

Bernard, J.-T., Khalaf, L., Kichian, M., and McMahon, S. (2015). The Convenience Yield and the Informational Content of the Oil Futures Price. *The Energy Journal*, 36(2):39–46.

Bildirici, M. E., Aykaç Alp, E., Ersin, Ö. Ö., and Bozoklu, Ü. (2010). *İktisatta Kullanılan Doğrusal Olmayan Zaman Serisi Yöntemleri.*

Breeden, D. T. (1979). An intertemporal asset pricing model with stochastic consumption and investment opportunities. *Journal of Financial Economics*, 7(3):265–296.

Breeden, D. T. (1980). Consumption Risk in Futures Markets. *The Journal of Finance*, 35(2):503 520.

Breeden, D. T. and Litzenberger, R. H. (1978). Prices of State-contingent Claims Implicit in Option Prices. *The Journal of Business*, 51(4):621–51.

Chevallier, J. (2013). Price relationships in crude oil futures: new evidence from CFTC disaggregated data. *Environmental Economics and Policy Studies*, 15(2):133–170.

Dusak, K. (1973). Futures Trading and Investor Returns: An Investigation of Commodity Market Risk Premiums. *Journal of Political Economy*, 81(6):1387–1406.

Elder, J., Miao, H., and Ramchander, S. (2014). Price discovery in crude oil futures. *Energy Economics*, 46(S1):S18–S27.

Fong, W. M. and See, K. H. (2002). A Markov switching model of the conditional volatility of crude oil futures prices. *Energy Economics*, 24(1):71–95.

Franses, P. H. and van Dijk, D. (2000). *Non-Linear Time Series Models in Empirical Finance.* Cambridge University Press.

Guidolin, M. and Timmermann, A. (2006). An econometric model of nonlinear dynamics in the joint distribution of stock and bond returns. *Journal of Applied Econometrics*, 21(1):1–22.

Hamilton, J. D. (1989). A New Approach to the Economic Analysis of Nonstationary Time Series and the Business Cycle. *Econometrica*, 57(2):357–384.

Kordnoori, S., Mostafaei, H., and Ostadrahimi, M. (2013). Modelling the fluctuations of Brent oil prices by a probabilistic Markov chain. *African Journal of Business Management*, 7(17):1648–1654.

Koy, A. (2017). International Credit Default Swaps Market During European Crisis: A Markov Switching Approach. In *Global Financial Crisis and Its Ramifications on Capital Markets*, pages 431–443. Springer.

Krolzig, H.-M. (2000). Predicting Markov-switching vector autoregressive processes. Department of Economics Working Papers 2000-W31, Nuffield College, University of Oxford.

Markov, N. (2010). A Regime Switching Model for the European Central Bank. Research Papers by the Institute of Economics and Econometrics 10091, Geneva School of Economics and Management, University of Geneva.

Medhioub, I. (2015). A Markov Switching Three Regime Model of Tunisian Business Cycle. *American Journal of Economics*, 5(3):394–403.

Perez-Quiros, G. and Timmermann, A. (2001). Business cycle asymmetries in stock returns: Evidence from higher order moments and conditional densities. *Journal of Econometrics*, 103(1-2):259–306. Studies in estimation and testing.

Rockwell, C. S. et al. (1967). Normal backwardation, forecasting, and the returns to commodity futures traders. *Food Research Institute Studies*, 7(1967):107–130.

Schwartz, E. and Smith, J. E. (2000). Short-Term Variations and Long-Term Dynamics in Commodity Prices. *Management Science*, 46(7):893–911.

Vo, M. T. (2009). Regime-switching stochastic volatility: Evidence from the crude oil market. *Energy Economics*, 31(5):779–788.

Working, H. (1949). The theory of price of storage. *The American Economic Review*, 39(6):1254–1262.

Zhang, Y.-J. and Zhang, L. (2015). Interpreting the crude oil price movements: Evidence from the Markov regime switching model. *Applied Energy*, 143(C):96–109.

Zlatcu, I., Kubinschi, M., and Barnea, D. (2015). Fuel Price Volatility and Asymmetric Transmission of Crude Oil Price Changes to Fuel Prices. *Theoretical and Applied Economics*, 22(4):33–44.

Figure 1: Crude Oil Futures Prices, Crude Oil Brent Futures and Differential Natural Logarithmic Prices

(a) Crude Oil WTI Futures

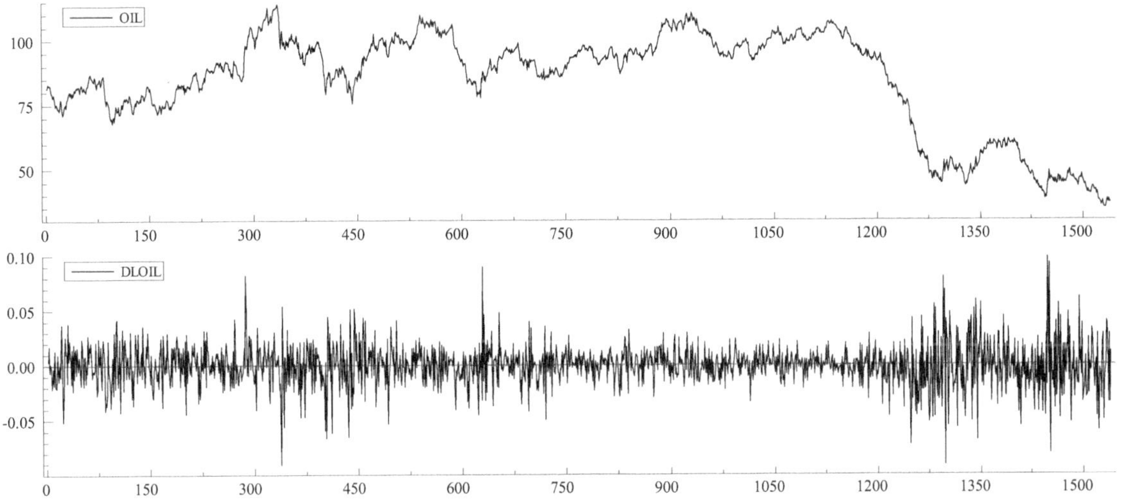

(b) Crude Oil Brent Futures

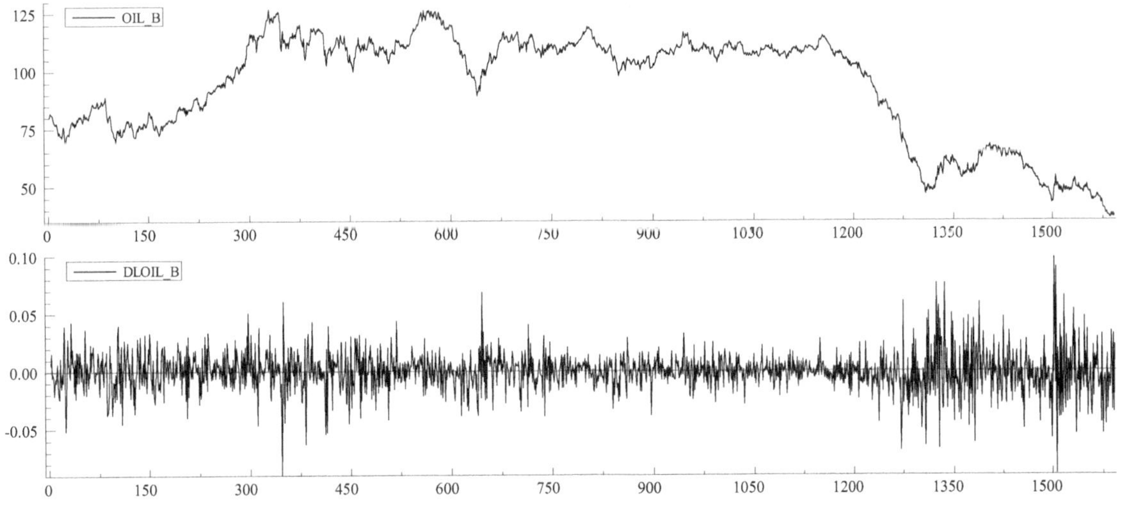

Figure 2: Regime Probabilities – Crude Oil WTI

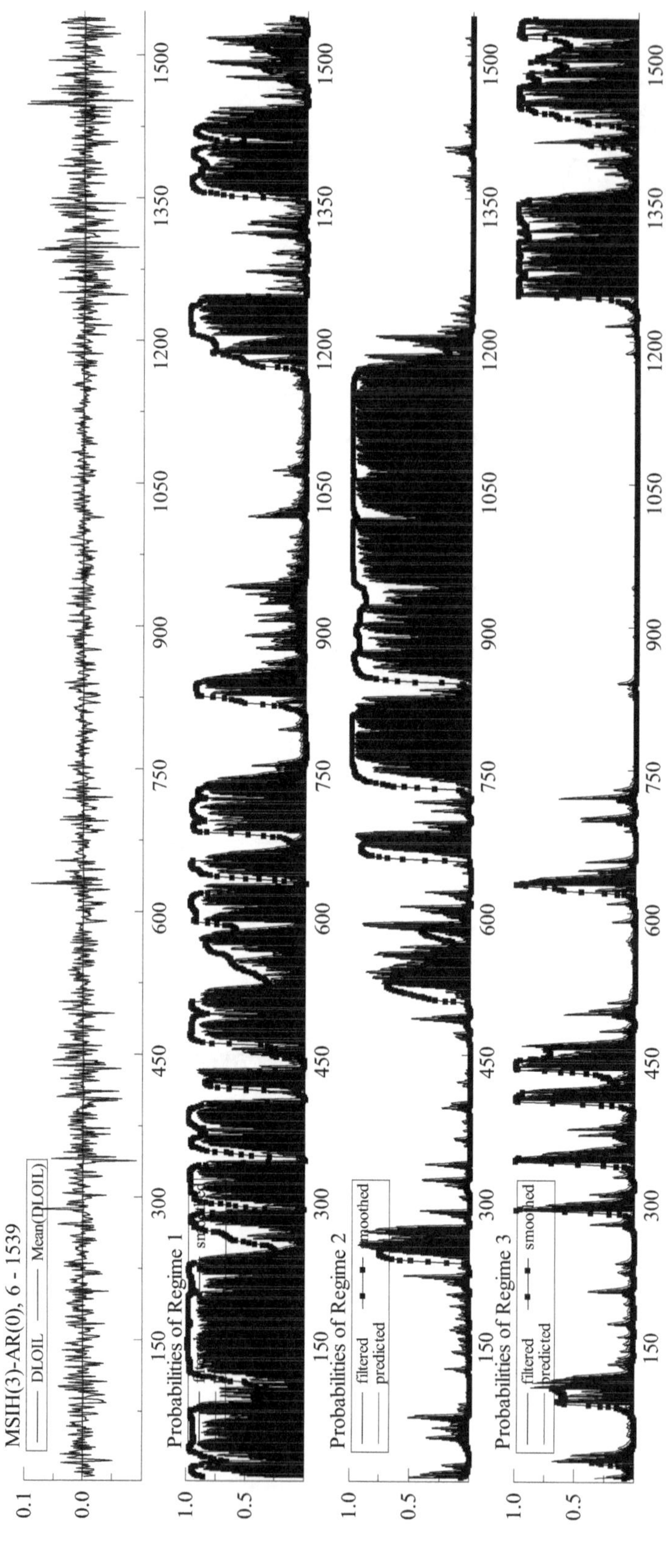

Figure 3: Regime Probabilities – Crude Oil Brent

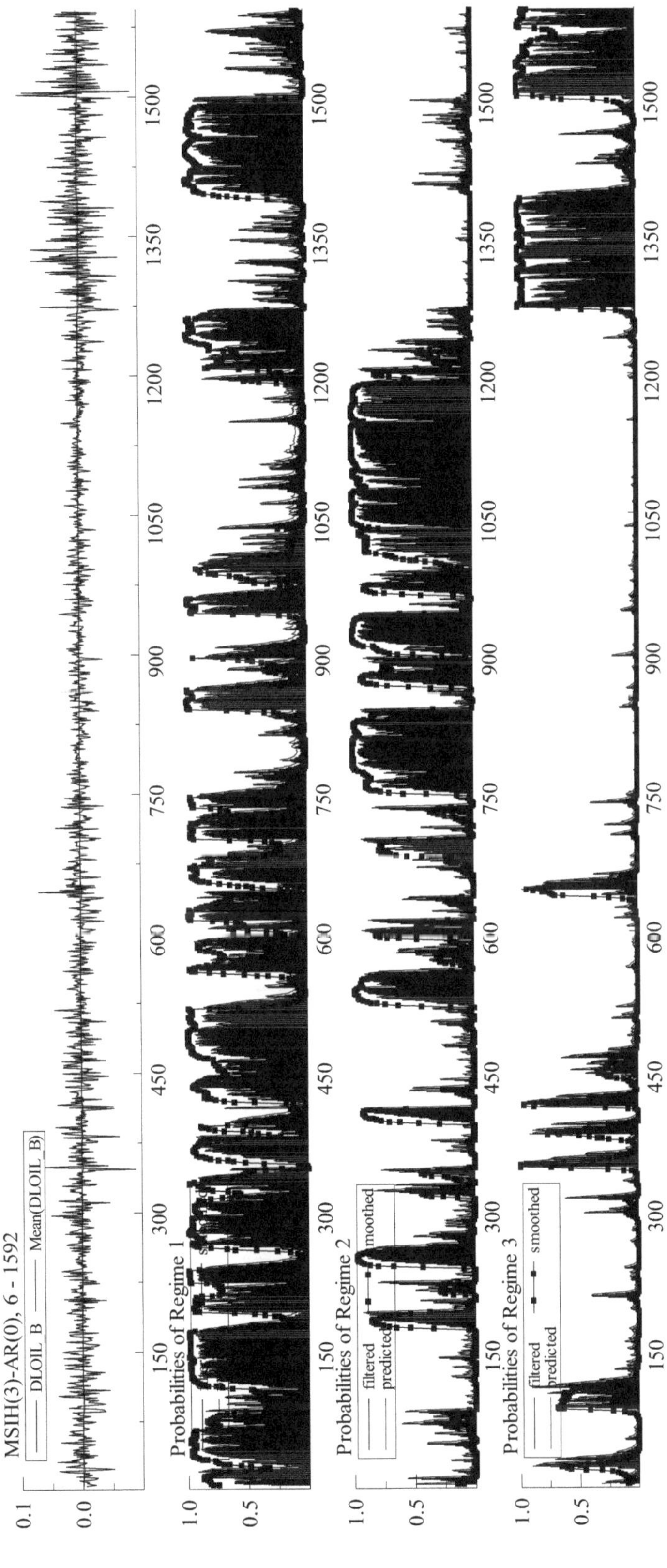

Table 1: Descriptive Statistics of Analyzed Variables

	WTI	BRENT
Mean	84.49617	94.91823
Median	90.80000	105.5400
Maximum	113.9300	126.6500
Minimum	34.73000	42.69000
Std. Dev	19.19545	21.55654
Skewness	-0.977078	-0.785413
Kurtosis	2.872541	2.333900
Jarque-Bera	245.9176	186.6795
Probability	0.000000	0.000000
Sum	130039.6	146079.2
Sum Sq. Dev.	566699.5	714684.8

Table 2: Information Criterion Values for Crude Oil WTI

Model	log-likelihood	AIC	HQ	SIC	LR linearity test	p-value of the Davies' test
MSI(3)-AR(0)	3991.8353	-5.1779	-5.1650	-5.1432	203.7858	0.0000
MSIH(2)-AR(0)	4045.4444	-5.2529	-5.2451	-5.2320	311.0041	0.0000
MSI(3)-AR(0)	4063.3734	-5.2821	-5.2666	-5.2404	370.1262	0.0000
MSI(3)-AR(1)	3991.1921	-5.1792	-5.1650	-5.1410	202.6508	0.0000
MSIH(2)-AR(1)	4043.0675	-5.2519	-5.2428	-5.2276	306.4016	0.0000
MSIH(3)-AR(1)	4073.5898	-5.2838	-5.2670	-5.2386	367.4462	0.0000
MSI(3)-AR(2)	3982.2975	-5.1764	-5.1609	-5.1347	201.8906	0.0000
MSIH(2)-AR(2)	4033.9452	-5.2490	-5.2386	-5.2211	305.1860	0.0000
MSIH(3)-AR(2)	4071.0222	-5.2826	-5.2645	-5.2339	367.2806	0.0000
MSI(3)-AR(3)	3982.3519	-5.1752	-5.1583	-5.1299	201.9004	0.0000
MSIH(2)-AR(3)	4034.0096	-5.2477	-5.2361	-5.2164	305.2158	0.0000
MSIH(3)-AR(3)	4067.9061	-5.2807	-5.2613	-5.2285	366.9508	0.0000
MSI(3)-AR(4)	3982.6001	-5.1742	-5.1561	-5.1255	202.3419	0.0000
MSIH(2)-AR(4)	4034.0103	-5.2464	-5.2335	-5.2116	305.1623	0.0000
MSIH(3)-AR(4)	4064.7701	-5.2787	-5.2580	-5.2231	366.6819	0.0000

Table 3: Coefficients for Models of Crude Oil WTI

	MSIH(3)-AR(0)		
	Coefficient	Standard Error	t-value
Constant (Regime 1)	-0.0005	0.0007	-0.7295
Constant (Regime 2)	0.0003	0.0005	0.6868
Constant (Regime 3)	-0.0019	0.0019	-0.9940
Standard Error (Regime 1)	0.0169		
Standard Error (Regime 2)	0.0104		
Standard Error (Regime 3)	0.0317		

Table 4: Matrix of Transition Probabilities for Crude Oil WTI

Model	Regime	Regime 1	Regime 2	Regime 3
MSIH(3)-AR(0)	Regime 1	0.9733	0.0085	0.0182
	Regime 2	0.0125	0.9875	0.0000
	Regime 3	0.0408	0.0000	0.9591

Table 5: Number of Observations for Crude Oil WTI

Model	Regime	Number of observations	Probability	Duration (days)
MSIH(3)-AR(0)	1	727.8	0.4709	37.51
	2	499.9	0.3197	79.74
	3	306.4	0.2094	24.46

Table 6: Information Criterion Values for Crude Oil Brent

Model	log-likelihood	AIC	HQ	SIC	LR linearity test	p-value of the Davies' test
MSIH(2)-AR(0)	4328.0040	-5.4468	-5.4392	-5.4265		0,0000
MSIH(3)-AR(0)	4374.2848	-5.4837	-5.4687	-5.4432	400.2764	0,0000
MSI(3)-AR(1)	4267.6265	-5.3644	-5.3505	-5.3272	204.0874	0,0000
MSIH(2)-AR(1)	4330.4120	-5.4485	-5.4397	-5.4248	329.6585	0,0000
MSIH(3)-AR(1)	4373.5604	-5.4850	-5.4687	-5.4411	398.1731	0,0000
MSI(3)-AR(2)	4267.6750	-5.3632	-5.3481	-5.3226	203.6919	0,0000
MSIH(2)-AR(2)	4330.7581	-5.4477	-5.4377	-5.4206	329.8582	0,0000
MSIH(3)-AR(2)	4371.2413	-5.4843	-5.4667	-5.4369	398.3565	0,0000
MSI(3)-AR(3)	4267.7990	-5.3621	-5.3457	-5.3181	202.9672	0,0000
MSIH(2)-AR(3)	4330.7605	-5.4465	-5.4351	-5.4160	328.8901	0,0000
MSIH(3)-AR(3)	4367.9474	-5.4823	-5.4635	-5.4316	397.0194	0,0000
MSI(3)-AR(4)	4268.7489	-5.3620	-5.3444	-5.3146	204.3794	0,0000
MSIH(2)-AR(4)	4030.7984	-5.4452	-5.4327	-5.4114	328.4784	0,0000
MSIH(3)-AR(4)	4364.8448	-5.4806	-5.4605	-5.4264	396.5712	0,0000

Table 7: Coefficients for Models of Crude Oil Brent

	MSIH(3)-AR(0)		
	Coefficient	**Standard Error**	**t-value**
Constant (Regime 1)	-0.0003	0.0007	-0.3893
Constant (Regime 2)	0.0003	0.0005	0.7071
Constant (Regime 3)	-0.0025	0.0018	-1.3949
Standard Error (Regime 1)	0.0160		
Standard Error (Regime 2)	0.0085		
Standard Error (Regime 3)	0.0293		

Table 8: Matrix of Transition Probabilities - Crude Oil Brent

Model	Regime	Regime 1	Regime 2	Regime 3
MSIH(3)-AR(0)	Regime 1	0.9629	0.0262	0.0109
	Regime 2	0.0363	0.9595	0.0042
	Regime 3	0.0335	0.0002	0.9663

Table 9: Number of Observations for Crude Oil Brent

Model	Regime	Number of observations	Probability	Duration (days)
MSIH(3)-AR(0)	1	781.5	0.4873	26.97
	2	518.1	0.3160	24.68
	3	291.4	0.1967	29.68

Table 10: Cycle Dates - Crude Oil WTI

Regime 1		Regime 2		Regime 3	
Date	**Probability**	**Date**	**Probability**	**Date**	**Probability**
11/01/2010 - 03/05/2010	[0.9087]	07/12/2010 - 31/12/2010	[0.6927]	04/05/2010 - 03/06/2010	[0.6017]
26/05/2010 - 06/12/2010	[0.9515]	17/01/2012 - 17/02/2012	[0.6258]	18/02/2011 - 23/02/2011	[0.7989]
03/01/2011 - 17/02/2011	[0.8146]	08/08/2012 - 13/09/2012	[0.8238]	04/05/2011 - 13/05/2011	[0.8618]
24/02/2011 - 03/05/2011	[0.9017]	26/11/2012 - 02/04/2013	[0.9497]	03/08/2011 - 22/08/2011	[0.8954]
16/05/2011 - 02/08/2011	[0.9002]	07/05/2013 - 18/08/2014	[0.9673]	19/09/2011 - 27/10/2011	[0.8197]
23/08/2011 - 16/09/2011	[0.7674]			21/06/2012 - 09/07/2012	[0.7755]
28/10/2011 - 13/01/2012	[0.8911]			25/11/2014 - 16/04/2015	[0.9660]
21/02/2012 - 20/06/2012	[0.7842]			07/08/2015 - 31/12/2015	[0.8432]
10/07/2012 - 07/08/2012	[0.8583]				
14/09/2012 - 23/11/2012	[0.9068]				
03/04/2013 - 06/05/2013	[0.8106]				
19/08/2014 - 24/11/2014	[0.8538]				
17/04/2015 - 06/08/2015	[0.8590]				

Table 11: Cycle Dates - Crude Oil Brent

Regime 1		Regime 2		Regime 3	
Date	Probability	Date	Probability	Date	Probability
11/01/2010 - 01/02/2010	[0.7954]	03/09/2010 - 27/09/2010	[0.7484]	02/02/2010 - 08/02/2010	[0.5973]
28/01/2010 - 03/05/2010	[0.8611]	06/12/2010 - 30/12/2010	[0.8899]	04/05/2010 - 04/06/2010	[0.6180]
07/06/2010 - 02/09/2010	[0.9535]	12/07/2011 - 02/08/2011	[0.8283]	03/05/2011 - 12/05/2011	[0.8499]
28/09/2010 - 03/12/2010	[0.8792]	06/01/2012 - 22/02/2012	[0.8962]	21/06/2011 - 28/06/2011	[0.6228]
31/12/2010 - 02/05/2011	[0.8515]	18/04/2012 - 02/05/2012	[0.7293]	03/08/2011 - 11/08/2011	[0.8642]
13/05/2011 - 20/06/2011	[0.8286]	21/08/2012 - 13/09/2012	[0.7152]	20/06/2012 - 06/07/2012	[0.7296]
29/06/2011 - 11/07/2011	[0.7349]	22/11/2012 - 01/04/2013	[0.9215]	26/11/2014 - 17/04/2015	[0.9685]
12/08/2011 - 05/01/2012	[0.8812]	07/05/2013 - 17/06/2013	[0.7661]	19/08/2015 - 31/12/2015	[0.9184]
23/02/2012 - 17/04/2012	[0.7995]	25/06/2013 - 23/08/2013	[0.9151]		
03/05/2012 - 19/06/2012	[0.7854]	23/09/2013 - 16/10/2013	[0.7434]		
09/07/2012 - 20/08/2012	[0.8487]	13/11/2013 - 29/08/2014	[0.9271]		
14/09/2012 - 21/11/2012	[0.8750]				
02/04/2013 - 06/05/2013	[0.9375]				
18/06/2013 - 24/06/2013	[0.6836]				
14/08/2013 - 20/09/2013	[0.9073]				
17/10/2013 - 12/11/2013	[0.7327]				
01/09/2014 - 25/11/2014	[0.8134]				
20/04/2015 - 18/08/2015	[0.9052]				

11

Using Nonperforming Loan Ratios to Compute Loan Default Rates with Evidence from European Banking Sectors

Dobromił Serwa[*♣ ♠]

[♣]Institute of Econometrics, Warsaw School of Economics
[♠]Financial Stability Department, Narodowy Bank Polski

ABSTRACT: This research is the first attempt to calibrate default rates of loan portfolios using raw data on nonperforming loans and some additional information on the maturity structure of the loan portfolios. We applied a simple model of loan quality, controlling for loan maturities and dynamics of loan supply. Results for nine national aggregate indices of nonperforming housing loans in the Czech Republic, Greece, Ireland, Hungary, Latvia, Poland, Portugal, Romania, and Spain revealed strong differences in the dynamics of calibrated default probabilities between countries. Calibrated default rates were correlated with macroeconomic factors, but the linkages depended on the markets investigated.

Keywords: NPL ratio, default rate, credit growth, housing loans, European banking sectors

[*]Corresponding Author. Email: dserwa@sgh.waw.pl

Introduction

This paper suggests a simple method to derive default rates (DR) of loan portfolios from the time series of nonperforming loans (NPL). The NPL ratio (i.e., the ratio of NPLs to total loans in the portfolio) is a standard measure of loan quality widely used in research analyzing performance of banking sectors and their customers (e.g., Meeker and Gray, 1987; Lízal and Svejnar, 2002; Hasan and Wall, 2004; Podpiera, 2006; Mendoza and Terrones, 2008; Aman and Miyazaki, 2009; Festić et al., 2009; Čihák and Schaeck, 2010; Whalen, 2010; Jin et al., 2011). The well-known problem of this measure is the mechanistic dependence of its values on the rate of growth of the loan portfolio, which often forbids cross-sectional and inter-temporal comparisons (Tornell and Westermann, 2002, p. 22; Coricelli et al., 2006). Another drawback of the NPL rate as a measure of loan quality is that it is a backward-looking variable (i.e., it evaluates the historical performance of the loan portfolio). NPLs often remain in portfolios for several quarters or even years, affecting the NPL ratio but having no effect on the current financial performance of credit institutions. In contrast, most analysts are interested in the present standing of the portfolio and the present performance of the debtors. The DR is one alternative variable that describes the current performance of loans and does not automatically depend on the dynamics of the loan.

The DR quantifies the rate at which borrowers default on the amount of funds they owe to the bank in a given (e.g., most recent) period. The DR is often weighted with the values of analyzed loans so that defaults of large loans weigh more in this measure. The historical DR may be used to predict further credit risk, and this is known as the probability of default (PD). Therefore, DRs are often used to predict values of loan portfolios. One important problem is the lack of publicly available data on the PDs and DRs of loan portfolios, while the time series of NPL ratios at the aggregate country level are published by international central banks and financial supervisory authorities.

The literature bears witness to just a few attempts to construct a DR of some loan portfolios using information contained in the NPL ratio. Pinto and Vivan (2013) constructed the implied NPL ratio, a new measure that controlled the changes in the portfolio growth rate during its average term to maturity. This measure took into account differences in the default distribution across time and the amount of time a past due loan remained in the balance sheet. Serwa (2013) derived another measure of loan quality: the adjusted NPL rate. This measure was similar to the DR because it was also robust to changes in the rate of growth of the loan portfolio.

This paper contributes to the literature by deriving the DR from the information contained in the NPL ratio. Moreover, we applied this measure in the analyses of stability in the aggregate loan portfolios in nine European banking sectors. We applied a simple method to calibrate the term structure of the loan portfolios proposed by Serwa (2013) and derived the time series of DRs from historical data of NPL rates in the Czech Republic, Greece,

Ireland, Hungary, Latvia, Poland, Portugal, Romania, and Spain. We found that the derived PDs for some countries provided valuable information about the state of the banking sector. However, for other countries we found the need for a better calibration of the method.

We focused here on the aggregate portfolios of housing loans because these loans are relatively uniform in comparison to other types of banking loans. The housing loans are long-term contracts, and something such as a bad quality mortgage can remain in the loan portfolio for a long period of time and have an influence the NPL ratio. Analyzing the aggregate DRs of housing loans provided valuable information about the average financial performance of households involved in mortgages.

The next section describes the method to calibrate the DRs, given minimum information on the term structure of the loan portfolio. Section 2 includes empirical results of estimated DRs for nine country-aggregates of housing loans, and the final section involves our conclusions.

1 Term-structure of loans and default rates

Our description of the model of a loan portfolio strictly followed Serwa (2013). Let n be the maximum maturity of a loan contract in a given portfolio. The loan portfolio $\boldsymbol{X}_t$ at time t consists of aggregated loan cohorts $x_{i,j,t}$ supplied to borrowers i periods ago and maturing in j periods, where $i = 0, 1, \ldots, n-1$ and $j = 1, 2, \ldots, n$, respectively. The NPLs are a part of this portfolio and the aggregated bad-quality (non-performing) loan cohorts are denoted as $b_{i,j,t}$. The tranches of good-quality loans $g_{i,j,t}$ are computed as $g_{i,j,t} = x_{i,j,t} - b_{i,j,t}$.

The NPL ratio is the share of bad loans in the portfolio:

$$NPL_t = \frac{\sum_{i=0}^{n-1} \sum_{j=1}^{n} b_{i,j,t}}{\sum_{i=0}^{n-1} \sum_{j=1}^{n} x_{i,j,t}}. \tag{1}$$

The following simplifying assumptions were introduced in order utilize the derivation of DRs. The important characteristics of loan contracts do not change while loans are present in the analyzed portfolio. Loans are only removed from the portfolio after reaching maturity. Good-quality loans pay interest while the NPLs do not. The interest paid on loans in each period is not included in the portfolio, and all new loans added to the portfolio at time t are of good quality. The good-quality loans are repaid by borrowers in equal tranches between each period, $g_{i,j,t}/j$, and the bad-quality loans are not repaid until maturity. Calculations assuming other repayment schedules do not change our general results, the above assumptions are the same as in Serwa (2013).

The recursive formula for the value of NPLs is as follows:

$$b_{i,j,t} = b_{i-1,j+1,t-1} + DR_{i-1,j+1,t-1} \cdot g_{i-1,j+1,t-1}, \tag{2}$$

where $DR_{i-1,j+1,t-1}$ is the average default rate between time $t-1$ and t for the loans that have belonged to the portfolio since $i-1$ periods and have been expected to mature in $j+1$ periods at time $t-1$. Because we aimed to construct a single index of DR, we computed an average DR for all cohorts of loans. To simplify computations, we assumed that $DR_{i,j,t} = DR_t$ was the same for all maturities and cohorts at time t. Now, the aggregate value of all NPLs is equal to the following:

$$\sum_{i=0}^{n-1}\sum_{j=1}^{n} b_{i,j,t} = \sum_{i=0}^{n-1}\sum_{j=1}^{n-1} b_{i,j,t-1} + DR_t \cdot \sum_{i=0}^{n-1}\sum_{j=1}^{n-1} g_{i,j,t-1}. \tag{3}$$

Also, the aggregate value of good-quality loans is equal to the following:

$$\sum_{i=0}^{n-1}\sum_{j=1}^{n} g_{i,j,t} = \sum_{j=1}^{n-1} g_{0,j,t} + (1-DR_t) \cdot \sum_{i=0}^{n-1}\sum_{j=1}^{n-1} g_{i,j,t-1} \cdot \frac{j}{j+1}. \tag{4}$$

Deriving DR_t from (3) and (4) was complicated by the fact that data for neither $\sum_{i=0}^{n-1}\sum_{j=1}^{n-1} b_{i,j,t-1}$, $\sum_{i=0}^{n-1}\sum_{j=1}^{n-1} g_{i,j,t-1}$, or $\sum_{j=1}^{n-1} g_{0,j,t}$ are publicly available.

One way to overcome the problem of unobservable cohorts of the portfolio's loans was to calibrate the term structure using information about the maximum available maturity of loans, the growth rate of loans, the NPL ratio, and the distribution of new loans entering the portfolio in each period. Then, the rate of default can be recursively computed from equation (3) as follows:

$$DR_t = \frac{\left(\sum_{i=0}^{n-1}\sum_{j=1}^{n} b_{i,j,t}\right) - \left(\sum_{i=0}^{n-1}\sum_{j-1}^{n-1} \tilde{b}_{i,j,t-1}\right)}{\sum_{i=0}^{n-1}\sum_{j=1}^{n-1} \tilde{g}_{i,j,t-1}}, \tag{5}$$

where $\tilde{b}_{i,j,t-1}$ and $\tilde{g}_{i,j,t-1}$ are the approximated values of true $b_{i,j,t-1}$ and $g_{i,j,t-1}$, respectively, derived from equations (3) and (4) for the time $t-1$. The initial values of $b_{i,j,0}$ and $g_{i,j,0}$ as well as the new loans $g_{0,j,t}$ should be either known or assumed. In the latter case, Serwa (2013) proposed to use some artificial distributions of initial loans in the portfolio and to perform robustness analysis afterwards.

We considered two distributions of new loans with respect to their maturity. The first approach assumed that all new loans were equally distributed across maturities. In this approach, the value of new one-year loans was equal to the value of ten-year loans. The second approach controlled for when new long-term loans were more frequent than new short-term loans and the distribution of new loans was triangular. The one-period loans were n times less frequent than the n-period loans, and the values of loans with respective maturities were all calibrated with the initial growth rate of a total loan portfolio and the initial ratio of the NPLs. The two distributions described here were used in our empirical analysis.

When calibrating the distribution of good and bad loans in the portfolio to match the initial ratio of NPLs, we recursively calculated the long-term levels of $b_{i,j,t}$ and $g_{i,j,t}$ for t approaching infinity assuming a steady state growth rate of the whole portfolio, a constant distribution of new loans with respect to maturity, and a constant rate of default of loans. In practice, 500 recursive computations of $b_{i,j,t}$ and $g_{i,j,t}$ from equations (3) and (4) lead to stable steady state values of these variables for all i and j independently of the initial values (cf., Serwa, 2013).

2 Default rates of housing loans in nine European economies

We looked at nine European banking sectors, and we were able to obtain information on NPL ratios, the growth rates of loans, and the values of maximum available (but realistic) maturity for all loans in each sector. We chose to focus on the aggregate portfolios of housing loans in each country, because these loans have long maturities and are more homogenous than other types of loans. The countries we analyzed were the Czech Republic, Greece, Hungary, Ireland, Latvia, Poland, Portugal, Romania, and Spain. The sample began in 2002 and ended in 2009 for the Czech Republic, and ranged from 2004–2010 for Hungary (both samples contain annual data). For other countries, the data are quarterly and equal: 2005 Q1-2011 Q4 for Greece; 2009 Q3–2011 Q3 for Ireland; 2007 Q3–2011 Q4 for Latvia; 2004 Q4–2011 Q4 for Poland; 1998 Q1–2012 Q2 for Portugal; 2008 Q3–2011 Q4 for Romania; 1999 Q1–2012 Q1 for Spain.

The data on NPL rates came from the central banks in each respective country. Unemployment rates, wage growth rates, and market interest rates (usually the short-term interbank rates in respective markets) were obtained from the International Financial Statistics database of the International Monetary Fund.

Figures 1–9 present fluctuations of the NPL ratios in time and the intermediate changes in the business cycles of respective economies. For most of the countries, we observed rising unemployment and slowing income growth during the global financial crisis of 2008–2009. In the calm periods wage growth was higher and the unemployment rate was lower. By observing NPL ratios, it was difficult to distinguish between crisis and non-crisis periods because they contained combined information about credit growth rates and credit DRs. These two combined factors provided rather noisy messages on credit risk. For instance, the pace of credit growth in many countries was still high at the beginning of the recent global financial crisis while the economic fundamentals were already weak and the credit risk was rising.

Loan DRs should react more rapidly to changing economic conditions than the NPL ratios. Figures 10–18 present changes in DRs for each analyzed country. These DRs were calibrated using the model presented in Section 1. The DRs shown in these figures are computed using of equation (5) and are valid for the two scenarios: (a) when all new loans are equally distributed across remaining maturities (DR1); (b) when more new loans have longer-term maturities (DR2). The differences between the two estimates were relatively small and they did not affect the general conclusions (other distributions of new loans in the portfolio were also possible, but they did not significantly change the results).

There were strong differences in the volatility and roughness of the calibrated DRs for different countries. For some countries such as Hungary, Latvia, or Spain, the estimates were relatively smooth. The series for Portugal and Poland were much rougher. These latter DRs may contain more economic information or they may simply contain more random noise. It is clear from the figures that large increases in DRs were observed during the global financial crisis of 2008–2009 for all the countries (this applied to Greece later as well). For some countries (such as Spain) the crisis period was also the most volatile in terms of changes in the DRs.

Surprisingly, DRs became very small values in calm periods for some markets (such as Latvia). The rates of default were also rather small for most portfolios, which seems unlikely even for developed economies in prosperous times. Therefore, the calibrated indices should be treated as proxies of credit risk rather than precise estimates of credit risk. Our new measures are likely to provide valuable information on changes of credit risk over the business cycle rather than the information on the levels of risk.

In the Czech Republic, the DRs are on average 50 percent lower before the crisis. A similar result was found in Hungary where the DR started to increase in 2008 and was six times higher in 2010 than it was in 2007. In Greece, the lowest rates of default were observed in the years 2006 and 2007. These rates doubled during the crisis of 2008–2009 and even quadrupled in the year 2011. In the short sample of Irish data, the DR grew steadily over the 2008–2009 crisis and in the post-crisis period, which suggests a negative effect on Irish households during the sovereign debt crisis in the euro zone. In Latvia and in Spain, one can observe the single peak of the rate of default in the middle of the global financial crisis. Such a peak was also apparent for Poland, but in a much noisier neighborhood of similar peaks in 2004, 2006, and 2011. In turn, the crisis period for Romania and Portugal was difficult to distinguish from other times when using the DR time series.

We investigated how our measure of credit risk was correlated with macroeconomic factors, and the results are shown in Table 1. We found that DRs were often strongly correlated with macroeconomic variables in the investigated samples. The patterns of correlation were not perfectly clear, however, and they strongly depended on the investigated countries. It is interesting to note that the DRs measured at time t were more correlated with the unemployment rates in the upcoming quarter (measured at time $t+1$) rather than those measured in the present quarter (at time t) in six out of nine cases. For the growth of wages, correlations were more negative between present defaults and the future growth of wages in five out of nine cases. Similarly, correlations were more negative between present defaults and the future interest rates in five out of nine cases. We expected a negative link between present DRs and future interest rates if central banks adjusted the interest rate to worsening or improving economic conditions proxied by DRs. We conclude that there is no strong evidence that proves DRs rates can predict macroeconomic variables very well; however, the contemporaneous linkages of credit risk and macroeconomic factors are strong in many countries.

We also tested for any evidence of pairwise Granger causality between macroeconomic variables and the DR. The results are presented in Table 2 only for the countries where enough time-series data were available. Our results confirmed the outcomes from the correlation analysis and suggested that there was no clear direction of lagged causality between the analyzed variables.

Conclusions

Deriving probabilities of default from raw indices of NPLs is a difficult task when only limited information is available. Depending on the country, the computed DRs are volatile or smooth, but are always more irregular than original NPL ratios. This may suggest that economic fluctuations and their effects on the loan quality are volatile. Banks tend to smooth their economic performance (and the NPL ratio) by controlling their loan supply. There are several factors that influence changes in the NPL ratios independently of the changing rates of default. For example, selling some parts of a loan portfolio will significantly affect the term-structure of the aggregate loan portfolios. Changing accounting regulations, and changing policies of banks with respect to new loan supply and old NPLs would also affect the results. In practice, more information about the structure of the loan portfolio improves the precision of calibrated DRs.

Further analyses should compare our proxy of credit risk for a loan portfolio with the true values of DRs in bank loan portfolios. This task is complicated by the fact that few banks publish estimates of PDs cyclically.

One direct extension of our results could be regression analyses of macroeconomic factors affecting credit risk in different countries. It is possible that the combined macroeconomic variables in regression models may explain a large share of credit-risk volatility. This may lead to more efficient models used to predict credit risk, and our Granger causality analysis represents a first step in this direction.

Acknowledgements

This research has been financed by the National Centre of Science (grant no. OPUS 2012/07/B/HS4/00361). We would like to thank seminar participants at the European Central Bank,

Narodowy Bank Polski, Warsaw School of Economics, FRAP 2015 conference participants in Steyr, and an anonymous referee for valuable comments to this paper.

References

Aman, H. and Miyazaki, H. (2009). Valuation effects of new equity issues by banks: evidence from Japan. *Applied Financial Economics*, 19(8):635–645.

Čihák, M. and Schaeck, K. (2010). How well do aggregate prudential ratios identify banking system problems? *Journal of Financial Stability*, 6(3):130 – 144.

Coricelli, F., Mucci, F., and Revoltella, D. (2006). Household Credit in the New Europe: Lending Boom or Sustainable Growth? CEPR Discussion Papers 5520, C.E.P.R. Discussion Papers.

Festić, M., Repina, S., and Kavkler, A. (2009). The Up-Coming Crisis and the Banking Sector in the Baltic States. *Swiss Journal of Economics and Statistics (SJES)*, 145(III):269–291.

Hasan, I. and Wall, L. D. (2004). Determinants of the Loan Loss Allowance: Some Cross-Country Comparisons. *Financial Review*, 39(1):129–152.

Jin, J. Y., Kanagaretnam, K., and Lobo, G. J. (2011). Ability of accounting and audit quality variables to predict bank failure during the financial crisis. *Journal of Banking and Finance*, 35(11):2811 – 2819.

Lízal, L. and Svejnar, J. (2002). Investment, Credit Rationing, And The Soft Budget Constraint: Evidence From Czech Panel Data. *The Review of Economics and Statistics*, 84(2):353–370.

Meeker, L. G. and Gray, L. (1987). A note on non-performing loans as an indicator of asset quality. *Journal of Banking and Finance*, 11(1):161 – 168.

Mendoza, E. G. and Terrones, M. E. (2008). An Anatomy Of Credit Booms: Evidence From Macro Aggregates And Micro Data. NBER Working Papers 14049, National Bureau of Economic Research, Inc.

Pinto, R. L. and Vivan, G. F. A. (2013). Converting the NPL Ratio into a Comparable Long Term Metric. Working Papers Series 309, Central Bank of Brazil, Research Department.

Podpiera, R. (2006). Does Compliance with Basel Core Principles Bring Any Measurable Benefits? *IMF Staff Papers*, 53(2):5.

Serwa, D. (2013). Measuring Non-Performing Loans During (and After) Credit Booms. *Central European Journal of Economic Modelling and Econometrics*, 5(3):163–183.

Tornell, A. and Westermann, F. (2002). Boom-Bust Cycles in Middle Income Countries: Facts and Explanation. NBER Working Papers 9219, National Bureau of Economic Research, Inc.

Whalen, G. W. (2010). Are Early Warning Models Still Useful Tools for Bank Supervisors? Economics Working Paper 2010-3, Office of the Comptroller of the Currency, Washington DC.

Figure 1: The NPL ratio and macroeconomic data for the Czech Republic

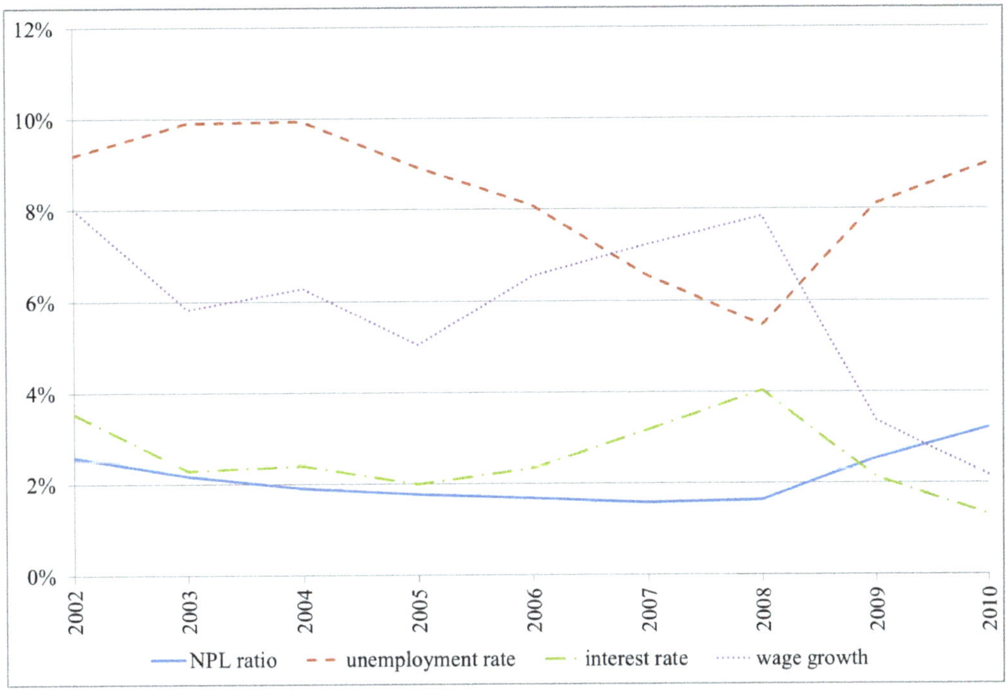

Figure 2: The NPL ratio and macroeconomic data for Greece

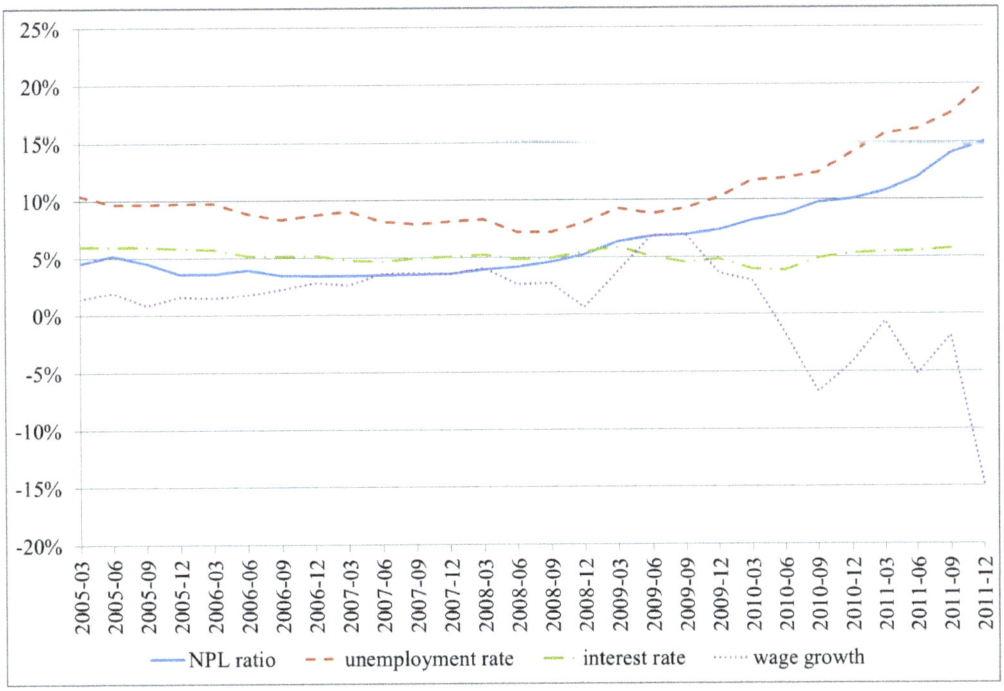

Figure 3: The NPL ratio and macroeconomic data for Ireland

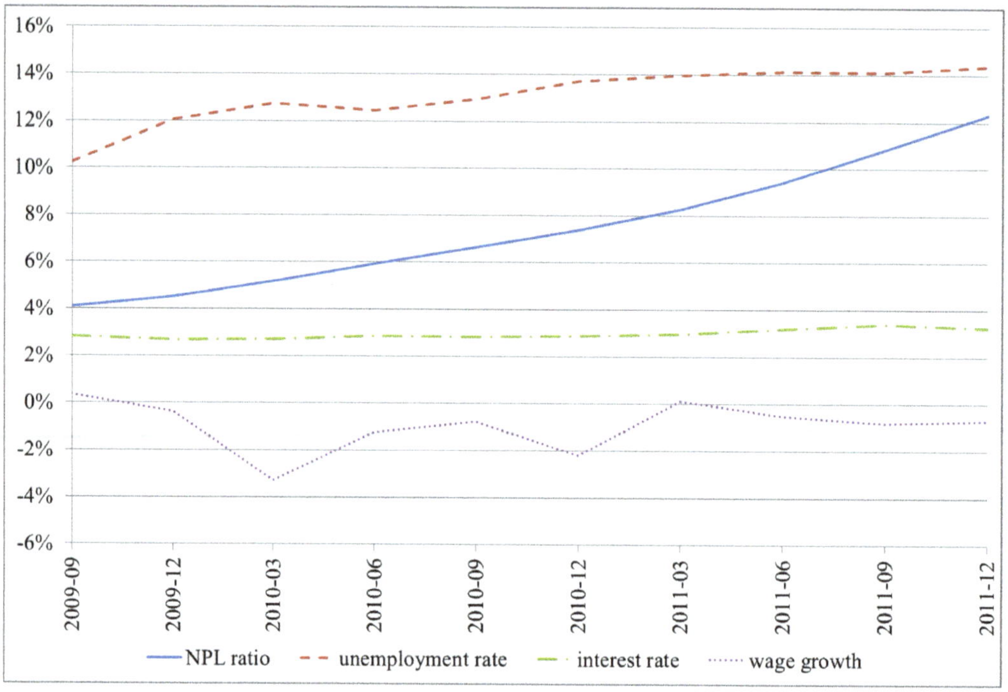

Figure 4: The NPL ratio and macroeconomic data for Hungary

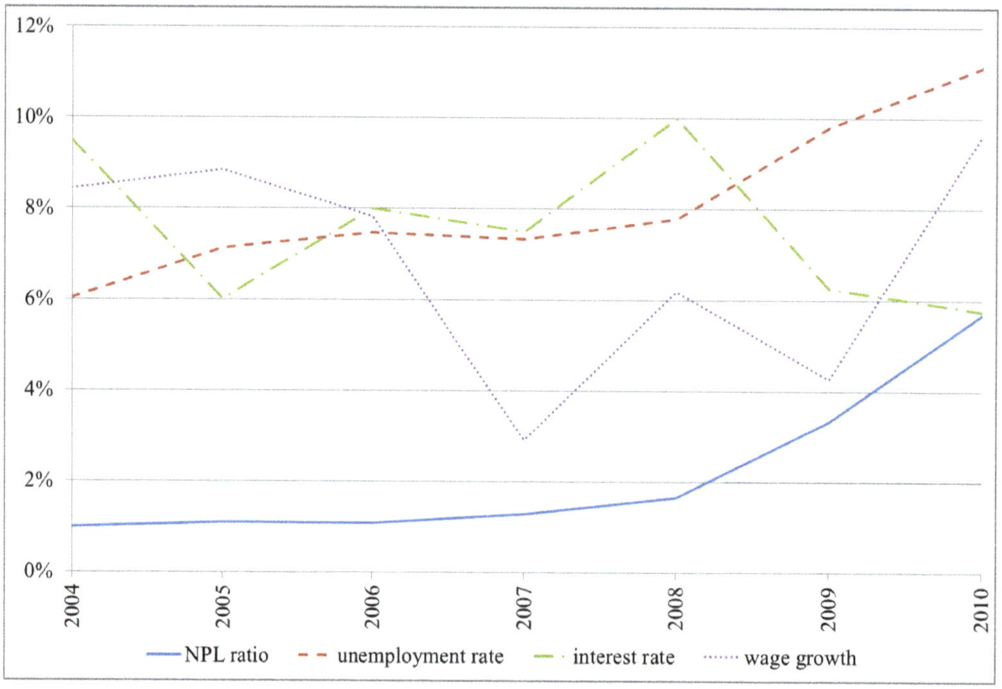

Figure 5: The NPL ratio and macroeconomic data for Latvia

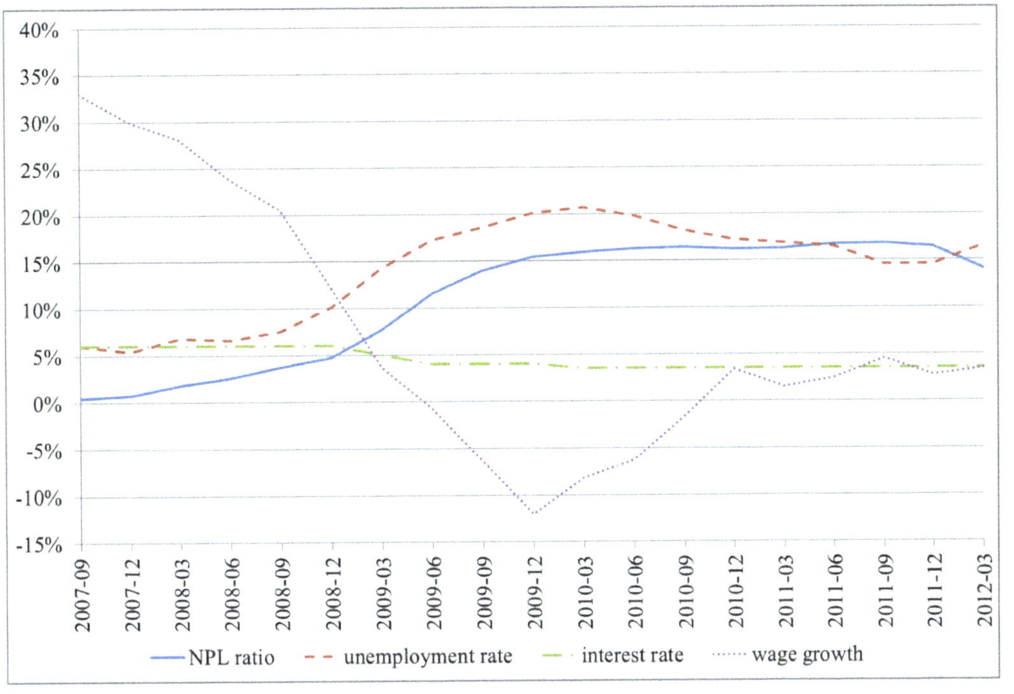

Figure 6: The NPL ratio and macroeconomic data for Poland

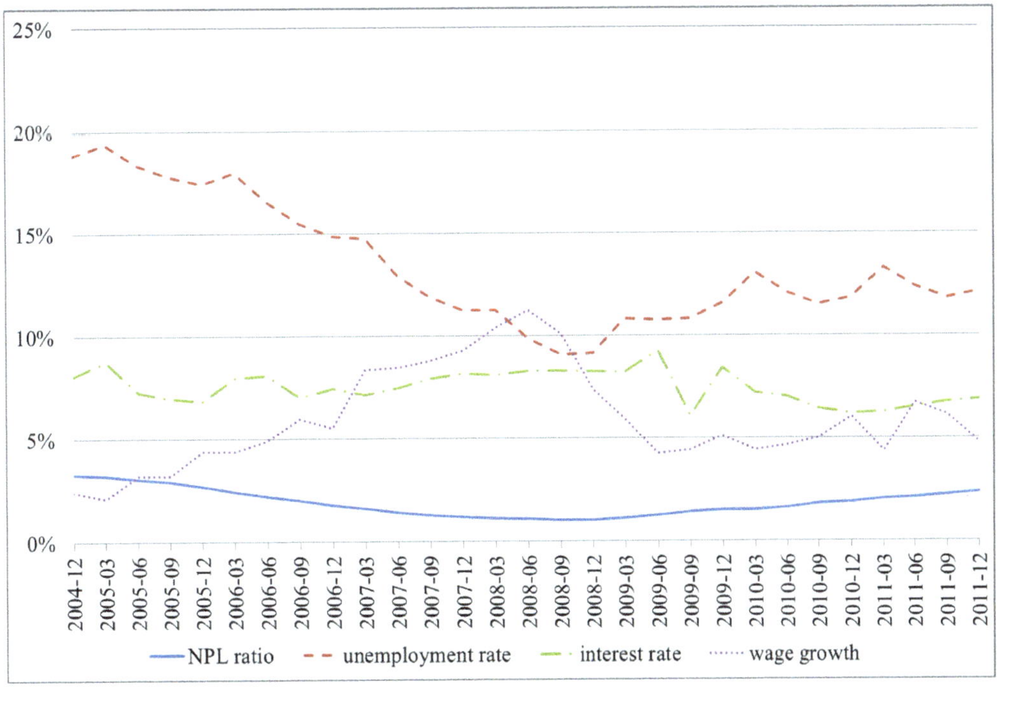

Figure 7: The NPL ratio and macroeconomic data for Portugal

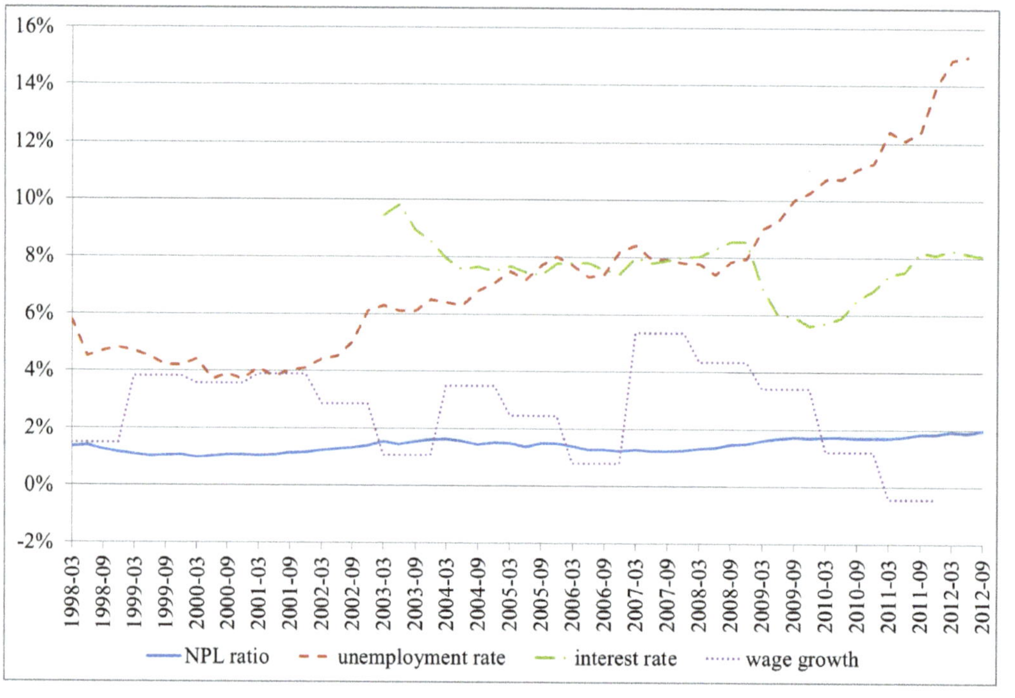

Figure 8: The NPL ratio and macroeconomic data for Romania

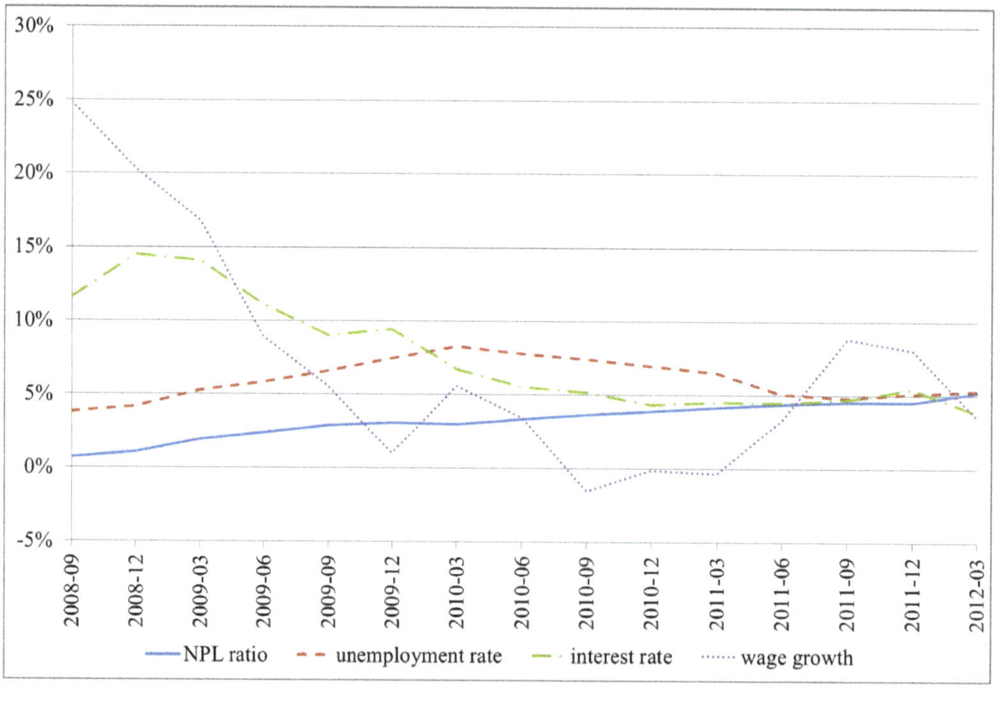

Figure 9: The NPL ratio and macroeconomic data for Spain

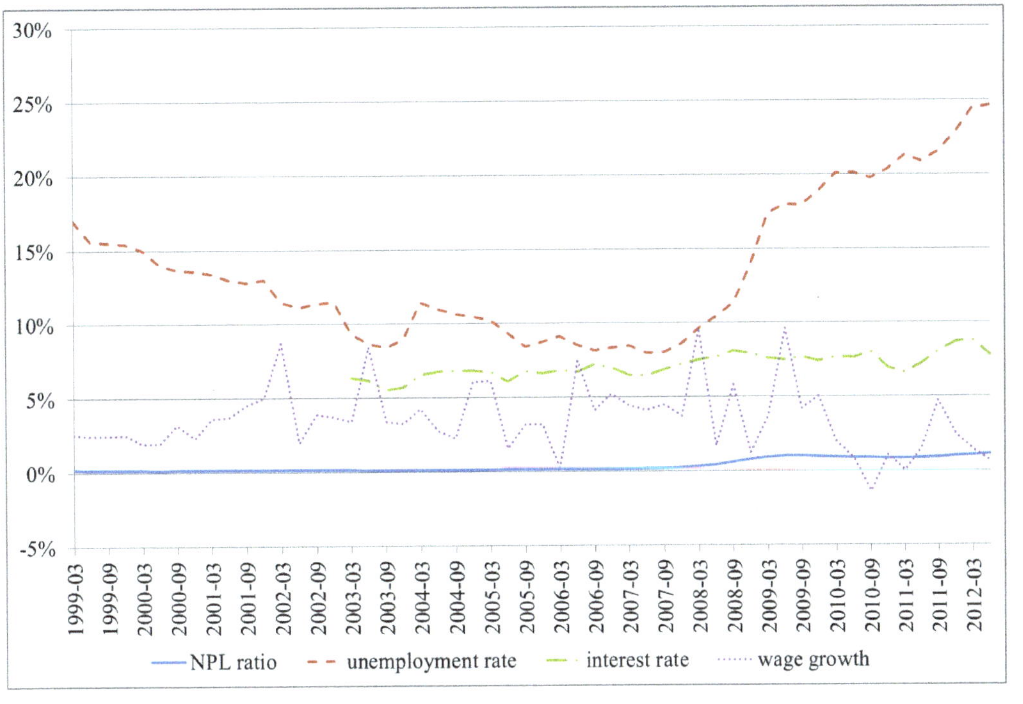

Figure 10: Calibrated DRs for the Czech Republic

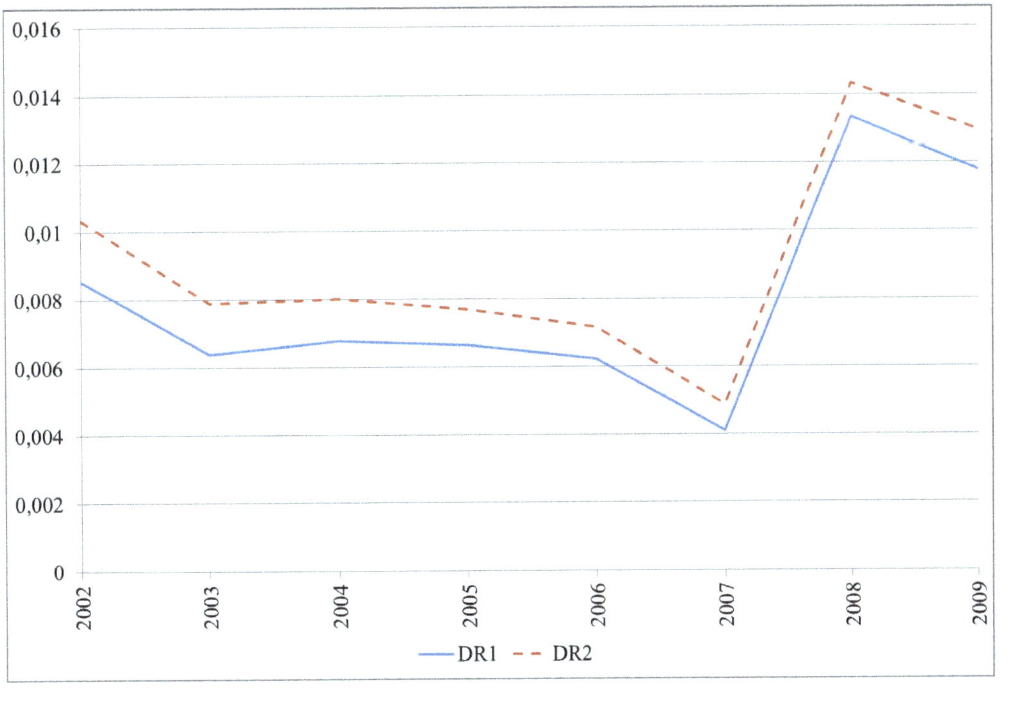

Figure 11: Calibrated DRs for Greece

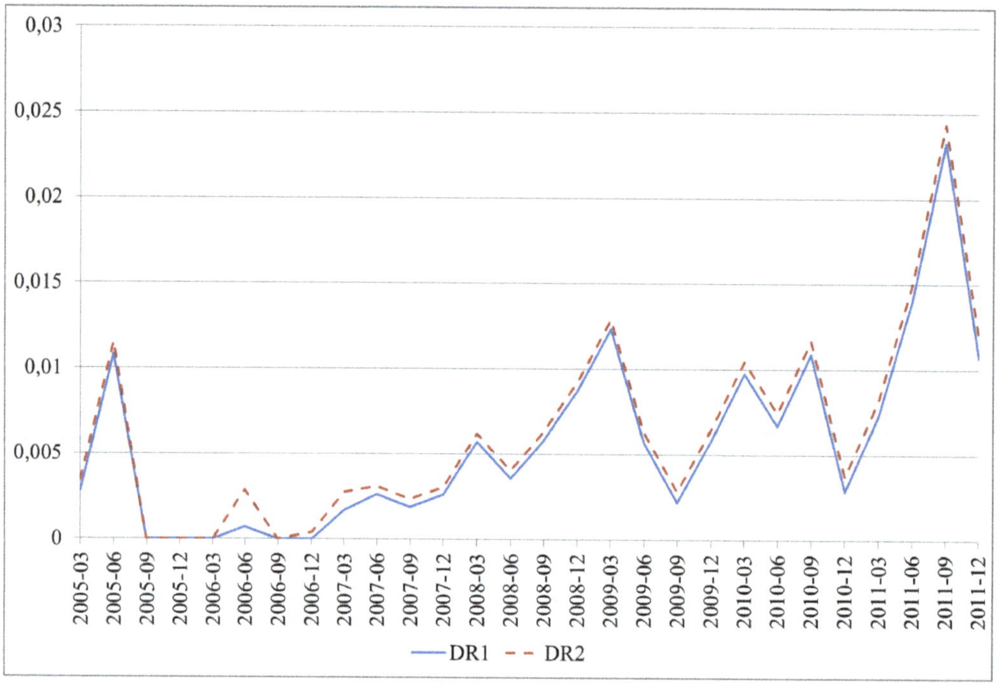

Figure 12: Calibrated DRs for Ireland

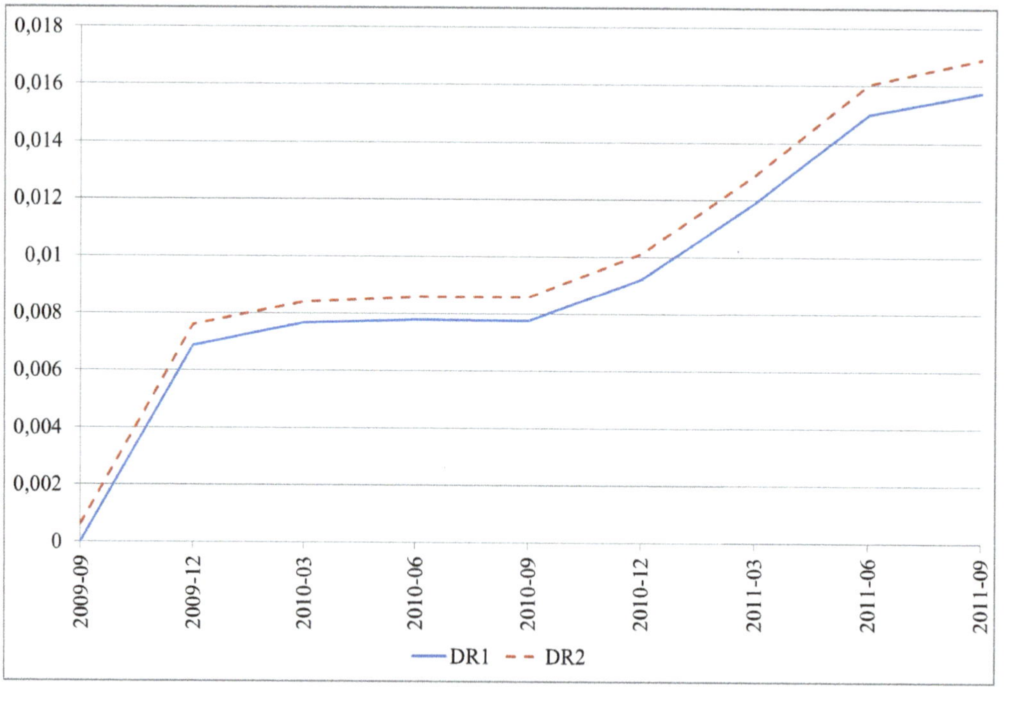

Figure 13: Calibrated DRs for Hungary

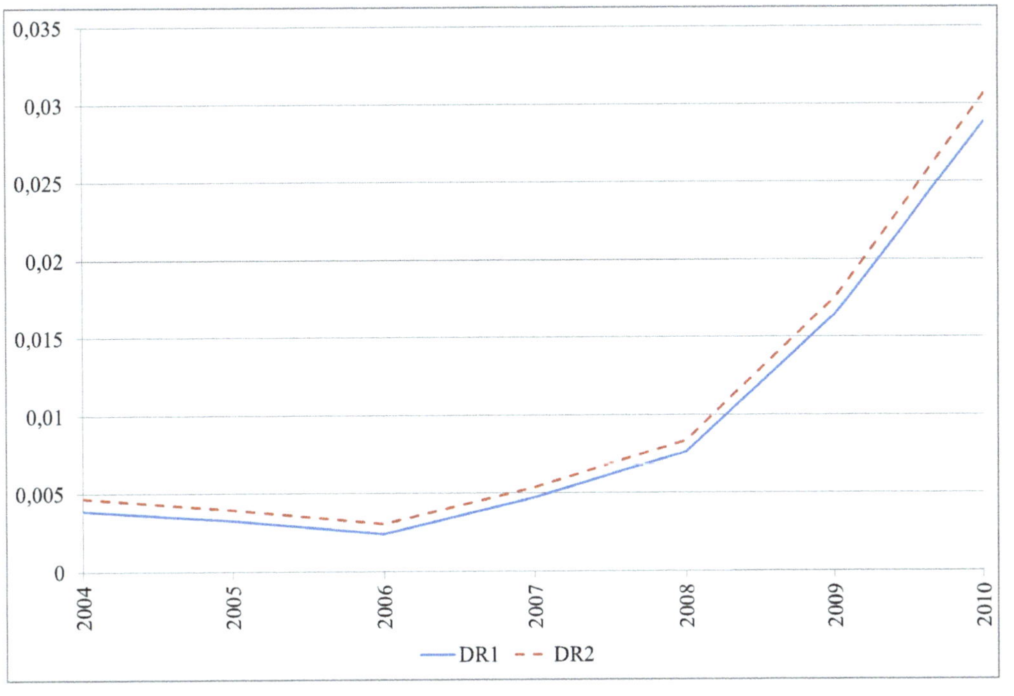

Figure 14: Calibrated DRs for Latvia

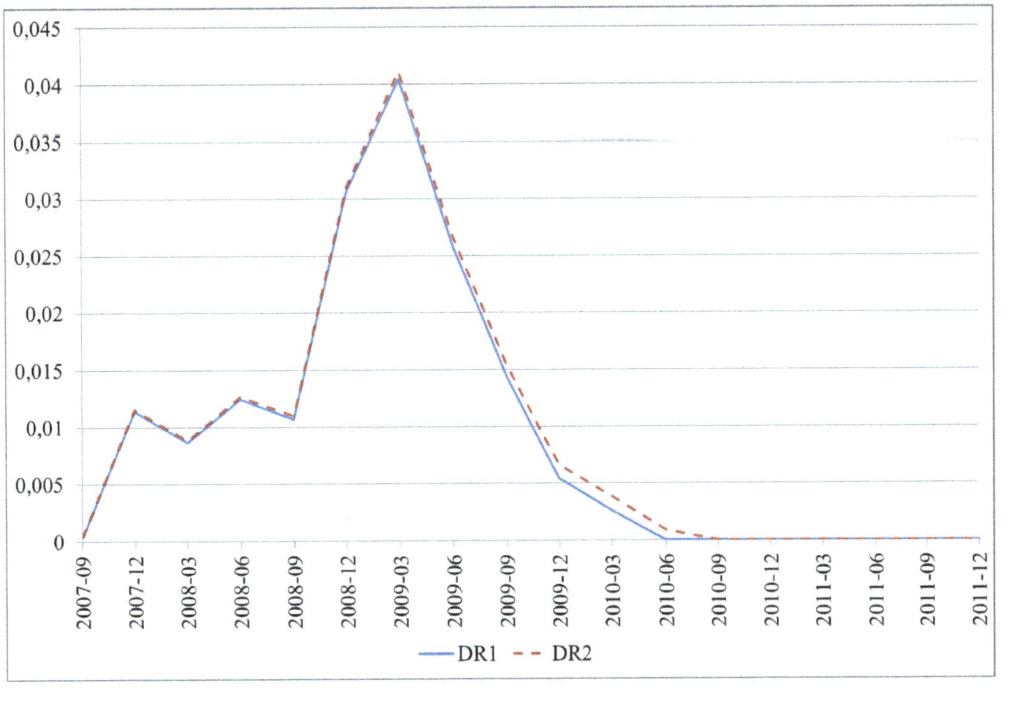

Figure 15: Calibrated DRs for Poland

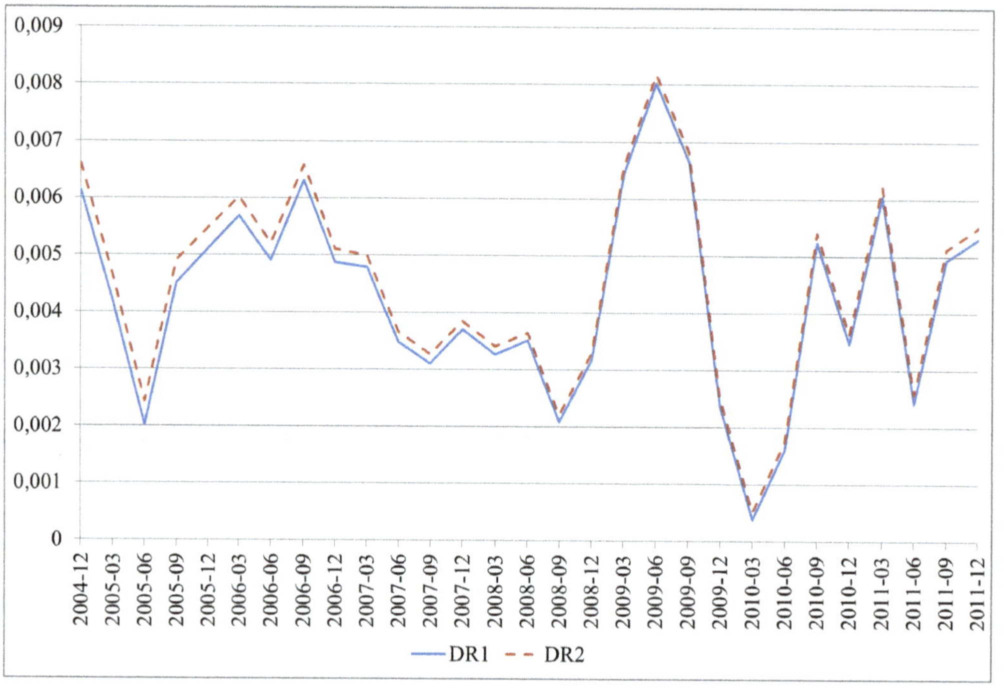

Figure 16: Calibrated DRs for Portugal

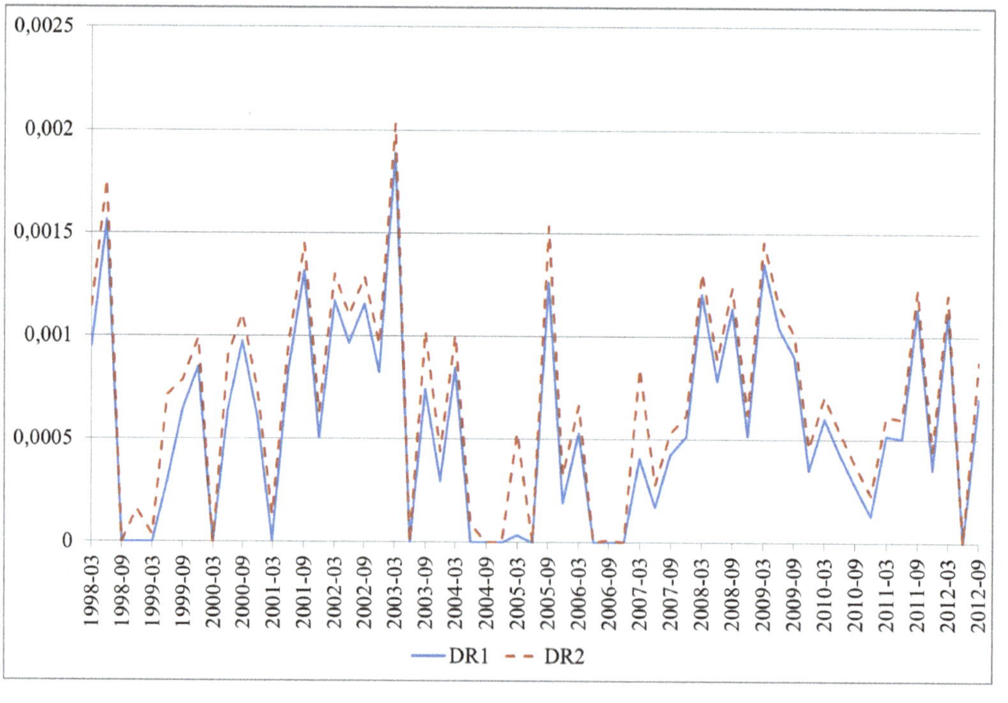

Figure 17: Calibrated DRs for Romania

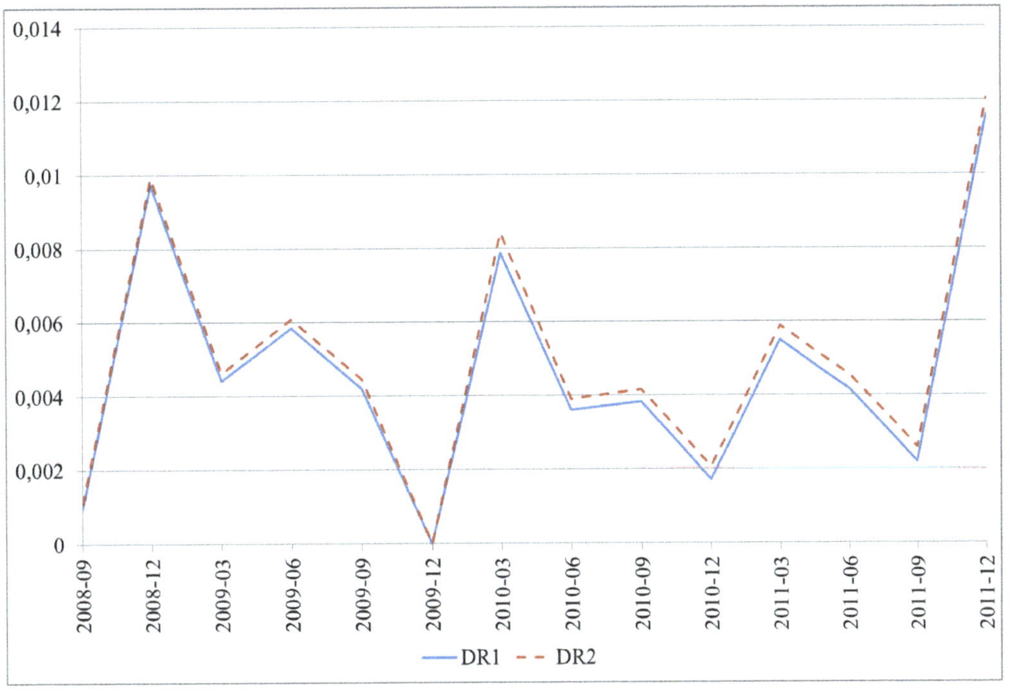

Figure 18: Calibrated DRs for Spain

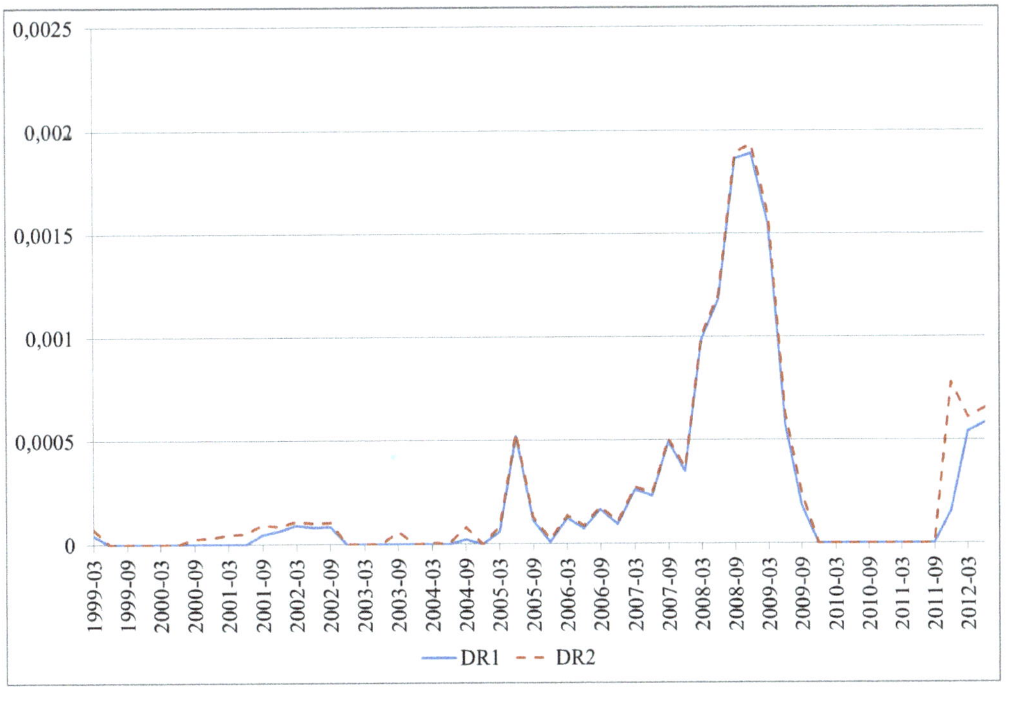

Table 1: Correlations of loan DRs with NPL ratios and macroeconomic variables

	NPL (t)	NPL ($t+1$)	unemployment rate (t)	unemployment rate ($t+1$)	wage growth (t)	wage growth ($t+1$)	interest rate (t)	interest rate ($t+1$)
Czech Rep.	0.32	0.87	-0.40	0.40	-0.10	-0.91	0.39	-0.72
Greece	0.75	0.77	0.62	0.65	-0.40	-0.62	0.10	0.04
Ireland	0.92	0.93	0.94	0.87	-0.07	0.15	0.79	0.91
Hungary	1.00	0.98	0.95	0.86	0.19	0.40	-0.53	-0.30
Latvia	-0.42	-0.26	-0.20	0.04	0.09	-0.12	0.45	0.24
Poland	0.17	0.14	0.17	0.20	-0.30	-0.18	0.00	0.08
Portugal	0.10	0.10	-0.07	-0.01	0.07	-0.01	0.10	0.10
Romania	0.03	0.20	-0.15	-0.16	0.16	0.01	0.10	-0.02
Spain	0.33	0.41	-0.01	0.06	0.10	0.15	0.42	0.37

Note: DRs are measured at time t while the other variables are measured at time t or $t+1$ (as denoted in the first row).

Table 2: Granger causality tests between macroeconomic variables and the DR

	unemployment rate	interest rate	wage growth
Greece	-		+
Latvia	- +	- +	- +
Poland			
Portugal			
Spain	+		

Note: The symbol + denotes Granger causality from the DR to the respective macroeconomic variable. The symbol - denotes Granger causality from the respective macroeconomic variable to the DR. Empty cells denote no causality in any direction. All tests use the 5% level of significance.

12

The Stock Market between Classical and Behavioral Hypotheses: An Empirical Investigation of the Warsaw Stock Exchange

Mostafa Raeisi Sarkandiz*♣, Robabeh Bahlouli♣

♣Department of Management and Economics, University of Tabriz, Iran

ABSTRACT: In empirical studies of the efficient market hypothesis using a classic approach, attention has generally been paid to the weak form of performance; other aspects of efficiency, such as informational efficiency, have not been addressed. Also, the study of alternative theories, such as behavioral hypotheses, is neglected. This article seeks to investigate not only the weak and informational forms of the efficient market hypothesis, but also to test the adaptive and fractal market hypotheses as two alternative theories by conducting an empirical study on the Warsaw Stock Exchange.

Keywords: efficient market hypothesis, informational efficiency, adaptive market hypothesis, fractal market hypothesis, Warsaw Stock Exchange

Introduction

Since Fama (1965) first introduced the concept of market efficiency, a considerable amount of economic investigation has been centered on whether to accept this hypothesis. Numerous definitions of market efficiency all emphasize a common notion that if the market is

*Corresponding Author. Address: Department of Management and Economics, University of Tabriz, 29 Bahman Boulevard 51666, Tabriz, Iran. Email: mostafa.raeisi.sarkandiz@gmail.com

efficient, asset prices will reflect existing information (Eakins and Mishkin, 2012). In other words, prices reflect the fundamental information about active companies in the market. This hypothesis therefore states that any price deviations are quickly corrected by arbitrageurs. Nonetheless, Shleifer (2000) asserts, in contrast to the efficient market hypothesis, that the behavioral finance theory indicates arbitrage is risky and therefore limited. The importance of establishing which of these two hypotheses is correct is that if the market is not efficient it can be argued that with limits on arbitrage, there is the possibility of creating asset bubbles. Therefore, prices have not followed their fundamental trend. With the continuation of deviations from the fundamental trend and an incremental increase of the bubble, there will probably be an economic crash.

After several periods of high price fluctuations in stock exchanges, the efficient market hypothesis was seriously questioned and Keynes' (1936) idea, which suggested the possibility of creating an asset price bubble, was again considered. Shiller (1979) introduced the variance bounds tests to investigate the existence of bubbles in the market and the possibility that the market hypothesis was rejected. In the following years, Diba and Grossman (1988) examined a cointegration relationship between the prices and dividends of stocks in line with the market efficiency hypothesis and the existence of a bubble when this hypothesis was violated. Subsequently, Evans (1991) introduced a different type of a bubble called "periodically collapsing bubble" and the cointegration method did not allow for the diagnosis of this bubble. Finally, Phillips et al. (2011) introduced the SADF test and Phillips et al. (2015) introduced the GSADF test, making it possible to detect more probable bubbles. In reviewing the numerous empirical studies that challenged the efficient market hypothesis, Peters (1994) introduced the fractal market hypothesis as an alternative which could better explain market characteristics. This hypothesis, unlike the efficient market hypothesis, declares that market agents respond to new information with delays and therefore prices follow a long memory process.

In 2004, Lo proposed the adaptive market hypothesis, which states that market performance has a dynamic trend: in some periods the market is efficient, but in other periods the market is inefficient. In other words, even if the market is not functioning efficiently in a given time period, it is likely that it behaves efficiently in some of its sub-intervals. The logic behind this hypothesis is based on the principles of behavioral economics, which argue that, in many cases, the behaviors of market agents are biased and people generally make their decisions based on past results. Hence, market efficiency can vary according to market conditions (Soteriou and Svensson, 2017). This hypothesis assumes that the behavior of market agents will be different during ascending and descending trends, and although this will not allow the market to be efficient for a long period, in some sub-periods the market will behave efficiently. Lo (2012) also states that the efficient market hypothesis is not an incorrect hypothesis, but is merely an incomplete model.

It is worth noting that examining the existence of a bubble in a market can be considered an indirect method of evaluating the efficient market hypothesis because, in the presence of a bubble, it is obvious that this hypothesis is violated. This paper focuses on direct methods of assessing the efficient market hypothesis. Furthermore, to obtain a more complete picture of markets and the behavior of their agents, the adaptive and fractal market hypotheses will also be tested.

The primary goal of this study is to achieve an appropriate hypothesis to explain the behavior of prices and active agents in the Warsaw Stock Exchange. Describing the behavior of the market with a coherent hypothesis can help with the analysis and prediction of market trends, and allow decision makers to apply their monetary policy with less uncertainty.

The structure of the paper is as follows. The data and descriptive statistics are introduced and presented in Section 1. In Section 2, the efficient, adaptive, and fractal market hypotheses are studied using econometric methods. In addition, some of the methods used in the empirical studies carried out in this area are critiqued. Finally, in Section 3, concluding remarks and suggestions for future research are presented.

1 Data

The data used in this research are the daily closing prices of the WIG20 index of the Warsaw Stock Exchange from January 2010 to May 2018. The WIG20 indicator is a weighted index of the 20 largest active companies in the Warsaw Stock Exchange. The statistical software packages JMulti, Eviews9, and Excel 2013 are used for the analyses.

Econometric methods require that the time series of returns be used instead of the time series of prices. In this regard, the logarithmic difference of prices has been used to calculate the time series of returns:

$$r_t = Log(p_t) - Log(p_{t-1}). \tag{1}$$

The trends of prices and returns are shown in Figures 1 and 2, respectively. The descriptive statistics for the returns are reported in Table 1.

The trend in the returns shows some fluctuations in the market, and the skewness of the data clearly indicates a deviation from the normal distribution. The Jarque and Bera (1980) normality test (J-B) also reveals that the distribution of the data does not follow a normal pattern, so at first glance, it seems that the market may be showing some sort of inefficient behavior.

The period under review, which is illustrated in Figure 1, relates to the post-2008 global economic crisis. An important point to be drawn from the chart is that, until 2016, the overall trend in prices is of decline and fluctuation; after 2016, which coincided with the depreciation of the world markets from the recession, we again see growth in prices. It seems that the Warsaw Stock Exchange, like many capital markets in the European Union, has a significant correlation with global economic fluctuations, which could be a reason for the development of Poland's economic incoherence in relation to the global economy. It should be noted that this is a hypothesis based on an empirical observation, thus to be confirmed or rejected through analysis, which is beyond the scope of this article.

2 Methodology and Discussion

In the first part of this section, we examine the weak form of the efficient market hypothesis using two methods: unit root tests and Shannon's entropy method. In the second part, we study the adaptive market hypothesis using the variance ratio test. In the third part, we examine the fractal market hypothesis using the Hurst index. We also been attempt to analyze common technical mistakes related to some empirical studies carried out in these areas.

2.1 Efficient Market Hypothesis

In this part, the efficient market hypothesis is tested based on unit root tests and Shannon's entropy method.

2.1.1 Unit Root Tests

From the econometric point of view, the weak form of the efficient market hypothesis means that prices follow a random walk process, making it impossible to forecast prices. Several empirical studies have been performed to establish whether this condition holds true in stock markets, including Dedunu (2017) in the Sri Lankan stock exchange, Ananzeh (2016) in Amman Jordan, Shaker (2013) in Finland and Sweden, Borges (2010) in the stock exchanges of several European countries, Dragota et al. (2009) in Bucharest, and Nagayasu (2003) in the Japanese stock exchange. The analysis process in these studies was based on unit root detection tests founded on the daily prices of stock indices.

Two technical flaws can be identified in these analyses. First, the existence of structural breaks in the markets were not examined in any of these studies. Perron (1989) indicated that the presence of a structural break in data with an increase in type 1 errors would lead to a reduction in the strength of diagnostic tests. This means that even if the null hypothesis is correct, the tendency to reject it increases. The second issue goes back to the tests employed: most studies have used the Dickey and Fuller (1981) test (ADF) along with the Phillips and

Perron (1988) test (P-P) and the variance ratio test presented in Lo and Mackinley (1988). In the case of the ADF test, when the autocorrelation of data is negative, taking advantage of the AIC and BIC criteria to determine test lag length can be deceptive and these criteria will select a shorter lag (Ng and Perron, 2001). In addition, the ADF and P-P tests use the same critical values table, both of them suffer from low diagnostic power, and they are often recognized as biased tests (Cochrane, 1991).

Unfortunately, in some instances, the Wald and Wolfowitz (1940) nonparametric test–known as the Runs test–was employed to conclude whether unit roots were present. But the rejection of the null hypothesis with the Runs test does not necessarily imply market inefficiency; the rejection may have other causes, such as the ARCH effect or structural changes in the time series.

The final point relates to the unit root tests used in the research cited above. Although these tests have a nonstationary null hypothesis, the alternative hypothesis does not state the static behavior of the time series. In order to obtain a precise characterization of the time series, in the absence of the unit root, the behavior of the time series must be specified. If the differential parameter is in the interval (0.5, 1), then the time series asymptotically has a unit root and will behave like a random walk process. If the differential parameter is in the interval (-0.5; 0.5), then the series has a long memory and its behavior will be stable through time (Shao and Wu, 2007). Thus, in addition to the unit root tests, it is also necessary to use the Kwiatkowski et al. (1992) test (KPSS). Unlike for the other tests, the null hypothesis of the KPSS test is stationary. If, after the rejection of the null hypothesis of other unit root tests, the null of the KPSS test is rejected, then it must be inferred that the differential parameter is a non-integer number and, thus, it will be necessary to estimate its value through existing methods. Therefore, to avoid the above-mentioned problems in this procedure, the probability of structural breaks has been investigated before undertaking any further analysis. For more accurate inferences, along with the common unit root tests, some other tests have also been used, which we will further discuss.

Before any analysis, the Runs test is performed on the data. In this test, the actual number of runs is being compared with the expected number of runs. So, we have:

$$\overline{R} = \left(\frac{2n_1 n_2}{n_1 + n_2}\right) + 1 \tag{2}$$

$$S^2 = \frac{2n_1 n_2(2n_1 n_2 - n_1 - n_2)}{(n_1 + n_2)^2(n_1 + n_2 - 1)} + 1 \tag{3}$$

where $\overline{R}$ denotes the expected number of runs, S^2 denotes the standard error of the expected number of runs, and n_1 and n_2 are the sums of the positive and negative runs, respectively. The test statistic is calculated as follows:

$$Z = \frac{R - \overline{R}}{S} \tag{4}$$

where R denotes the actual number of runs. The critical value for the test is based on the standard-normal Z table. The null hypothesis indicates that the time series is randomly distributed. The results of this test are reported in Table 2.

As the results show, at a significance level of 5%, the null hypothesis of this test is not rejected. In other words, from the perspective of this test, the market is efficient.

To identify the potential structural breakpoints in the data, the Bai and Perron (1998, 2003) test has been employed. The motivation for using this test is that, unlike traditional tests such as proposed by Chow (1960), it does not require prior information about probable breakpoints. Additionally, this test calculates the exact time of breakpoints. The results of this test are shown in Table 3.

As can be deduced from Table 3, the time series has no breakpoints. These results imply that significant structural changes in the performance and regulations of the Warsaw Stock Exchange have not been made, and that external shocks from macroeconomic adjustments in Poland have also not affected the market. Therefore, without any concern about misspecification, we can use unit root tests. To investigate the existence of a unit root, along with the traditional ADF and P-P tests, the Elliott et al. (1996) test (known as the DF-GLS) has likewise been employed because in statistical simulations, the DF-GLS test has greater power than the ADF test (Wu, 2010). The multiple variance ratio test proposed by Chow and Denning (1993), which is robust to heteroscedasticity, has also been used. Likewise, we use the KPSS test to detect the time series features. The results of these tests at a 5% significance level are shown in Tables 4 and 5.

The results of the unit root and variance ratio tests clearly indicate that the time series returns do not follow a random walk process and, therefore, the efficient market hypothesis does not apply throughout the study period. This means that prices have a predictable trend, and it is feasible for shareholders to gain unusual profits (over market performance) by using available information because stock price variations are not random.

2.1.2 Shannon's Entropy

The concept of informational efficiency declares that prices contain information from companies active in the market, and changes in information flow will change trends in prices. In other words, new information will quickly affect the behavior of market actors and cause price changes. However, the key point is that the market agents with access to prices can access all the information. Beaver (1981), in a descriptive definition, states that the market would be efficient with respect to a set of information if disclosure of this information to all market players did not lead to a change in equilibrium prices.

In this section, we will discuss the Warsaw Stock Exchange in terms of informational efficiency. It should be noted that in the previous section, the weak performance of the market was examined and this hypothesis was not confirmed. In this study, to measure the informational efficiency of the stock market, Shannon's (1948) entropy equation is used.

In the first step, we use the following function to transform the returns series into a binary series:

$$S_t = \begin{cases} 0 & r_t < 0 \\ 1 & r_t \geq 0 \end{cases} \tag{5}$$

where r_t denotes the returns series. We consider the ratio of the number of zeros to the whole numbers equal to P. It is obvious that this ratio will be equal to $1 - P$ for the ones. Therefore, based on the method presented in Risso (2008), we will have:

$$H_s = -\{P \cdot log_2 P + (1 - P) \cdot log_2(1 - P)\} \tag{6}$$

where H_s denotes Shannon's entropy index. H_s is a value in the interval $[0, 1]$ and the maximum value is obtained when $P = \frac{1}{2}$. In the latter case, when the maximum value is obtained, we say that the market is efficient. Therefore, for values less than one, the market will not be efficient.

In order to obtain stable values, the rolling-recursive window method, with two initial windows containing 50 and 100 data elements, has been used to calculate the desired index. In this paper, contrary to the approach outlined in Phillips et al. (2011) in the selection of steps for the rolling-recursive window method, each of which adds new data to the previous dataset, the steps add 50 or 100 data elements. The reason for this is that Phillips et al. (2011) used monthly data, and within a month (as much as the length of a step), it is possible to change the behavior of the market somewhat. In this study we use daily data, and a one-day increase to the previous dataset will not lead to a significant change in the data process, whereas these changes can be significant over 50 or 100 days of trading. So, steps of 50 and 100 data points, a 50-window and 100-window, respectively, have been selected for use in this research.

The descriptive statistics of the H_s values are given in Table 6. The mean of the values is used as the desired index. The values obtained are close to 1, so we need to test their equality with 1. The one-way t-test is used for this purpose. It is clear that in the case of the 100-window, the distribution of data is normal, but this is not true for the 50-window.

A one-way t-test for examining the mean of a sample requires the normal assumption because this test is highly sensitive to large skewness and heavy-tailed distributions (Cressie and Whitford, 1986). Unfortunately, in many applications of this test, the assumption of normality is not taken into account and, therefore, the statistical inference is generally inaccurate. To solve this problem, we use the Hall (1992) method, which is known as the trimmed t-statistic. The statistics used in this method are calculated as follows:

$$H_{t_w} = \left\{ (\overline{X_t} - \mu_t) + \frac{\widehat{\mu_w}}{(6\ f\ \widehat{\mu_w}^2)} + \widehat{\mu_w}\frac{(\overline{X_t} - \mu_t)^2}{3\widehat{\sigma_w}^4} + \frac{\widehat{\mu_w}^2(\overline{X_t} - \mu_t)^3}{27\widehat{\sigma_w}^8} \right\} / (\frac{\widehat{\sigma_w}}{\sqrt{f}}) \quad (7)$$

If n is equal to the sample size and $e = [\beta n]$, $0 \leq \beta < 0.5$ and $2e$ is the trimmed value from the ordered data, then $f = n - 2e$ will be the effective sample size. So, we have:

$$\overline{X_t} = \frac{1}{f} \sum_{i=e+1}^{n-e} X_i \qquad \textit{Sample Trimmed Mean} \quad (8)$$

$$Z_i = \begin{cases} X_{e+1} & X_i \leq X_{e+1} \\ X_i & X_{e+1} < X_i < X_{n-e} \\ X_{n-e} & X_i \geq X_{n-e} \end{cases} \quad (9)$$

$$\overline{X_w} = \frac{1}{n} \sum_{i=1}^{n} Z_i \qquad \textit{Sample Winsorized Mean} \quad (10)$$

Therefore, we can write:

$$\widehat{\sigma_w}^2 = \sum_{i=1}^{n} \frac{(Z_i - \overline{X_w})^2}{f-1} \qquad \textit{Squared Standard Error of Sample Trimmed Mean} \quad (11)$$

$$\widehat{\mu_w} = f \sum_{i=1}^{n} \frac{(Z_i - \overline{X_w})^3}{(f-1)(f-2)} \qquad \textit{Unbiased Trimmed Third Central Moment} \quad (12)$$

Also, μ_t is the default value under the null hypothesis. The critical value of this statistic is calculated according to the standard table of the Student's t-distribution.

Therefore, for the 100-window, we use the standard t-test, but for the 50-window, we employ the trimmed t-test. The trimming factor is 10% because after trimming the distribution of the data follows the normal distribution (the J-B probability for the trimmed sample is 0.915). The null hypothesis is $H_0 : \mu = 1$ and the alternative is $H_1 : \mu < 1$. The test results are reported in Table 7.

The t-test results indicate that the null hypothesis is rejected for both windows. That is, the index value will be less than 1, and therefore the informational efficiency hypothesis is also rejected.

The rejection of the informational efficiency hypothesis implies that new information in the market is not immediately reflected in the prices. This could be due to a lack of access to corporate information. Informational inefficiency can likewise be due to a lack of professionalism among traders such that they do not respond quickly to new information. If the efficient market hypothesis was rejected, it could be possible to acquire excess returns in the Warsaw Stock Exchange.

It is worth noting that the results of the Runs test indicate market efficiency, but the other two methods have rejected this hypothesis. Hence, as mentioned at the beginning of this section, the Runs test cannot be a good benchmark for examining the efficient market hypothesis.

2.2 Fractal Market Hypothesis

The failure to validate the efficient market hypothesis leads us to analyze an alternative hypothesis to explain the behavior of prices in the stock market. In this regard, the fractal market hypothesis is tested as a model based on the principles of behavioral economics. This hypothesis states that the returns follow a long memory process. For this purpose, the Hurst index is used to examine market behavior. This index is a numerical value that is in the range of (0, 1). If $H = 0.5$, then the series has a random walk behavior. If $0.5 < H < 1$, then the time series has a positive correlation and will display long memory behavior. Finally, if $0 < H < 0.5$, then the time series has a negative correlation and will show mean-reverting behavior (Peters, 1994).

Several studies have been conducted on market behavior using the Hurst index (for example, Van Quang, 2005; Panas and Ninni, 2010; Morales et al., 2012; Oprean et al., 2017), but some of these studies have flaws. First, due to the possible structural breaks in the data and the lack of stability of the trends, the Hurst index must be estimated using the rolling-recursive window method, but in some studies the calculation of the parameter was made once and over the entire time period. Second, despite the use of the rolling-recursive window method, in some cases the analysis is presented based on the calculated value, but because this index is an estimate, it requires a statistical inference. In other words, this value should be subjected to statistical testing. Finally, in some studies, only one window has been used, but in order to ensure the results achieved, it is advisable to use at least two different windows. Therefore, in this study, for calculating Hurst index values, similar to the calculation of Shannon's entropy, the rolling-recursive window method was used based on two different windows with steps of 50 and 100, and the optimum amount was ultimately tested.

The method used to estimate the Hurst index is the (R/S). Again, similar to the calculation of Shannon's entropy, this method also requires that the time series of returns be used instead of using the time series of prices. It is also necessary that the return series have no unit roots. According to the unit root test results in Subsection 2.1.1, this condition is clearly established and, therefore, the Hurst index can be employed.

The index, first introduced by Hurst (1951), is estimated as follows:

$$H = Log(R/S)/Log(T) \tag{13}$$

Here, the presentation of the calculation method (R / S) has been avoided and we refer the reader to Resta (2012).

The descriptive statistics of the obtained Hurst values are given in Table 8. The mean of the values is used as the parameter and, therefore, its meaningful test is based on the t-test.

As can be seen, in both of the above categories, the data distribution has a nonparametric positive skewness, which means that the mean is greater than the median. Also, the calculated skewness is clearly greater than the skewness of the normal distribution. In addition, at a 5% significance level, the null hypothesis of the J-B test was rejected, so the distribution of the calculated Hurst values is abnormal. So, again, we must use trimmed t-statistics. The trimming of the sample by 10%, by adjusting the skewness and kurtosis of the data, led to their normal distribution and, therefore, the statistical inference based on the trimmed t-statistic would be efficient. The results of the J-B test for the trimmed sample are reported in Table 9.

The tests of the Hurst values for the 50-window and 100-window with the null hypothesis $H_0 : \mu = 0.5$ against the alternative $H_1 : \mu < 0.5$ are considered. The test results are described in Table 10. Clearly, for both of the windows, the null hypothesis is rejected. Therefore, the efficient market hypothesis is also rejected. The important point is that if the standard t-statistic was used, the null hypothesis for the 100-window would not be rejected. Also, the calculated parameter is in the range of $(0, 0.5)$ and so the behavior of the series is not long memory. Likewise, $0 < H < 0.5$ indicates that any increase in any of the series terms will entail its decrease at the next moment in time. Therefore, the fractal market hypothesis is also rejected during the entire period.

2.3 Adaptive Market Hypothesis

As noted above, the adaptive market hypothesis states that in some of the sub-periods, market efficiency may be possible. The volume of empirical studies carried out in this area is not comparable to those of the efficient market hypothesis, but some of the most important studies in this field are: Todea et al. (2009), Neely et al. (2009), Kim et al. (2011), Charles et al. (2012), Hiremath and Narayan (2016), Gyamfi (2018). The methods used in these studies emphasize the autocorrelation tests, both linear and non-linear. The results of most research in this field have confirmed the validity of the adaptive market hypothesis, but the main point in all this research is that there is no proper mechanism for determining the sub-intervals, and the method used is generally based on the rolling-recursive window. It is worth noting, however, that the present study does not propose a specific method. Also, in order to study the adaptive market hypothesis, in this study the multiple variance ratio test was used. Because the market did not work efficiently throughout the entire study period, finding at least one sub-period in which market behavior was efficient would be sufficient to confirm the adaptive market hypothesis.

In determining the sub-intervals, not only has the rolling-recursive window method been used with 50-step data, but also, to separate the intervals that have more fluctuations than others, the entire period is divided into several sub-intervals with data volumes of 100, 150, 300, 350, 700, and 1,050. The results of the analyses of these 95 intervals are reported in Tables 11 and 12.

As can be clearly derived from the results, among all the subperiods studied the market behaved efficiently only between January 2, 2014, and May 27, 2014. Therefore, it can be stated that throughout the study period, the adaptive market hypothesis has been validated in the Warsaw Stock Exchange. This indicates that individual trading strategies change over time and do not occur according to a fixed and specific pattern. Further, market agents are comprised of both beginners and experts, and cannot be classified as a homogenous collection (as assumed in the efficient market hypothesis). Accordingly, the behavioral economics approach is substantially better than traditional approaches for interpreting the behavior of the stock market and its agents.

3 Concluding Remarks

This study examines the existing assumptions about the behavior of prices in the Warsaw Stock Exchange. Before undertaking the analysis, the presence of structural changes was investigated using the structural breaks test. The results confirmed there were no structural breaks in this data. In order to investigate the efficient market hypothesis, four different unit root tests—ADF, P-P, DF-GLS, and KPSS—were used, along with the variance ratio test. The results of these tests showed that the market is not efficient at a 5% significance level. For a more detailed analysis, Shannon's entropy index was evaluated using a rolling-recursive window method to investigate market informational efficiency; the results of this test confirmed the market inefficiency. To obtain a better understanding of market performance, the fractal market hypothesis was tested as an alternative to the efficient market hypothesis. To this end, the Hurst index calculated with a rolling-recursive window method was used. The results show that at some intervals prices followed a long memory process, but in most of the intervals they followed a mean reverting process. However, throughout the period under review, the desired time series followed a mean reverting process and so the fractal market hypothesis was rejected. In contrast to the efficient market hypothesis, the adaptive market hypothesis states that although a market can be inefficient throughout the entire period, there will be intervals in which market behavior is efficient. To test this hypothesis, the multiple variance ratio test was performed using the rolling-recursive window method. Additionally, in order to study the time series more precisely, the entire time period was divided into sub-intervals where the fluctuations of returns are different. The results of the analysis of the 95 study periods showed that in just one of these intervals, the market was efficient. As there exists at least one sub-period in which the market was efficient, the adaptive market hypothesis was confirmed.

In general, it can be stated that during the period under consideration, it was possible most of the time to earn returns greater than the market yield on the Warsaw Stock Exchange. Also, the market trend in most of the sub-periods was mean-reverting and so there was a downtrend following an uptrend in prices, and vice versa. In the sub-periods where the long memory process was followed, an uptrend was followed by another uptrend and, similarly, a downtrend was succeeded by another downtrend.

It should be noted that, in testing the adaptive market hypothesis, the results are sensitive to the choice of sub-intervals and, therefore, the results of this research are limited to the selected intervals. Consequently, this study does not rule out the possibility of more sub-periods in which the hypothesis may be validated. Therefore, in order to carry out future research, it will be helpful to use an effective method for determining the maximum possible number of sub-intervals.

Ultimately, it is worth noting that in this paper, conventional econometric techniques are employed to examine the hypotheses. However, the authors are considering two approaches to future investigations of the Warsaw Stock Exchange. The first approach is based on the use of chaos theory to study the nonlinear, dynamic, and chaotic nature of stock prices. In the second approach, due to the lack of evidence to support an efficient market hypothesis and therefore, the possibility of price bubbles forming in the market, the diagnosis and detection of such bubbles applying the latest tools, such as the SADF, GSADF, and BSADF tests, will be addressed.

Funding Sources

This research did not receive any specific grants from funding agencies in the public, commercial, or not-for-profit sectors.

References

Ananzeh, I. (2016). Weak Form Efficiency of the Amman Stock Exchange: An Empirical Analysis (2000-2013). *International Journal of Business and Management*, 11(1):173–180.

Bai, J. and Perron, P. (1998). Estimation and Testing Linear Models with Multiple Structural Changes. *Econometrica*, 66(1):47–78.

Bai, J. and Perron, P. (2003). Computation and Analysis of Multiple Structural Change Models. *Journal of Applied Econometrics*, 18(1):1–22.

Beaver, W. H. (1981). Market Efficiency. *Accounting Review*, 56(1):23–27.

Borges, M. R. (2010). Efficiency Market Hypothesis in European Stock Markets. *The European Journal of Finance*, 16(7):711–726.

Charles, A., Darne, O., and Kim, J. H. (2012). Exchange Rate Return Predictability and the Adaptive Market Hypothesis: Evidence from Major Foreign Exchange Rate. *Journal of International Money and Finance*, 31(6):1607–1626.

Chow, G. C. (1960). Tests of Equality Between Sets of Coefficients in Two Linear Regressions. *Econometrica*, 28(3):591–605.

Chow, K. V. and Denning, K. C. (1993). A Simple Multiple Variance Ratio Test. *Journal of Econometrics*, 58(3):385–401.

Cochrane, J. H. (1991). A Critique of the Application of Unit Root Tests. *Journal of Economics Dynamics and Control*, 15(2):275–284

Cressie, N. A. C. and Whitford, H. J. (1986). How to Use the Two Sample t-test. *Biometrical Journal*, 28(2):131–148.

Dedunu, H. H. (2017). Weak Form Efficiency of the Sri Lankan Stock Market From 2010-2014. *IOSR-Journal of Economics and Finance*, 8(3):75–81.

Diba, B. T. and Grossman, H. I. (1988). Explosive Rational Bubbles in Stock Prices. *American Economic Review*, 78(3):520–530.

Dickey, D. A. and Fuller, W. A. (1981). Likelihood Ratio Statistics for Autoregressive Time Series with a Unit Root. *Econometrica*, 49(4):1057–1072.

Dragota, V., Ciobanu, A., Cotarama, D., Semenescu, A., and Lacatus, C. (2009). Minority Shareholders' Protection: The Romanian Experience. *Theoretical and Applied Economics*, 2(2):35–48.

Eakins, S. and Mishkin, F. (2012). Financial Markets and Institutions . Massachusetts.

Elliott, G., Rothenberg, T. S., and Stock, J. H. (1996). Efficient Tests for an Autoregressive Unit Root. *Econometrica*, 64(4):813–836.

Evans, G. (1991). Pitfalls in Testing for Explosive Bubbles in Asset Prices. *American Economic Review*, 81(4):922–930.

Fama, E. F. (1965). The Behavior of Stock-Market Prices. *The Journal of Business*, 38(1):34–105.

Gyamfi, E. N. (2018). Adaptive Market Hypothesis: Evidence from the Ghanaian Stock Market. *Journal of African Business*, 19(2):195–209.

Hall, P. (1992). On the Removal of Skewness by Transformation. *Journal of the Royal Statistical Society Series*, 54(1):221–228.

Hiremath, G. S. and Narayan, S. (2016). Testing the Adaptive Market Hypothesis and its Determinants for the Indian Stock Market. *Financial Research Letters*, 19(C):173–180.

Keynes, J. M. (1936). *The General Theory of Employment, Interest, and Money.* Macmillan.

Kim, J. H., Shamsuddin, A., and Lim, K. P. (2011). Stock Returns Predictability and the Adaptive Market Hypothesis: Evidence from Century-Long U.S. Data. *Journal of Empirical Finance*, 18(5):868–879.

Kwiatkowski, D., Phillips, P. C., Schmidt, P., and Shin, Y. (1992). Testing the Null Hypothesis of Stationary Against the Alternative of a Unit Root. *Journal of Econometrics*, 54(1-3):159–178.

Lo, A. W. (2004). The Adaptive Markets Hypothesis: Market Efficiency from an Evolutionary Perspective. *The Journal of Portfolio Management*, 30(5):15–29.

Lo, A. W. (2012). Reading about the Financial Crisis: A Twenty-One-Book Review. *Journal of Economic Literature*, 50(1):151–178.

Lo, A. W. and Mackinley, C. A. (1988). Stock Market Prices Do Not Follow Random Walks: Evidence from a Simple Specification Test. *The Review of Financial Studies*, 1(1):41–66.

Morales, R., Matteo, D., T., G. R., and Aste, T. (2012). Dynamical Generalized Hurst Exponent as a Tool to Monitor Unstable Periods in Financial time series. *Physica A: Statistical Mechanics and its Applications*, 391(11):3180–3189.

Nagayasu, J. (2003). The Efficiency of the Japanese Equity Market. Working Paper WP/03/142, International Monetary Fund, Washington, D.C.

Neely, C. J., Weller, P. A., and Ulrich, J. M. (2009). The Adaptive Market Hypothesis: Evidence from Foreign Exchange Market. *Journal of Financial and Quantitative Analysis*, 44(2):467–488.

Ng, S. and Perron, P. (2001). Lag Length Selection and the Construction of Unit Root Tests with Good Size and Power. *Econometrica*, 69(6):1519–1554.

Oprean, C., Tanasescu, C., and Bucur, A. (2017). A new proposal for efficiency quantification of capital markets in the context of complex nonlinear dynamics and chaos. *Economic Research-Ekonomska Istraživanja*, 30(1):1669–1692.

Panas, E. and Ninni, V. (2010). The Distribution of London Metal Exchange Prices: A Test of the Fractal Market Hypothesis. *European Research Studies Journal*, 13(2):192–210.

Perron, P. (1989). The Great Crash,The Oil Price Shock,and the Unit Root Hypothesis. *Econometrica*, 57(6):1361–1401.

Peters, E. E. (1994). *Fractal market analysis*. Wiley, New York.

Phillips, P. C. and Perron, P. (1988). Testing for a Unit Root in Time Series Regression. *Biometrika*, 75(2):335–346.

Phillips, P. C., Shi, S.-P., and Yu, J. (2015). Testing for Multiple Bubbles: Historical Episodes of Exuberance and Collapse in the S&P 500. *International Economic Review*, 56(4):1043–1078.

Phillips, P. C., Wu, Y., and Yu, J. (2011). Explosive Behavior in the 1990s Nasdaq: When Did Exuberance Escalate Asset Values. *International Economic Review*, 52(1):201–226.

Resta, M. (2012). Hurst Exponent and its Applications in Time-series Analysis. *Recent Patents on Computer Science*, 5(3):211–219.

Risso, W. A. (2008). The Informational Efficiency and the Financial Crashes. *Research in International Business and Finance*, 22(3):396–408.

Shaker, A. M. (2013). Testing the Weak-form Efficiency of the Finnish and Swedish Stock Markets. *European Journal of Business and Social Sciences*, 2(9):176–185.

Shannon, C. E. (1948). A Mathematical Theory of Communication. *Bell System Technical Journal*, 27(3):379–423.

Shao, X. and Wu, W. B. (2007). Asymptotic Spectral Theory for Nonlinear Time Series. *The Annals of Statistics*, 35(4):1773–1801.

Shiller, R. (1979). The Volatility of Long-term Interest Rates and Expectations Models of the Term Structure. *Journal of Political Economy*, 87(6):1190–1219.

Shleifer, A. (2000). *Inefficient Markets: An Introduction to Behavioural Finance.* Clarendon Lectures in Economics. OUP Oxford.

Soteriou, A. and Svensson, L. (2017). *Testing the Adaptive Market Hypothesis on the OMXS30 Stock Index: 1986-2014 (Master Thesis).* Jönköping International Business School, Jönköping.

Todea, A., Ciupac-Ulici, M., and Silaghi, S. (2009). Adaptive Market Hypothesis: Evidence from Asia-Pacific Financial Markets. *The Review of Finance and Banking*, 1(1):7–13.

Van Quang, T. (2005). The Fractal Market Analysis and its Application on Czech Conditions. *Acta Oeconomica Pragensia*, 13(1):101–111.

Wald, A. and Wolfowitz, J. (1940). On a Test Whether Two Samples are from the Same Population. *Annals of Mathematical Statistics*, 11(2):147–162.

Wu, S. (2010). Lag Length Selection in DF-GLS Unit Root Tests. *Communications in Statistics-Simulation and Computation*, 39(8):1590–1604.

Figure 1: Time series of daily WIG20 prices

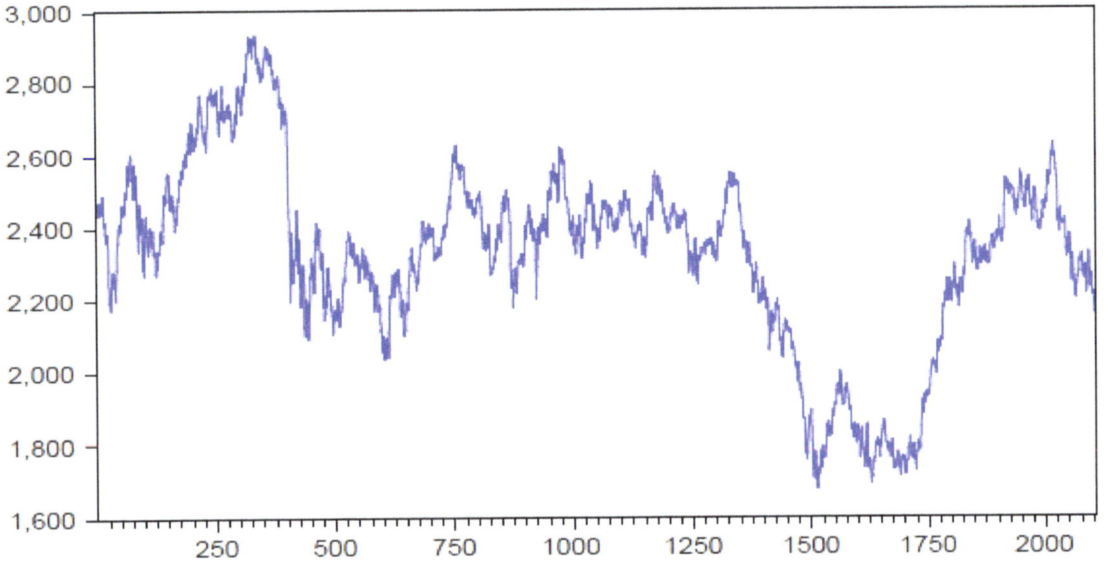

Figure 2: Time series of daily WIG20 returns

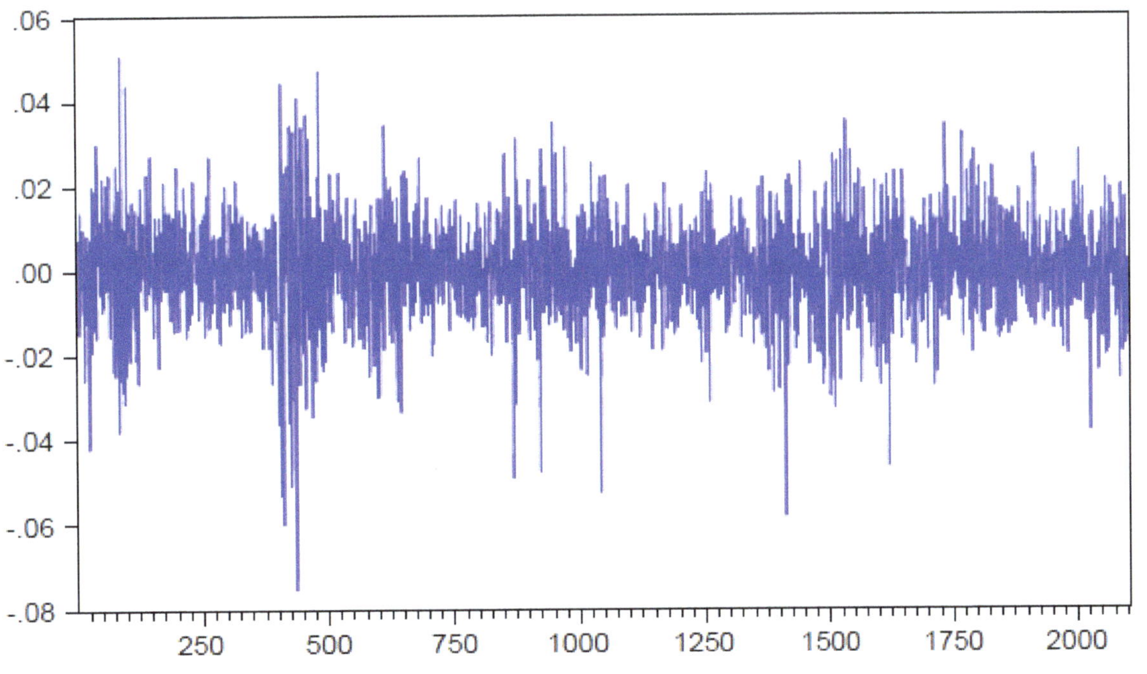

Table 1: Descriptive Statistics

Mean	-4.63e-05	Standard deviation	0.011615
Skewness	-0.391367	Kurtosis	5.918638
J-B statistic	798.9732	J-B probability	0.00000

Table 2: Results of the Runs Test

Test Value	Number of Runs	Z-Statistic	Probability
The Mean of Data	1085	1.52	0.129

Table 3: Structural Breaks Test

Break type: Bai and Perron tests of L+1 vs. L-Sequentially Determined Breaks Standard Errors & Covariance Breaks: No Breakpoints Selected			
Variable	Coefficient	t-statistic	Prob
C	-4.63E-05	-0.1933	0.8467

Note: Break selection is based on trimming 0.15; significance level: 0.05.

Table 4: Unit Root Test Results

		ADF	P-P	DF-GLS	KPSS
Intercept	Statistic	-33.93	-44.00	-4.27	0.04
	Critical Value	-2.86	-2.86	-1.94	0.46
Intercept and Trend	Statistic	-33.93	-43.99	-12.74	0.03
	Critical Value	-3.41	-3.41	-2.89	0.14

Note: The significant level is 5%.

Table 5: Variance Ratio Test Results

Joint Test			
Statistic	Value	df	Probability
$Max\,\|Z\|$ (at Period 2)	13.68	2099	0.00
Individual Tests			
Period	Var. ratio	Z-Statistic	Probability
2	0.55	-13.68	0.00
4	0.26	-13.03	0.00
8	0.13	-10.30	0.00
16	0.06	-7.74	0.00

Table 6: Shannon's Entropy Index Estimation

	50-Window	100-Window
Mean	0.9986	0.9987
Median	0.9987	0.9988
Max	0.9999	0.9999
Min	0.9953	0.9969
Std. Dev	0.0008	0.0008
Skewness	-1.2230	-0.4733
Kurtosis	5.8807	2.9108
J-B (Statistic)	24.9936	0.7911
J-B (Prob)	0.0000	0.6732

Note: The significant level is 5%.

Table 7: t-Test Results

	Standard t	Critical Value ($\alpha = 1\%$)	Trimmed t	Critical Value ($\alpha = 1\%$)
50-Window	-9.801 (41)	2.423	-10.020 (33)	2.457
100-Window	-6.971 (20)	2.528	—	—

Note: The values in parentheses indicate the degrees of freedom.

Table 8: Hurst Index Estimation

	50-Window	100-Window
Mean	0.473	0.470
Std. Dev	0.067	0.067
Median	0.463	0.465
Max	0.673	0.673
Min	0.379	0.379
Skewness	1.097	1.192
Kurtosis	4.315	4.785
J-B statistic	11.455	7.769
J-B probability	0.003	0.020

Table 9: Trimmed Sample Normality Test

	50-Window	100-Window
J-B (Statistic)	2.213	1.075
J-B (Prob)	0.330	0.584

Table 10: t-Test Results

	Standard t	Critical Value ($\alpha = 1\%$)	Trimmed t	Critical Value ($\alpha = 1\%$)
50-Window	-2.558 (41)	2.423	-3.281 (33)	2.457
100-Window	-2.011 (20)	2.528	-2.664 (16)	2.583

Note: The values in parentheses indicate the degrees of freedom.

Table 11: Variance Ratio Test Results / Part I

Length	Stat	Prob	Length	Stat	Prob	Length	Stat	Prob
50	3.24	0.00	750	8.69	0.00	1450	11.18	0.00
100	3.78	0.00	800	8.95	0.00	1500	11.30	0.00
150	4.47	0.00	850	9.09	0.00	1550	11.54	0.00
200	4.95	0.00	900	9.39	0.00	1600	11.74	0.00
250	5.47	0.00	950	9.49	0.00	1650	12.00	0.00
300	5.86	0.00	1000	9.85	0.00	1700	12.08	0.00
350	6.41	0.00	1050	9.79	0.00	1750	12.23	0.00
400	6.85	0.00	1100	9.93	0.00	1800	12.42	0.00
450	5.98	0.00	1150	10.03	0.00	1850	12.60	0.00
500	6.87	0.00	1200	10.17	0.00	1900	12.87	0.00
550	7.23	0.00	1250	10.32	0.00	1950	13.09	0.00
600	7.54	0.00	1300	10.42	0.00	2000	13.26	0.00
650	8.21	0.00	1350	10.56	0.00	2050	13.50	0.00
700	8.50	0.00	1400	11.03	0.00	2100	13.68	0.00

Note: Length indicates window length and Stat indicates variance ratio statistic.

Table 12: Variance Ratio Test Results / Part II

Range	Statistic	Prob	Range	Statistic	Prob
1-100	3.78	0.00	901-1050	3.05	0.00
101-200	4.22	0.00	1051-1200	4.71	0.00
201-300	3.98	0.00	1201-1350	3.92	0.00
301-400	4.74	0.00	1351-1500	4.02	0.00
401-500	3.60	0.00	1501-1650	4.10	0.00
501-600	4.20	0.00	1651-1800	4.21	0.00
601-700	4.91	0.00	1801-1950	5.40	0.00
701-800	4.56	0.00	1951-2100	4.21	0.00
801-900	2.77	0.02	1-300	5.86	0.00
901-1000	3.46	0.00	301-600	5.12	0.00
1001-1100	2.22	0.10*	601-900	6.53	0.00
1101-1200	3.41	0.00	901-1200	3.96	0.00
1201-1300	3.37	0.00	1201-1500	5.22	0.00
1301-1400	4.17	0.00	1501-1800	5.69	0.00
1401-1500	2.86	0.01	1801-2100	6.60	0.00
1501-1600	3.43	0.00	1-350	6.41	0.00
1601-1700	2.95	0.01	351-700	5.94	0.00
1701-1800	3.65	0.00	701-1050	4.82	0.00
1801-1900	4.37	0.00	1051-1400	6.56	0.00
1901-2000	4.17	0.00	1401-1750	5.79	0.00
2001-2100	3.60	0.00	1751-2100	7.08	0.00
1-150	4.47	0.00	1-700	8.50	0.00
151-300	4.90	0.00	701-1400	7.16	0.00
301-450	3.27	0.00	1401-2100	8.58	0.00
451-600	4.79	0.00	1-1050	9.79	0.00
601-750	5.57	0.00	1050-2100	10.59	0.00
751-900	3.71	0.00			

Note: Range indicates the range of data in the interval based on their order in the original returns series. Also, * indicates significance at the 5% level.

Permissions

All chapters in this book were first published in ERF, by SGH Warsaw School of Economics, Collegium of Economic Analysis; hereby published with permission under the Creative Commons Attribution License or equivalent. Every chapter published in this book has been scrutinized by our experts. Their significance has been extensively debated. The topics covered herein carry significant findings which will fuel the growth of the discipline. They may even be implemented as practical applications or may be referred to as a beginning point for another development.

The contributors of this book come from diverse backgrounds, making this book a truly international effort. This book will bring forth new frontiers with its revolutionizing research information and detailed analysis of the nascent developments around the world.

We would like to thank all the contributing authors for lending their expertise to make the book truly unique. They have played a crucial role in the development of this book. Without their invaluable contributions this book wouldn't have been possible. They have made vital efforts to compile up to date information on the varied aspects of this subject to make this book a valuable addition to the collection of many professionals and students.

This book was conceptualized with the vision of imparting up-to-date information and advanced data in this field. To ensure the same, a matchless editorial board was set up. Every individual on the board went through rigorous rounds of assessment to prove their worth. After which they invested a large part of their time researching and compiling the most relevant data for our readers.

The editorial board has been involved in producing this book since its inception. They have spent rigorous hours researching and exploring the diverse topics which have resulted in the successful publishing of this book. They have passed on their knowledge of decades through this book. To expedite this challenging task, the publisher supported the team at every step. A small team of assistant editors was also appointed to further simplify the editing procedure and attain best results for the readers.

Apart from the editorial board, the designing team has also invested a significant amount of their time in understanding the subject and creating the most relevant covers. They scrutinized every image to scout for the most suitable representation of the subject and create an appropriate cover for the book.

The publishing team has been an ardent support to the editorial, designing and production team. Their endless efforts to recruit the best for this project, has resulted in the accomplishment of this book. They are a veteran in the field of academics and their pool of knowledge is as vast as their experience in printing. Their expertise and guidance has proved useful at every step. Their uncompromising quality standards have made this book an exceptional effort. Their encouragement from time to time has been an inspiration for everyone.

The publisher and the editorial board hope that this book will prove to be a valuable piece of knowledge for researchers, students, practitioners and scholars across the globe.

List of Contributors

Małgorzata Pawłowska
Szkoła Główna Handlowa w Warszawie and Narodowy Bank Polski, Economic Institute

Rolando Gonzales Martínez
School of Business and Law, University of Agder, Norway

Aleksandra Wójcicka
Poznań University of Economics and Business

Giovanni De Luca and Danilo Carità
Università degli Studi di Napoli "Parthenope"

Giampiero M. Gallo
Università degli Studi di Firenze

Eric Fosu Oteng-Abayie
Department of Economics, Kwame Nkrumah University of Science and Technology, Ghana

Anthony Affram and Henry Kofi Mensah
School of Business, Kwame Nkrumah University of Science and Technology, Ghana

Badry Hechmy
University of Tunis el Manar, Faculty of Economic Sciences and Management of Tunis

Leonardo Augusto Tariffi
University of Barcelona, Department of Economics

Afees A. Salisu
Centre for Econometric and Allied Research, University of Ibadan, Nigeria
Department of Economics, Obafemi Awolowo University, Nigeria

Idris A. Adediran
Centre for Econometric and Allied Research, University of Ibadan, Nigeria

George-Jason Siouris, Despoina Skilogianni and Alex Karagrigoriou
Lab of Statistics and Data Analysis, Department of Statistics and Actuarial-Financial Mathematics, University of the Aegean

Ayben Koy
Istanbul Ticaret University, Department of Banking and Finance

Dobromił Serwa
Institute of Econometrics, Warsaw School of Economics
Financial Stability Department, Narodowy Bank Polski

Mostafa Raeisi Sarkandiz and Robabeh Bahlouli
Department of Management and Economics, University of Tabriz, Iran

Index

www.ingramcontent.com/pod-product-compliance
Lightning Source LLC
LaVergne TN
LVHW080725210926
848485LV00003B/521